THE FUNCTION OF MIMESIS
AND ITS DECLINE

*For all my good friends
at Carmel with
appreceation.*

*In Xto,
John Boyd. S.J.*

*Mt. Carmel
1981*

THE FUNCTION OF
MIMESIS
AND ITS DECLINE

JOHN D. BOYD, S.J.

New York
FORDHAM UNIVERSITY PRESS
1980

Printed in the United States of America

FOR MY MOTHER AND FATHER
In Memoriam

CONTENTS

PREFACE

My aim in these pages is to study a single critical concept in its tradition, namely *the function of mimesis,* of poetry or literature looked upon as an imitation of life. The scope of such a study, however, is potentially vast. Conceptually it should include all the elements discussed by the critics dealing with poetry or literature (the two words are interchangeable throughout for our purposes), for they all had a bearing on the function of mimesis. Historically it should cover the twenty-three centuries of this theory's hegemony, from fifth-century Classical Greece to eighteenth-century England. But a study of such scope would be both prohibitively elaborate and, indeed, of dubious worth. Yet the subject matter does demand a somewhat spacious scope if its importance is to be appreciated; it calls for a discussion that is compressed without being distorted, and substantial without being diffuse.

Hence, to insure a unity that is at once ample and incisive, I have centered my attention on two focal points, which, however, do not constitute in any sense separate "parts" of the study. Rather, they are interrelated centers of attention, constantly pertinent to each other in the argument. The first focus is a discussion, in its context, of Aristotle's contribution to the subject, which in all antiquity best accounts for the basic features of the mimetic literary tradition—indeed is minimally required by this tradition—and best reveals the premises of the culture from which it grew. The second focus is the discussion, in its context, of the problem at the close of this tradition in England. Each discussion is necessary for the other; these "two eyes [must] make one in sight" if this critical notion is to be properly understood inside its tradition.

In approaching the problem in this fashion I have assumed the validity of Eliot's notion of a literary tradition, that individual works, germane in their cultural origin, form a simultaneous and mutually modifying order or whole, though spread out over a long period of time. Even more germane to my purpose is Wellek's analogous concept of how best to shape a literary theory with respect to history and practical criticism. While eager to avoid dogmatic theorizing, Wellek rightly claims that history, theory, and criticism should so energize each other as finally to render a theory that supersedes "historicism." He quotes with approval Ernst Troeltsch, who, he says, struggled more than any other historian with the problem of historicism: " 'The Absolute is in the relative, though not finally or fully in it.' " Wellek concludes that theory, though needfully rich in literary, critical, and historical induction, should ultimately assert "man's . . . victory over impermanence, relativity and history."[1] In the light of these two readily acceptable positions I take it that a tradition as a unit, or a significant part of a tradition, is a legitimate center of literary and critical attention, and that one can form reasonably accurate notions about such a tradition.

My purpose, then, is to discuss a single critical notion in the context of its tradition, and to evaluate it. Hence this is primarily a study in critical theory. From the outset, then, I wish it to be clear that I am not writing detailed history of this critical notion, much less a history of literary criticism or theory either in antiquity or in the eighteenth century.

1. René Wellek, *Concepts of Criticism*, ed. Stephen G. Nichols (New Haven: Yale University Press, 1963), pp. 1-20, especially p. 20.

Yet each of the focal points mentioned above is at once historical and theoretical. All pertinent historical factors have been related to the notion in question, but ultimately subordinated to a better understanding of it. For example, in discussing Aristotle's contribution to the tradition, I have related to it Plato's and Horace's treatment of the problem, partly because of the influences of antiquity they represent, and partly because of their enormous impact upon the later development of the tradition. Similarly, in discussing the eighteenth-century critics I have absorbed what Medieval and Renaissance influences had entered the critical mainstream by then; and I have discussed these critics in the context of the radically new cultural climate of their time. Again, in line with this approach, in order to fasten attention on our central concern I have treated eighteenth-century critical opinion in a topical fashion, though in context, rather than presenting each critic's view as a whole, with the notable and understandable exception of Samuel Johnson. But the evidence, deriving from some thirty critics who span the entire century, is plentiful. Hundreds of passages and references have been assembled in this topical fashion, and their cumulative effect reveals clearly and strongly the decline of a critical tradition and not just the end of a period of time.

Independent of theoretical comment, and prior to it, literature in Classical antiquity and in the Western tradition deriving from it down to the end of the eighteenth century was predominantly mimetic. This is to say that it was characteristically "objective," object-oriented, outward-going, especially by comparison with what followed in the nineteenth century and after. Hence when Plato and Aristotle spoke of literature and the arts as imitative of human life, they were making explicit the fundamental and long-standing characteristic of their entire culture. Similarly, though Horace did not use the word "imitation" in this sense, both the literature he knew and his critical premises shared this basic orientation. The tradition that later developed from their lead still spoke of imitation, though with varying emphases and understanding of the word, and looked at the world of culture, *mutatis mutandis,* from this fundamental vantage point.

Further, the mimetic critical tradition spoke of poetry with the audience very much in mind. If it was an imitation of human life, its meaning must be of serious interest to its audience. After Horace's time his please-and-teach formula became the stock phrase for summing up this function. But the matter went much deeper. Practically every aspect of criticism had at least an oblique reference to one's view of the function of poetry. Hence I have thought it necessary to delve behind the ready use of the formula, to find out what critics really meant by it, and thus to study their oblique treatment of the function of poetry in what they had to say of the other aspects of criticism and critical theory. Opinions will be found to vary within the polarity of autonomous, pleasurable contemplation outlined by Aristotle and the notion of pleasure as a means of persuasion espoused by the far greater majority of the critics studied. Behind this serious discrepancy lie two fundamentally different views of poetry itself, one of which sees it as an autonomously meaningful structure, and the other, more rhetorically conceived, which views it as an instrument for molding opinion or moving an audience to action.

Because Aristotle's view of the nature and function of mimesis best reflects the actual literary achievement in this tradition, I have thought it wise, and indeed necesssary, to develop the discussion according to the very large lines of his contribution. What he has to say, at the level at which I use his ideas, shows a vital coherence necessary for accurate understanding of the problem of our study. There is no question, then, of arguing from authority—"as the philosopher says." In fact, a failure to understand Aristotle's *Poetics* was one of the reasons why the mimetic tradition came to an end when it did. Of this, history is the best judge.

A detailed discussion of certain of Aristotle's fundamental ideas has been necessary to give our problem adequate treatment. All the eighteenth-century critics employed the framework of the *Poetics* in their discussion of poetry and its function; and both then and now this document has been understood in a variety of ways. One may ask how legitimate it is to judge eighteenth-century critics by a kind of Aristotelianism of which they apparently had little notion, as, for example, that of Else and Randall. For one thing, it seems necessary to judge the basic concepts of the *Poetics* for what they are, and not to limit ourselves to the imperfect understanding of many of the critics studied. This kind of historicism, I agree with Wellek, has little value. Secondly and more importantly, the critical ideas being dealt with are so fundamental, and their interpretation so pertinent to a proper understanding of the mimetic tradition, both literary and critical, that no sense can be made of it without them. Finally, those who had a more adequate sense of the deeper demands of mimesis—Johnson and Twining, for example— were constantly and intuitively very close to Aristotle's notions, despite the distortions of others in the tradition.

In the second focus of attention, the eighteenth century, some thirty critics of varying stamp and acumen have been quoted with more or less frequency. Many more passages could have been cited, but there seemed little need for piling up repetitive evidences of similar attitudes beyond a reasonable point. For example, practically every critic of the time used the Horatian formula frequently and as a matter of course. Also, I have not limited my selection to those critics who wrote in the early half of the century, the period conventionally referred to as Neoclassical, as distinguished from the latter half, when the newer premises of taste, sense, and feeling were gradually supplanting that of reason as a prime framework of criticism. All the critics cited spoke of imitation and of how they understood its function, though with varying kinds and degrees of perception and conviction. I have frequently noted the influence of these newer premises, but my main interest in the critics who discuss them is in how the notion of imitation and its function fared with them. I have not thought it necessary to assess their systems. This would bring me far afield from mimesis; and the work of Brett, Crane, Hooker, Marsh, McKensie, Monk, and Wasserman in this area is well known.

Studying the critical notion of the function of mimesis, then, inside its tradition, with a special unifying focus at each end of its historical duration, seems both necessary and valuable. If we change the image employed earlier from one of sight to one of sound, this tradition resembles the physical phenomenon called "the whispering gallery," found in St. Paul's in London and in the Capitol in Washington. A word whispered at a certain spot can be heard several yards away, an occurrence impossible in normal conditions. Yet it happens in this situation because of an elliptical convergence of the sound waves upon the place where they are heard. Aristotle's voice, as heard in the eighteenth century, was to some extent still identifiable, though distorted by Platonic and Horatian overtones; and the acoustics suffered much interference from the cultural milieu of the time. A proper knowledge of both the sending and the receiving ends of this system involves an adequate sense of the waves' transit in between. The tradition is one, but at the eighteenth-century end it is surely in decline; and this can be appreciated only by careful reference to its origins. The tradition was no longer viable in itself, though its better values were very much alive in a giant such as Johnson, and in a lesser way in others. These values really transcend historical limitations, though they were developed in this specific tradition.

Our study helps us understand better the importance among these values of a poetic contemplation based upon a transcendently mimetic quality vital to all kinds of poetry. In this way we may at least approach Wellek's goal of a theory of poetry that supersedes historicism. But more of this later. It is hoped that these pages will show the immense difference between poetic contemplation and its all too prevalent rhetorical parody, moralistic suasion, a difference which the best literature of the tradition makes amply clear.

J. D. B.

May 1968

PREFACE TO
THE SECOND EDITION

It is more than a decade since the first edition of this study appeared, and it has been out of print the past few years. Given its generous critical reception, it has seemed good to make it available once again, especially since it is, to my knowledge, the only thoroughgoing modern analysis in English of the mimetic theory of poetry and its function, viewed in its long, complex history and cultural context. This edition includes a few corrections and some minor helpful revisions. In reissuing the book, while I have in mind my colleagues' interest in this important subject, I am further thinking of the book's use to younger students of the Classical and Neoclassical tradition. It has already been found valuable to graduate students of literary criticism and to serious undergraduates seeking more than a superficial approach to the questions raised by critics from Plato, Aristotle, and Horace down to those of eighteenth-century England. In fact, there is serious reason to believe that the time is ripe for affirming the essentially mimetic dimension of all literature, no matter in what age it was written, and hence of all criticism itself. Not a little modern criticism and the theories supporting it have neglected the mutually nourishing affinities of literature and life that keep both healthy. This problem calls for a further study in itself, to which I plan next turning my attention. Meanwhile it may prove fruitful to many to re-examine the rich tradition in which mimesis was first developed.

J. D. B.

June 1980

1
FORM: THREE VIEWS
AND THREE PHASES

The literature of Classical antiquity from Homer onward was centrally concerned with presenting and interpreting human values. By the end of this tradition in the eighteenth century, much English literature had a strong and explicit ethical purpose. We need only think of the *Spectator* and *Rambler* papers, Pope's *Essay on Man,* the growth of sentimental comedy, and the widespread development of satire. Even the novels of Richardson and Fielding were valued as conduct books. It is quite natural to expect that the critical opinion of this long tradition should parallel its central poetic concern by discussing the humane function of literature. Aristotle's view of literature as mimesis, or an imitation of human life, best stated the fundamental nature of the Classical literary achievement, and his view of its function for the audience as pleasurable contemplation most faithfully reflected the minimal demands of such literature. But Horace's view of what it should achieve for its audience, conceived of in the Hellenistic rhetorical tradition, was decidedly more influential from his own day down to the tradition's end. The Horatian formula, which held that literature was most successful when it blended what was useful with what was pleasant, when it both taught and pleased its audience, was everywhere in evidence. This book attempts to study the critical concept of the function of mimesis within its tradition, its characteristic and minimal demands, and their implications in context, especially as conceived of by Aristotle, and as they appeared during the decline of this concept in eighteenth-century England.

Some find it awkward to associate literature and a concern for man's moral well-being, to speak of ethics and aesthetics in the same breath. The conflict, as frequently posed, is often more imaginary than real. Desire to forward a theory of art for art's sake has frequently destroyed straw-man opposition. On the other hand, "moralists" have at times been their own worst enemies in claiming for literature and the arts a function hard to reconcile with the nature of art itself. Again, Classical and Neoclassical positions on the subject have not always been given fair expression and hearing. This is so partly because of historical prejudice, which is best remedied by the change in perspective afforded by the passing of years, and partly because the full implications of any theory are seldom realized when formulated. The best theories take time to unfold, and the protection of a friendly cultural climate often hides their limitations and inconsistencies.

It would be unwise, then, to discuss the ethical implications of this critical tradition by hastily resorting to a formula. In such matters formulae often have a way of saying too much by saying too little. Again, if some find the Horatian formula a bit philistine, it is just as interesting to note with Harry Levin that nowadays we most readily associate the claim of art for art's sake with the roar of the M.G.M. lion for more profits! One can view with much sympathy the claims of theorists of art for its own sake and yet agree with F. L. Lucas when he says: "Since literature influences, can we wholly forget that influence?"[1] That the poet is a seer is a very old idea, and it still has attraction for such critics as Tate, Eliot, and in a different way, Winters.

1. F. L. Lucas, *Literature and Psychology,* rev. American ed. (Ann Arbor: University of Michigan Press, 1957), p. 233.

W. J. Bate has observed: "Conceptions of the nature and purpose of art closely parallel man's conceptions of himself and of his destiny. For art, in one of its primary functions, is the interpreter of values, and aesthetic criticism, when it rises above mere technical analysis, attempts to grasp and estimate these values in order to judge the worth of the interpretation."[2] It seems wise, then, to approach the problem of this study with caution, with historical awareness, and with an alert sense of the larger premises of the Western Classical tradition.

Where the eighteenth-century English critics are concerned, I have assembled the opinions of some thirty of them, some prominent, others more obscure. Some were the professional critics; several wrote textbooks for the youthful scholars of the time; but all were in one way or another influential and bear witness to the temper of their critical milieu. It has been of much value to try to penetrate behind the façade of the Horatian formula when studying these authors. Because a critic of the day was expected to subscribe to it as a matter of course, one can hardly hope to know what he meant by it unless one knows what his deeper and related premises were. Often an oblique statement about one of these premises lights up his ideas of the purpose of literature more effectively than any mere adherence to the formula.

For this reason I have taken what, for the want of a better word to describe the process, may be called a *noetic* approach to the problem. I mean to discuss it against the background of the general psychological and cultural orientation of the critic's thought and of his age. To call this approach "philosophic" might be misleading. Although philosophic elements are involved, most of the critics in question were not philosophers in any systematic sense of the word. "Noetic" is also

2. W. J. Bate, *From Classic to Romantic: Premises of Taste in Eighteenth-Century England* (Cambridge: Harvard University Press, 1949), p. 1.

meant to suggest the spontaneous attitudes of one's mind, one's characteristic psychological and prephilosophic habits of thought.

Such an approach is imperative if we are to be realistic in this study. The long tradition out of which eighteenth-century theory grew underwent several important changes because of the cultural milieus through which it passed and in which it developed. Aristotelian and Platonic philosophies, Alexandrian and Hellenistic cultures, the rhetorical tradition, old as Western Europe, the exigencies of Roman culture and civilization, and finally, the eighteen highly varied centuries of Christianity naturally had a profound effect upon this tradition and upon its vital moral center. It would indeed be a fossil were it not nourished by these various springs.

Further, if poetry is to please and teach, it is important for us to know what is being taught and how it affords pleasure. Is what is known conceived of as empirical, metempirical, idealistic? How does it influence moral persuasion and action? What is the more ultimate meaning of morality and art to the critics concerned? All this and more is suggested by the word "noetic" as it is used throughout these pages, in the hope that a tolerably accurate idea will emerge of the Classical moral concern with literature and its decline in eighteenth-century England. It is hoped, too, that some larger implications for the critical tradition will suggest themselves, for the West is still heir to Greece, Rome, and Christendom despite the far-reaching cultural changes of the past two centuries.

FORM

Because of the complications of the tradition involved in our study, one might easily get lost in details. And yet the details are very important. We fortunately have a homing point in the Greek notion of *form* to help order and unify

4

our discussion. Aristotle, for example, used μορφή and εἶδος (form) to specify what was ultimately both real and intelligible in things. His mind and the Greek mind generally were outward-going. They lived in an object-centered world which, for all its irony and mystery, was considered ordered, substantial, and stable. It was deemed intelligible in its very objectivity, and hence it demanded of the mind a transcendent loyalty. At this basic point of departure, though they differed sharply in their premises and methodologies, Plato and Aristotle both reflected an old and prephilosophic Greek conviction at the heart of Greek art, letters, science, and philosophy. Poetry, then, for both Plato and Aristotle was in one way or another an imitation of this objective form, some kind of mimetic knowledge. Literary theory in the West up until the end of the eighteenth century hovered about this same conviction. Hence it would be well in this study to focus attention upon the multiple changes undergone by this concept of poetry until its demise and upon the many shades of meaning that lie between form and formalism.

Three views of form in poetry and in its function for the reader were important in Classical criticism and highly influential in the eighteenth century. These were the views of Plato, Aristotle, and Horace. Given the objective orientation of the Classical mind, they tend to constitute three polar positions in poetic theory and to exhaust the basic possibilities of looking at the arts as imitative. In a very general way, for the moment, Plato's view was idealist, Aristotle's realist, and Horace's pragmatic.

Because the Greeks thought of poetry as a kind of mimetic knowledge, it is natural that their poetic theory should relate it to actual life both as its source and as its goal or function. For them, the art process was something like closing an electric circuit between the audience and nature imitated, especially since nature imitated was properly human nature, with the rest of the world considered meaningful only as a context

5

for human life. The Greek sculptor busied himself with the human form as the corporeal expression of the person; the Greek tragedian wrestled with the dark angel of human fate; and the greatest accomplishment of Greek philosophy beginning with Socrates centered upon the whole tangle of the human mystery. Socrates thought of knowledge as moral virtue and consequently judged literature in directly ethical terms. Plato came under his influence in this as in other basic notions; and even Aristotle, who differed from both in this matter, reflected the general Greek conviction that the arts were valuable in educating the young, and that the ideal of humanism which they helped nourish could be both aesthetic and ethical in nature without any conscious dichotomy. Ethical humanism, then, was practically a synonym for Classical Greek culture.[3] When literary theory began with the pre-Socratics, poetry was naturally thought of as oriented toward actual human life.[4] And even Plato and Aristotle with their more critical terminology, although they distinguished between the fine and practical arts much as we do today, used the undifferentiated term τέχνη for both. By this word they understood any of the several activities that reduce knowledge of doing or making from the realm of ordered understanding to actual accomplishment.[5] This tends to confirm the orientation of even the fine arts of the time to actual life.

PLATO

Plato and Aristotle were the first in the West to treat the problem of this study philosophically at any length. From

3. *Ibid.*, p. 2.

4. Rupert C. Lodge, *Plato's Theory of Art* (London: Routledge and Kegan Paul, 1953), pp. 11–12.

5. John Wild, *Plato's Theory of Man* (Cambridge: Harvard University Press, 1948), pp. 46 ff.

them stem two fundamentally opposed attitudes which continue to appear throughout the tradition. Plato was the first to challenge the intrinsic human value of poetry by condemning what he considered its metaphysical, educational, and moral hazards, an indictment which F. L. Lucas calls the distrust of poetry as unreal, unrighteous, and unrestrained.[6] Yet he approved of an idealistic kind of poetry because he found it useful for his utopian moral purposes. His judgment, made in the light of his fundamental philosophic premises, and with a strong ethical finality in mind, is an odd mixture of an idealist absolutism and a moral pragmatism, a more limited phase of his larger philosophic purpose of propounding a moral *modus vivendi* based on absolute truth. The subject of Plato and the poets has often been discussed pro and contra. It is admittedly complicated, but I think it is best understood against the background of his well-known theory of knowledge. What may loosely be called the Platonic tradition in criticism is surely centered here.

It is suggested that Plato's attack on poetry and the poets was partially conditioned by the decline of tragedy at the time and by the prevalence of a kind of comedy which, because it purveyed morbidity, sensationalism, undiscipline, horseplay, vice, and flattering rhetoric, he viewed as dangerous (*Republic,* 395-397).[7] But in a larger way he was dissatisfied with what he considered the disproportionate place held by the poets, including Homer, in the education of youth (*Republic,* 606-607). He saw in philosophy a much more potent and secure pedagogy, whereby reason, unshackled by feeling, passion, and the other agencies of mat-

6. Lucas, *Literature and Psychology,* p. 269. In discussing these objections I have changed the order of their treatment both from that of Plato's in the *Republic* and from Lucas' because this helps the clarity of my argument.

7. Plato, *The Dialogues of Plato,* trans. Benjamin Jowett (New York: Random House, 1937), I, 658-661. All further references to Plato in English are taken from this version.

ter, might more effectively form and liberate the human spirit. His philosophic convictions, then, about the nature of knowledge best explain Plato's judgment of poetry. They are, I think, more fundamental than any attendant circumstance of his argument, even more than the special pleading in behalf of philosophy as the leading educator, of which Atkins makes so much.[8]

Plato's search for wisdom drove him beyond the changing universe of experience, ordered though it seemed, to a more ultimate reality behind it, which gave it its meager and, by comparison, shadowy being. The world met by the senses imitated the world of real, transcending forms. These were the true beacons of the mind and the only substantial realities.[9] In his system all forms of knowledge were imitations, better or worse in direct proportion to the immediacy and thoroughness with which they reflected the eternal and absolute forms. Hence imitation is an important and functional word for Plato in both the real and the conceptual order, a word of itself universal in scope and indeterminate of application, receiving ultimate definition from his dialectic in particular contexts.[10]

When reality is conceived of as the substantially ideal (substantial and real inasmuch as it is ideal or intelligible rather than vice versa), it is natural enough to find Plato establishing the hierarchy of value in both the real and the conceptual order inversely according to the degree of imitation involved and the consequent distance from the forms. It follows that imitation in both orders is centered in *content* rather than in *structure,* because it is primarily an analogue of the intel-

8. J. W. H. Atkins, *Literary Criticism in Antiquity* (London: Methuen, 1952), I, 47 ff.

9. Plato's theory of knowledge and its origins is developed in many of his dialogues, especially in the *Phaedo,* the *Republic,* and the *Parmenides.*

10. Richard McKeon, "Literary Criticism and the Concept of Imitation in Antiquity," in *Critics and Criticism, Ancient and Modern,* ed. R. S. Crane (Chicago: University of Chicago Press, 1952), p. 149.

ligible. This will be of the first importance later, when discussing the account he gives of poetry and the fine arts. The hierarchy of imitation in the conceptual order—1) philosophic or ideal knowledge, 2) belief and opinion, which are largely the product of sensation, and 3) imagination—correspond roughly to 1) the forms, 2) natural things of experience, including the products of the practical arts such as a bed, and 3) the products of the fine arts, such as a tragedy. It is eminently logical, then, that knowledge be measured by philosophy as an overruling norm. Collingwood has well said that imitation for Plato does not express resemblance between two real things, nor one more or less real, but between appearances and reality. McKeon in his compact discussion of the word says much the same thing.[11]

It is easy to see what Plato meant when he claimed that poetry was unreal. If the world of experience is an imitation of the true world of forms, and poetry, in turn, an imitation of the world of experience, it is clear that poetry is inferior to philosophy both in dignity and in educational value, for philosophy rises to the eternal forms themselves. And so a telling blow was scored against poetry. An imitation of an imitation was twice removed from reality, further from the "truth" than a carpenter's table or bed, which more directly imitated its archetype. Poetry and the poet obviously knew less of reality than the philosopher; how then could the poet be a better teacher (*Republic,* 595–602)? An interesting corollary of this first objection to poetry is that mimetic impersonation in the drama is bad for the actor, since it weakens his character and impairs single-mindedness and integrity. Plato feared that the Greeks with their natural liking for posing would become characterless, being absorbed into a "second nature," the character of those impersonated (*Republic,* 395). This unreal occupation was also deemed

11. *Ibid.,* p. 154; R. G. Collingwood, "Plato's Philosophy of Art," in *Mind,* n.s., 34 (1925), 160-161.

unrestrained, the second fault he found with poetry, because it dealt too freely with human emotion, which Plato fundamentally distrusted.

This distrust is itself a consequence of his notion of reality. Emotions arise from and are directly concerned with matter, the obviously dark and unreal element in life. Reason not only tries to escape matter, but must, as well, dominate and silence the psychological inroads into the human personality made by it. In the *Republic* we read that the sympathy awakened by drama stirs the passions that were better suppressed: "In all of them [plays] poetry feeds and waters the passions instead of drying them up. She lets them rule, although they ought to be controlled if mankind are ever to increase in happiness and virtue" (*Republic,* 606; see also 387). Commenting on the *Ion* (535c), Grube remarks: "Ion is made to insist upon the violence of his emotions when he recites, and upon his success in communicating these emotions to his audience. We have here a fundamental belief of Plato's, and one which lies at the very root of his attitude to art, namely that successful art depends upon a stream of emotion which flows from poet to actor, and from actor to audience."[12] The empirical picture of disordered human conduct has always contained a large share of emotional disturbance.

Plato also feared pleasure, an element usually directly associated with emotion (while happiness for him was a more comprehensive concern), though he is surely aware of its charm. "The fairest music is that which delights the best and the best educated, and especially that which delights the one man who is pre-eminent in virtue and education. And therefore the judges must be men of character, for they will require both wisdom and courage" (*Laws,* 659). The same theme is repeated some paragraphs later, as poets are censured

12. G. M. A. Grube, *Plato's Thought* (London: Methuen, 1935), p. 181.

who offer vulgar and licentious songs. They have not appealed to truth but to fickle pleasure (*Laws,* 700–701).[13]

Thirdly, Plato objected to poetry because it was unrighteous: the poets told lies about the gods. This was closely related both to the first objection, in that all poetry told lies in proportion to its distance from the vision of philosophy, and to the second, in that these special lies, by treating the gods anthropomorphically, attributed to them more than a modicum of emotional foibles and vices. Although Plato's rational philosophy helped to purify contemporary concepts of religion and morality, he seems here to miss the rich potential of myth for illuminating the mysterious areas of human belief, though elsewhere he trusts its dim light very readily. Here he concentrates on what he considers the likely scandal of youth in so sacred and sensitive an area, to the neglect of the peculiar educational efficiency of myth which he elsewhere acknowledges. "For a young person cannot judge what is allegorical and what is literal; anything that he receives into his mind at that age is likely to become indelible and unalterable; and therefore it is most important that the tales which the young first hear should be models of virtuous thoughts" (*Republic,* 378). One can sympathize with this perennial problem, yet Plato seems here again to neglect the precisely imaginative nature of poetry and the values involved in the tradition of myth.

But his treatment of poetry was not entirely one of censure. In the *Laws* he genuinely admired an ideal poetry, which sought to reveal the forms, the perfection of human life as it should be lived. Because it resembled philosophy to this ex-

13. Linked with this second objection is Plato's attribution of poetic inspiration to madness and frenzy (*Apology,* 22; *Ion,* 534). This is possibly best taken not too solemnly, but as part of his special pleading against the poets; or it may be a modified assertion of the origin of the element of wonder in most art (θέλξις); or again, he may be trying to explain the origins of poetic imagination somewhat in analogy with his theory of pre-existence and the origin of ideas.

tent, such poetry was a good propaedeutic to it and had a practical moral value for the commonwealth as well. He considered the tragic poets at their best when they imitated the finest and noblest life. In this they were lawgivers and benefactors of the community (*Laws*, 817). A long discussion in the *Republic* (Book III) of the role of music in education shows a similar appreciation. Again, in the *Laws* (790) he ventures a theory of homeopathic treatment of emotion, possibly a forerunner of Aristotle's theory of katharsis. In *Philebus* (47–48) he observes that painful emotions are enjoyed when given full rein, reflecting the critical problem of why we enjoy tragedy despite its painful subject matter. He also remarked that comedy treats of self-conceit in one powerless to injure (else it would cause fear). The laughter evoked is a "malicious joy," not unlike Hobbes' sudden glory over another's weakness. Yet this joy is sympathetic and devoid of ridicule and personal satire (*Philebus*, 48–49; *Laws*, 935). Further, his detailed remarks on literary style reveal a serious interest in the arts of writing, reflecting the fine artist that he was (*Gorgias* and *Phaedrus, passim*). And a notable contribution to aesthetic doctrine is his insistence upon organic unity in a piece of art, governing and uniting style and content (*Phaedrus*, 264).

Plato's temper was anything but philistine. Rather his epistemological, ethical, and civic interests drew him to an ideal kind of poetry which would enshrine the large and permanent values of the race. Poetry was expected to open men's spirits to beauty and nurture them to ideal goodness, insensibly drawing "the soul from earliest years into likeness and sympathy with the beauty of reason" (*Republic*, 401). Mere pleasure would be precluded as the end of such poetry, since pleasure ranked low in his scale of goods (*Philebus*); otherwise this would put it in the one class with pastry cooking and sophistry (*Gorgias*, 463 ff.; *Republic*, 373).

Again, "Those who seek for the best kind of song and music, ought not to seek for that which is pleasant, but for that which is true; and the truth of imitation consists, as we were saying, in rendering the thing imitated according to quantity and quality" (*Laws,* 668). This, we may presume, would be equally true of poetry.

In reviewing many of these passages, Atkins says: "That there is an innate charm in poetry he is prepared to admit; but that the communication of this charm was the main business of the poet he stoutly denies. To him the real and ultimate end of poetry was none other than the influencing and moulding of human character; the bringing out of the best that was latent in the soul; thus enabling men to better their lives and to rebuild the world 'nearer to the heart's desire.' "[14] Whether he approves of the poetry of ideal beauty and perfection or disapproves of the other kinds, the world of experience is not for him the realm of intellectual traffic or moral motivation. Against this background we read his guarded welcome of censorship offered to foreign poets in the *Laws* (817): "First of all, show your songs to the magistrates, and let them compare them with our own, and if they are the same or better we will give you a chorus; but if not, then, my friends, we cannot."

A word now about Plato's notion of morality, because it is so evidently involved in the function of poetry for him. Morality usually comprehends the pattern of correct human living, measured by the good or value which is considered the goal of human existence. For Plato, moral goodness was a blend of the ultimate attainment of the ideal, the Good, and the gradual participation in it during one's lifetime, the latter to be understood, however, in the context of the good political process of the well-ordered state. This goal, achieved

14. Atkins, *Literary Criticism in Antiquity,* I, 61.

largely through contemplation, constituted happiness. The idea that knowledge was moral virtue attracted Plato strongly.

This attraction was natural enough in a system which centered on the real as substantial ideality. A more "realistic" system would look rather to action as the ultimate area of morals. For one thing, in this way it could make room for the "irrational" in man. Plato, of course, was aware of the discrepancy between his doctrine and its imperfect application in the life about him. In his most developed understanding of the matter he thought that *nous*, a very noble kind of insight and wisdom, perceived values under momentary illumination of the forms in such a way that one could desire nothing else while the illumination lasted.[15] It is easy, at all events, to understand Plato's insistence upon knowledge, especially knowledge of the forms, as the heart of moral goodness. Pleasure and pain could have no organic relationship with its quest. The forms had an exemplary and attracting influence upon the mind, and virtue consisted mainly in assimilating this influence. Here, again, given Plato's fundamental and pervasive idealistic premise, we find good reason for his ascetical withdrawal from matter and the dark emotions and his concomitant distrust of pleasure.

If knowledge tended to be virtue, and if poetry supplied one kind of knowledge, its only human function would be to draw the mind to the ideal forms. Plato had to be, first and last, a moralist, though his own kind of moralist, when discussing poetry. McKeon has well remarked: "criteria of [philosophic] truth and morality are applied as a natural course to the poet's work."[16]

15. Grube, *Plato's Thought,* pp. 216-258, presents a very sensitive treatment of the problem from the perspective of the evolution of Plato's view of the problem.
16. McKeon, "Literary Criticism," p. 158.

Many have attempted to defend Plato's judgment of the poets or to explain it away. But in the last analysis his epistemology and subsequent ontology must be the deciding factors. For all the love Plato as man and artist may have shown for poetry, his system simply does not allow him to judge it favorably. I have not been able to find any refutation of this claim. Although historical and political factors urged him toward the special pleading in behalf of the philosophers, a point of which Atkins makes much, the epistemological and systematic problem still remains. The same must be said about his praise of poetry of the ideal in the *Laws*. The sole systematic rule of the philosopher's knowledge lies behind the ridicule of the rhapsode in the *Ion* and the norm of judgment exercised in the *Sophist*, where some have thought Plato caught the idea of artistic transformation when he speaks of a sculptor's use of perspective. One may say that Plato was larger than his system, which in a sense is true of every thinker. But his system and its dialectic were intended as universal, and we are concerned in this study with his theory precisely as theory, because that is the way in which it was most influential. His idealistic noetic pervaded his teachings on poetry and had significant effect on the Platonic and Neoplatonic traditions of poetic theory.

The position assumed here has long since been ridiculed by R. G. Collingwood in his "Plato's Philosophy of Art." Yet nowhere in this stimulating article does Collingwood face this ultimate epistemological test. He says that Plato thinks of art as a symbol of truth which appeals to the mind through emotion. The truth is veiled, and the important struggle is to resist the emotional appeal while penetrating to the meaning! It is hard to see how this view can be considered appreciation or praise of poetry. Collingwood seems to confirm this judgment when describing the lower Platonic grades of reality, better called appearances, of which poetry is one: "So far as it is anything, it is a *confused* and *perverted* version of the highest grades; and so far as we can understand or apprehend it at all, we can do so only by thinking of it as such a *confused* version of the real" (italics mine). Actually, Collingwood's defense looks more to his own position as a modern idealist when he speaks of poetry as a symbolic presentation of the truth, a suspicion confirmed by his criticism of Plato's epistemology of art as being too objective for a thoroughgoing idealist.[17]

Where the status and value of imitation are judged solely by how faithfully the absolute truth is reflected in the content of the image or imitation, there is no place for poetry. (The contribution of modern idealism to poetic theory has come via the poet's active, creative imagination.) The Platonic notion of poetry lacks a sense of the *need of structure*. We shall presently see that recognizing this need was Aristotle's pregnant contribution. Through artistic transformation (as we would explain it today), an intense sense of the actuality of our experience, of its individual, concrete, and empirical character, is firmly secured in the self-identity of the plot, which thereby comes into existence as a thing of meaning. But a realism of some sort is needed to explain such a claim to poetic creativity, much as it is needed to account for ontological creation, the structured self-identity of many beings, when God himself exhausts Being. Further, a sense of analogy, rather than a sense of appearances-versus-reality, is necessary to appreciate this prior need of realism for truly guaranteeing structure. Analogy has always been a friend of the poets.

Platonic influences on the poetic theory of the Renaissance and the eighteenth century came in great part through Neoplatonism. From its third-century progenitor, Plotinus, Neoplatonism had inherited a firmer sense of the analogy of beauty in creation. Yet this need not detain us here, because

---

17. Collingwood, "Plato's Philosophy of Art," pp. 160-163.

the basic Platonic attitudes toward the forms and imitation and a relative lack of a sense of structure lie together with an idealistic moral orientation at the center of this critical tradition as well.

It would be foolish to ignore or deny the "other Plato," whose tremendously rich thought has nourished all the ages since his time. I do not wish to. Poets, philosophers, and civilizations in the large have truly been footnotes to his wisdom. Yet we must face the widely recognized paradox of Plato the poet, the philosopher of the dramatic dialogue, who never successfully coped with the place of the arts in his own system. Though part of the difficulty was due precisely to the demands of system, this is not the only or ultimate source of the trouble. Aristotle, immensely more systematic than his master, was able to give a reasonable account of them. Rather, I think, the trouble was Plato's basic mistrust of the concrete, together with the dark overtones of this deep mistrust and its consequent effects upon his systematic epistemology. I believe all forms of idealism suffer limitation from this mistrust. But the thoroughgoing Greek of *nous* and θεωρεῖν, for whom knowing was looking and seeing, ultimately had to be an empiricist in the only valuable sense of the word: one who was genuinely, though not merely, interested in concrete experience. Plato's thought lacks this orientation, despite its otherwise thoroughgoing, objective character. Without this interest in what is concrete, the shape of what is real in experience can too easily pale beside the thought of it. Surely in poetry and its theory poetic structure will be neglected, when the content of ideas substitutes for or even absorbs interest in the thing made, that is meaningful. This has been the tendency in both Classical and Modern idealist traditions, especially in the case of poetic theory. A blurring of the stubborn yet pliant lines that separate poetry from philosophy, art from life, intimately related though these interests are, in the long run serves none of them well.

One reason why the mature Yeats was a better poet than theorist was his operative sense of the stubborn demands of language. By the same token, Plato has served the cause of poetry in many ways, but not through his theory of it. It is not that I love Plato less, but a reasonable view of poetry more!

In summary, then, Plato's idealistic noetic tended to downgrade poetic imitation. Judging it mainly by its content, and hence as mere appearances, and assessing its value by its presumed dominantly moral function, Plato was logically forced, in the last analysis, to reject much of the poetry of the Greek tradition. Though one may sense some ambiguity and regret in this decision, his tradition of criticism reflects two of its important consequences. The first is that it never comes to grips with the actual in experience as an essential ingredient of poetry. Secondly, this lack of realism consistently occasions a nonliterary judgment of the function of literature. Poetry tends to become philosophy and ethics, instead of holding its own ground.

ARISTOTLE

What organic union there is in the Western critical tradition of poetry's needed realism and autonomy is largely derived from Aristotle. His methodology, sometimes simplistically considered as merely mechanical, reflects the realistic and empirical orientation of his mind. He characteristically viewed reality *as becoming*. He was content to watch man developing: as man, in gradually attaining his *entelechy*, that is, his goal or full stature; as artist, in achieving his work of art; and as audience, in enjoying this art. From the data of experience, Aristotle tried to draw the likely conclusions about the goals to which man's activities pointed. Though these goals beckoned to him from outside, once achieved they were the built-in fulfillment of his person, for they had been potentially present in him from his earliest state, as the flower is present in the seed. Werner Jaeger speaks of this compact system as dominated at every step by a sense of purpose whose meaning is not merely biological but "logical and ontological." This purpose is gradually being realized by one's inner power (δύναμις) "which now remains latent and now becomes active (ἔργον), attaining its end . . . only in this activity (ἐνέργεια)." "With reference to motion the form is the entelechy (ἐντελέχεια), inasmuch as in its form each thing possesses the end of motion realized within itself."[18] The organic realism which characterizes Aristotle's critical methodology, despite its limitations, lies at the heart of what is best in the tradition of Western realism.

For Aristotle, as well as for Plato, poetry was mimetic, imitative of nature, but any discussion of the precise meaning of this term should be seen against the background of his epistemology and ontology. The forms which Plato had postulated as the ultimate principles of reality and its intelligibility, and which he claimed transcended experience, were for Aristotle immanent in matter, shaping and achieving the concrete reality. Objects of experience, the human person above all, were constituted by an intimate and dynamic union of these two principles. Form needed matter to express its full potential and grow to maturity; and matter needed form for determination and stability. The forms were available to the active mind through a multiple induction from sense experience. The subsequent intentional union of the mind with the world about it was direct, in the sense that things were known in themselves and not merely as shadows; hence poetry, a special kind of imitative knowledge, was proportionately direct, unlike Plato's imitation of an imitation.

18. Werner Jaeger, *Aristotle: Fundamentals of the History of His Development*, trans. Richard Robinson, 2nd ed. (Oxford: Clarendon, 1948), pp. 383-385.

We have been used to Butcher, Bywater, and others translating the *Poetics* speaking of the *poem* as an *imitation*. More recently Gerald Else in his scholarly and stimulating study, *Aristotle's Poetics: The Argument*, insists that the imitating referred to is the *poet's activity*, the operation of τέχνη referred to above, the activity that reduces knowledge of doing or making from the realm of ordered understanding to actual accomplishment. But without discussing the merits of this controversy in the present context, one may simply use the qualifier *imitative* instead of the substantive *imitation* with respect to the poem. This is not merely a semantic compromise, because Else's illuminating remarks about the mimetic action in Aristotle apply at least reducibly and deductively to the poem. If it is precisely the poem that is the product of the poet's mimetic activity, its lineaments will automatically have this peculiar character. Indeed with this in mind the substantive *imitation* may also be used with the poem without doing violence to Else's claims.[19]

But apart from its presumed philological contribution, Else's approach is valuable in making explicit the most significant way in which Aristotle's view of the mimetic is an advance over Plato's. This is in the matter of structure. It was certainly involved in the earlier approach of Butcher and Bywater, but Else's explicit statement redefines our approach to Aristotle's contribution to a very central question: How is art imitative?

19. Ἀριστοτέλους Περὶ ποιητικῆς. *Aristotle On the Art of Poetry*, ed. Ingram Bywater (Oxford: Clarendon, 1909); S. H. Butcher, *Aristotle's Theory of Poetry and Fine Arts*, ed. John Gassner, 4th ed. (New York: Dover, 1951); Gerald F. Else, *Aristotle's Poetics: The Argument* (Cambridge: Harvard University Press, 1957), pp. 1-6. I have regularly cited Butcher's English translation of the *Poetics*, since it is generally more familiar, though on occasion Else's is explicitly preferred. I have used *The Works of Aristotle*, trans. W. D. Ross (Oxford: Clarendon, 1921-1928), in citing other treatises of Aristotle, with the exception of the *Rhetoric* for which I have used *The Art of Rhetoric*, ed. John H. Freese (Cambridge: Harvard University Press, 1952).

A poet, then, is an *imitator* in so far as he is *a maker,* viz. of plots. The paradox is obvious. Aristotle has developed and changed the bearing of a concept which originally meant a faithful *copying* of preexistent things, to make it mean a *creation* of things which have never existed, or whose existence, if they did exist, is accidental to the poetic process. Copying is after the fact; Aristotle's *mimesis* creates the fact. It is clear that his use of the word in such a way can only be accounted for historically: that is, that such a redefinition of a simple concept can only be understood as the end-product of a long, gradual development. Without Plato especially, and a considerable development of the idea in him, Aristotle's use of *mimesis* would be inconceivable.[20]

Earlier, however, with the distinction between copying and creating in mind, he stresses the differences between Plato's and Aristotle's use of the word: "It becomes in his [Aristotle's] hands a really new idea, having little more than the name in common with Plato."[21]

If the poet is an imitator precisely as a maker, then the product of his making, his poem, is imitative precisely in being a structure. (We are reminded that the Greek word for poet, ποιητής, and his poem, ποίημα, were derived from the word for making or constructing, ποιεῖν.) The poem, then, is something constructed. Though Aristotle was speaking primarily of tragedy, his poet was a maker of plots; yet the analogy with other kinds of art is frequently drawn in the *Poetics.* Hence at this general level it is fair enough to speak interchangeably of poem and drama.

But taking the plot as typical of Aristotle's concept of structure, we see that its coherence as a *thing made* depends upon what he calls "probability or necessity." Further, before we can discuss what this probability or necessity means, we must understand that drama is outward-going in the sense outlined earlier. It gets its start from form found in the real

20. Else, *Aristotle's Poetics,* p. 322.
21. *Ibid.,* p. 13.

world, that is, in the ontologically meaningful element in human life. Chapter II, for instance, begins with ". . . the objects of imitation are men in action" (1448a), and this idea is repeated throughout the *Poetics*. In a minimal way, this can only mean that to be viable as structure a drama must present, *be about,* significant human action; for the forms of probability derive ultimately from life. The drama must treat of the human quest for fulfillment, for achieving the *entelechy* spoken of above, this quest providing the clue to meaning in human life (though, of course, tragedy treats of the failure of this quest). But while drama looks to the ontologically real world, it does not present facts, that is, actions which really occurred, in the way history does (chapter IX). Rather, concerned with presenting action according to probability or necessity, it tells "what may happen," "how a person of a certain type will on occasion speak or act" (1451b). Here Aristotle is saying that the poet shapes his material into a kind of action that will reveal in a distilled way what is at stake, including the working out of human motivation, when one seeks a given, significant goal. A poet must not try to imitate the entire life of his subject, but only a single, significant action that can be presented as unified and coherent. In the eighth chapter we read: "The imitation is one when the object imitated is one, so the plot, being an imitation of an action, must imitate one action and that a whole, the structural union of the parts being such that, if any one of them is displaced or removed, the whole will be disjointed and disturbed" (1451a).

If, then, a poem or drama is imitative precisely in being structured, it can be such only if this structure presents, and hence imitates, an action of human import, which, in turn, is seen by the poet to be such by his familiarity with the human scene, where action is the cue to human significance. Hence for Aristotle a poem is not an imitation in the sense that it is factually like what it talks about or presents. This would make it merely a mirror, actually the same as a Platonic copy, where likeness consists mainly in a similarity of the poem's "content" with the material imitated. And yet the poem would not be a poem at all, unless its entire fiber were woven of human meaning, ultimately derived from the world of real action. The poet is an imitator, then, inasmuch as he is a maker of plots, but it is essential to his mimetic shaping that he present a meaning distilled from the human scene, and to this extent itself mimetic. The poet imitates nature by shaping the action of his play toward its goal, in somewhat the same way nature shapes our ends in real life, but this involves an orientation toward the arena of human struggle and quest. If a poem is more beautiful than it is true, it is so *only in and through being true*. But the truth in question here is not factual or reportorial, nor is it the truth of philosophy. Rather, it is the truth of poetry, which we variously call truth-to-life or the poetic universal. It is the truth which Aristotle saw as more universal than history because it embodied knowledge of what was probable or necessary, given what it is to be human. Because this is precisely the kind of knowledge of life contained in the theme of any successful poem or drama, we might think of calling it *thematic truth* as well. Though speaking from an entirely different background, Aristotle could well agree with MacLeish: "A poem should not mean/But be"; but he would be quick to add: "Its entire being is to mean, and realistically!" It can be, for Aristotle, a *thing made,* only by being a *thing of meaning* that reflects human life, and vice versa. A poet cannot be either a seer or a maker exclusively, but must be each in being the other. Hence, in explaining Else's paradox that a poet is an imitator insofar as he is a maker, we must add to it another, that he is a maker insofar as he is an imitator of human meaning as well.

The fuller development of Aristotle's view of poetry will be the subject of much that follows in this study. Here, however, we should stress that, in making what is imitative in poetry essentially a structural concept, Aristotle turned the notion of mimesis in a fresh and new direction. Though the word can have some misleading overtones, art is now implicitly, at least, *creative,* because it is no longer considered merely a mirror, but a structure shaped by an interpretative point of view. This point of view achieves the structure and the structure shapes what is cognitve in the poem or drama; yet in a way that implies an active influence of what is cognitive, as befits an "objective" sensibility. "Aristotle," says Else, "is a Greek, for whom creation means *discovery* (εὕρεσις), the uncovering of a true relation which already exists somehow in the scheme of things."[22] Yet this is not the same thing at all as scientific or philosophic research, but the mysterious insight into things which we associate with the truly gifted poet. Nonetheless, it comes about only in and through the poem's structure. The mutual interaction of structure and meaning makes any separation of "form" and "matter" a critical heresy as early as the *Poetics.*

The meaning of a poem has a special character for Aristotle. It is realistic in the sense that it presents a comment on human action that goes beyond the surface of life, a comment in some ways resembling his philosophic realism. "Realism" thus understood has a validity of literary reference, despite the vogue since the nineteenth century of applying the word almost exclusively to literature that deals largely with techniques akin to the photographic. This is far from Aristotle's brand of realism. For him, the poet searches into human action whose meaning, as we have seen, is ultimately specified by its goal. As we have said, his process in this resembles that of nature, where the concrete forms mold, guide, and develop matter in accordance with their purposeful pattern. Something of the sort takes place in a

22. *Ibid.,* p. 320.

poem, where the molding and shaping follows the pattern of probability or necessity. The poem, and Else would prefer to say the poet, seizes what is important in human life and molds it in accordance with its structural exigencies.

This process is sometimes described as distilling the form or meaning of some human event, releasing it from the accidental hindrances it may encounter in its quest for concrete fulfillment or perfection. For example, we are not told the color of Oedipus' sandals, for this has no relevance to the play's development. This idea can be of service, provided the process is not confused with the formation of an Aristotelian philosophic essence, or with the Platonic desire that poetry present only an ideal view of life. One might better use the word "ideating," rather than "idealizing," to describe the heightening process involved in forming "the probable." Here the stress is on finding the meaning involved in human experience and activity presented in drama and poetry, not on finding its ideal archetype. The word "ideate" is used here in analogy with "aerate," which describes a process of purifying water. As water is made more itself, and made fit for human use, by having air pass through it, so the poet's creative intelligence finds the potential of meaning in human activity by seeing the struggle for goals in the very concrete and unfinished process that inspires his composition. This is why Aristotle's view of poetry is essentially dramatic and ongoing. The distinction just made between idealizing and ideating suggests, too, that one should look for the "significant" rather than the "universal" as more characteristic of Classical art, though the latter, of course, has a valid enough reference. We should not let the dramatic fusion of meaning and experience, so central to the objective sensibility of the Greeks, run the risk of evaporating into philosophy.

And yet for Aristotle poetry is philosophic, is more "significant," as we have seen, than history or chronology (*Poetics,* 1451b). Nevertheless it is not abstract and skeletal. A later, more subjective philosophical milieu has accustomed criticism to the paradoxical concrete universal. Aristotle leaves us with more generic and less nuanced hints in the same direction, yet it is clear that because a poem is structured, it is neither the singular of history nor the abstract philosophic universal, but a transformation of both. Jacques Maritain, somewhat an heir to Aristotle's ways of thought, sees the poetic universal as breaking down the walls of concept, of genus and species, that limit rational analysis, and hinting at the plenitude of existence in each moment of realized experience. At all events, in speaking of poetry's peculiar kind of meaning Aristotle is answering Plato's objection to poetry as "unreal." The heightening and selective process involved in the probable approaches the deeper reaches of reality in a way that, although different from philosophy, rivals it in dignity and value.[23]

We can now draw some conclusions about what Aristotle thought of the value and function of poetry. In chapter XIV of the *Poetics* he says that every kind of poetry affords its own pleasure (ἡδονὴν ... τὴν οἰκείαν) (1453b), derived from the inner structure of the poem. Again, in chapter IV, in relating the enjoyment of poetry to structure and to the deep human instincts for imitation and harmony fulfilled in the poem, he accounts for our enjoyment of poetry by the or-

23. Recent scholarship has tended to stress Aristotle's empirical methodology, and to warn against any too easy a tendency to interpret the *Poetics* in too metaphysical a sense. Else denies that Aristotle gave an ultimate answer to Plato on this count in terms of metaphysics. See Else, *Ibid.*, pp. 303-305, and Jacques Maritain, *Creative Intuition in Art and Poetry* (New York: Pantheon, 1953), pp. 125-126. I may also note here that a poem "means," rather than "contains knowledge." I have found it easier, however, to speak regularly of poetic knowledge, partly because of its contrast with factual, scientific, and philosophical knowledge, and partly because of a wish to stress what is precisely cognitive in poetry. This expression parallels the common enough usage of calling a poet a *seer*, when actually we might be more comprehensive, if clumsier, calling him a *meaner*.

ganic relationship of knowing with the pleasure it affords: "to learn gives the liveliest pleasure, not only to philosophers but to men in general" (1448b). Here we can see Aristotle's characteristic approach to knowledge, reflected in his famous opening of the *Metaphysics,* where he asserts the premise that all men by nature desire to know. Further, what he says about the function of poetry must be set in the all-pervading context of teleology which we spoke of earlier. When specifying proper or particular finalities, he is not speaking of abstract or isolated acts but of human persons. Jaeger reminds us that for Aristotle, every kind of reality was an intelligible, ongoing process, determined at every step by its own end, but most of all by the highest operative end in the process.

What interests him is the fact, not that something *is coming to be* [as if through a blind life-force without intelligible determination], but that *something* is coming to be; something fixed and normative is making its way into existence . . .

In Aristotle's teleology substance and end are one, and the highest end is the most determinate reality there is.[24]

J. H. Randall speaks of the overriding goal of this teleology as the fullest development of *nous,* the human mind. "Sheer nousing, sheer knowing" is the aim that transcends and absorbs all human desire—a Platonic note, to be sure, but only in target, not in weapons. (Will, as we shall see in a moment, is for him the specific center of ethical activity.) "Thus for Aristotle the fullest and most intense activity of man's characteristic function, the completest fulfillment of man's distinctive 'nature,' is the operation of *nous,* of reason, in knowing."[25]

24. Jaeger, *Aristotle,* pp. 384-385.
25. John H. Randall, *Aristotle* (New York: Columbia University Press, 1960), pp. 270-271.

It is quite legitimate, then, to make more explicit what is inevitably and imperatively implied in Aristotle's view of the organic union of pleasure with poetic contemplation, namely that poetry is one of the formative agents both in education and in mature life, and has power to enlarge and deepen the human person. Butcher, arguing from a parallel with music in chapter VIII of the *Politics,* says quite legitimately, I think, of all art, including literature: "Art in its highest idea is one of the serious activities of the mind which constitute the final well-being of man. Its end is pleasure, but the pleasure peculiar to that state of rational enjoyment in which perfect repose is united with perfect energy."[26] One can become too solemn when speaking of the value of poetry, especially when reading Aristotle with the hindsight of more than twenty centuries. Yet Butcher's claim is not exaggerated. And whether Aristotle is speaking of educational or of more leisurely experience of the arts, his all-embracing sense of teleology and the organic harmony it achieves in evaluating human experience must always be kept in mind. In fact, the sanest and most fruitful view in our critical tradition of the function of poetry and the arts is his notion of pleasurable contemplation as the end of mimesis. This organic claim has found deeper, more subtle and sophisticated development since his time, but its telling accuracy and balance have never been surpassed.

Aristotle's view of pleasure as the end of mimesis contrasts markedly with Plato's disapproval of it and his desire to dry up the pleasurable emotions that art involves. In the passage in chapter VIII of the *Politics* which Butcher had in mind above, Aristotle writes: "Intellectual enjoyment is universally acknowledged to contain an element not only of the noble, but of the pleasant, for happiness is made up of both" (1339b). The pleasures proper to each kind of poetry of

26. Butcher, *Aristotle's Theory,* p. 201.

which he speaks in the *Poetics* (1453b) do not foster an idle hedonism. Because they arise from viewing the structure of the poem, they are organic with the activity of knowing, a sign of a healthy mind. They fit the larger context of his ethical theory: "Pleasure completes the activity not as the corresponding permanent state does [habit, that is], by its immanence, but as an end which supervenes as the bloom of youth does on those in the flower of their age" (*Nic. Eth.*, 1174b). Just before this he had observed that a human faculty in its best condition and joined with its most proper object experiences the most pleasure. Accordingly, the mind properly involved with the arts will operate in its most perfect and disinterested manner, in contemplation; and the concomitant pleasure is a sign that the mind is developing, being formed and matured according to its nature. The human mind in operating normally turns toward the significant. For Aristotle the arts, along with other knowledge, were meant to create an adequate answer to this natural instinct. And the concomitant pleasure was a sign of the authenticity of the mind's satisfaction.

Aristotle was aware that there are higher and lower pleasures available in life. The latter are such as accrue from mere pastimes and recreation (*Politics*, 1339b). But among the former was the pleasure he envisaged for worthwhile art, a pleasure he associated with wisdom in the *Metaphysics* (981b), because it is more autonomous than the uses derived from the practical arts. He knew well that unbridled pleasure can warp human judgment, as Helen's presence affected that of the elders of Troy. But he insisted that there are true objects of worthy pleasure, proportioned to a man's nature, and that intelligent people should be educated to appreciate them. The pleasure deriving from poetry, then, is a sign of the deeper formative effect and harmonious personal development deriving from the contemplation of reality through structured imitation. His theory reflects the deep Greek conviction that art brings an awareness, whereby the audience, naturally attuned to reality, is perfected by a heightened mimetic view of it. Implicit here, of course, is the pervasive effect of the interpreting human mind of the artist, who enhances reality without falsifying it. Pleasure, the sign of this effective awareness, is the light that is lit when the circuit is closed for the object-centered mind. This organic union of knowledge and pleasure, in which one cannot exist without the other, is a far cry from the later formulations of pleasure and teaching as the functions of poetry, and even further from the idea that life is too serious for poetry. In all of this, Aristotle was explicating in part the Greek program of liberal education, *paideia,* the rearing of children, and its fulfillment in adult contemplation, the "nousing" of which Randall speaks.

Because I shall treat the problem of Aristotelian κάθαρσις in Chapter 3, I shall merely say here that it must have been in some way or other consistently related to the function we have just considered. There are many interpretations of this enigmatic term. But we can presume it is in theoretical harmony with the larger formative and pleasurable claims he made for art. These are far too pervasive in his entire way of thinking to be denied simply to solve the pragmatic problem he was dealing with; they are too important for the autonomy of the arts to be sacrificed to any merely affective theory of poetry.

Aristotle's view of morality and how it relates to poetry also shows his generally realistic and organic procedure. The ultimate good to be attained, while intellectually perceived through contemplation, was achieved through activity of the will (see, however, below, pp. 224–225). This goal was in the order of experience, rather than in any transcendent order: "Even if there is some one good which is universally predicable of goods or is capable of separate and independent existence, clearly it could not be achieved or attained by man;

but we are now seeking something attainable" (*Nic. Eth.,* 1096b). This supreme good is to be identified with politics. "It would seem to belong to the most authoritative art and that which is most truly the master art. And politics appears to be of this nature; for it is this that ordains which of the sciences should be studied in a state, and which each class of citizens should learn and up to what point they should learn them; and we see even the most highly esteemed of capacities to fall under this, e.g. strategy, economics, rhetoric; so that this end [the political good] must be the good for man" (*Nic. Eth.,* 1094a–b).

To attain this goal constitutes happiness. "Now such a thing happiness, above all else, is held to be; for this we choose always for itself and never for the sake of something else" (*Nic. Eth.,* 1097a–b). This is further defined as action: "Human good turns out to be activity of soul in accordance with virtue, and if there are more than one virtue, in accordance with the best and most complete" (*Nic. Eth.,* 1098a). This, he continues, is a lifetime's work, "For one swallow does not make a summer, nor does one day." The action which attains to happiness derives from a disposition of soul called "virtue," determining the choice according to the prudent man's judgment, "the mean." This activity, in turn, strengthens the disposition of virtue.

How does the finality of poetry fit into this scheme of morality? Because for Aristotle poetry enshrines serious human values, it naturally becomes a formative agent of the human person. Concretely speaking, the mind's enrichment arising from the contemplation of a poem will naturally better one's personality and may even at times help in motivating the good and noble life. But this is quite different from the professedly didactic function envisaged by Plato or in a more narrow fashion by later, more pragmatic critics. For Aristotle, in the line of immediate finalities derived from the nature of things, poetry is autonomous. It is meant to give pleasurable contemplation and should not be bent to the purposes of moral rhetoric or persuasion to conviction and action, where pleasure is a goad rather than a sign of fulfillment. To be sure, this finality of poetry is proximate and relative in the larger scheme of things. Art is a human possession and hence subordinate to the "uses" of man, but never at the cost of its own natural and proximately autonomous function. Aristotle saw, as did all Greeks, that poetry could have value as an educator; but its main end for him was a pleasurable contemplation akin to wisdom. What further effects it had were outside the precincts of poetry as such and sprang from the larger psychological and ontological constitution of the person.

Poetry's function of pleasurable contemplation, then, fits organically into Aristotle's methodology or thought. His noetic may rightly be called realistic and metempirical. From this vantage point he can answer Plato's idealistic strictures on poetry. Poetic knowledge is realistic, direct, and beyond merely empirical report, hence poetry is not "unreal." Pleasure is organically and naturally a function of this real knowledge, hence poetry is not "unrestrained." Poetry deals with the larger truth of human nature and is of value only if it is "true to nature" rather than to merely contingent facts. Hence it is not "unrighteous," if it presents a valid picture of human weakness even in the anthropomorphic gods. This last point, of course, is a less explicit answer to Plato than the other two.

The Platonic and Aristotelian noetics and their consequent critical approaches are reflected in various ways throughout the entire critical tradition of the West. Coleridge has said that everyone is either a Platonist or an Aristotelian in his fundamental habits of thought. In its own way this is true of theorists of poetry and critics. Surely we should not expect either of these giants to defend every use which has been made of their germinal attitudes toward any problem, poetry included. Yet one can find among the critics significant affinity for one or the other precisely because of these germinal attitudes toward poetry and its function. With this in mind, these suggested hypotheses may be worth testing as this study develops.

From Aristotle's realistic noetic, his conception of structural realism, and his notions of the organic union of insight and pleasure for the audience of poetry stems all Western realistic critical theory down to the demise of the Neoclassical tradition. But this theory is rarely completely realistic. The pristine meaning of the *Poetics* was lost at an early stage, filtered for later centuries through Alexandrian and Roman interpretations. The document itself was not known to the Medieval Schoolmen. Had it been available, their poetic theory might not have been so rhetorical, because the realism of many of them in ontological and theological speculation was certainly germane to the realism of the *Poetics*. It is very frequently lacking in the theoretical work of those critics we shall deal with, with the exception of Johnson and Twining. It is more evident in the better practical criticism, and, of course, in the actual literature. Though transformed by several intervening influences, this same critical spirit is present in the work of Bate, Brooks, Fergusson, Tate, Wellek, and Wimsatt, to mention only a few contemporary critics.

We do find in earlier critics a kind of formalism, deriving indeed from the Peripatetic tradition, but too readily characterized as exclusively the Aristotelian critical tradition. Much of the true Aristotelian realism has been drained from it in its passage through Alexandrian, Roman, and Ramist rhetorical traditions, where formalism and moralism are parodies of structure and of the organic union of insight and pleasure Aristotle thought of as the function of literature for the audience. This unhappy critical tradition is too quickly linked by some with the "authoritarian Aristotle," deemed wisely rejected by the more enlightened modern mind. It lacked a philosophic sense of "the probable" in mimesis.

Actually the former of these two traditions has been the more fruitful among critics even up until modern times. It has surely shown a strong staying power among them. Despite the obvious and very valuable advances made through theories of imagination derived from nineteenth-century idealism and later subjective philosophies, Aristotelian realism has been most helpful in keeping alive a sound view of the function that literature should have for its audience, as well as a healthy sense of how literature and life relate to each other. At any rate, this Aristotelian realism serves as a good gauge in judging eighteenth-century critics: the more thoroughgoing the realism, the more organically is the union of insight and pleasure viewed.

On the other hand, from the idealistic noetic of Plato and his nonorganic conception of the role of pleasure and profit stem two peripheral traditions. One of them is a moralism of poetry for profit's sake, with pleasure as an extrinsic bait of honey on the cup of severe moral doctrine. It derives from Plato's moral idealism, which as we have seen is the source of his reasons for rejecting certain poets and for accepting those he thought fit for the Commonwealth. His concept of imitation, which does not distinguish between poetic and scientific knowledge, has the same source in his idealism. Hence it also feeds this moralistic conception of the function of poetry, in judging the value of the knowledge achieved in proportion to its power of leading to his morally conceived goal. Much Patristic and Medieval commentary, which looked to poetry as a propaedeutic to moral philosophy or theology, is in this tradition. So is Sidney, in spite of himself, and many moralistic critics of the Renaissance and the eighteenth century. Poetry is asked to perform a task for which it was not meant and of which it is not capable.

The second peripheral tradition derives more exclusively from Plato's interest in ideal beauty. Though in his conception of it such poetry as imitated the ideal forms was meant for profitable knowledge, we find in later versions, ironically enough, a more or less irresponsible interest either in technique or in beauty or in aesthetic pleasure, quite independent of the more realistic aspects of art as a concrete possession of the race. His interest in ideal beauty is thus reflected in the varying forms of art for art's sake. His failure to make the real of experience the focus of poetic and critical interest is a key to the Platonism of Shaftesbury, Shelley, and much French aestheticism of the nineteenth century. This tradition, of course, was greatly influenced by the new idealism in the nineteenth century, but still it had an ironic and genuine origin in Plato.

Although these judgments may seem highly controversial, they can at least serve as working hypotheses in the ensuing pages. We shall frequently see various tendencies in this critical tradition disrupt the organic unity of profit and pleasure as the function of imitation, originally implicit in the precritical tradition of the Greeks at its best, and later theoretically outlined by Aristotle. Enlightenment critics rarely saw it firmly. Stylistic formalism or a moralism of rhetoric tended to claim their allegiance in the final analysis. We shall see that this was due in great part to a waning or even a complete lack of both the realistic noetic of the *Poetics* and the practice of Greek classical art at its best. It took specific form in the pragmatic rhetorical tradition stemming at least from Alexandrian times. Much of this tradition was crystallized in the immensely influential *Ars Poetica* of Horace.

HORACE

Horace's view of the function of poetry is the third to be considered here. His influence on subsequent critics in this matter was the most explicit of the three. Although most Renaissance critical treatises were fashioned on the framework of the *Poetics,* their spirit more often than not was Horatian. This was especially true concerning the question of the function of poetry. The please-and-teach formula derived from him was regularly grafted onto commentaries on the *Poetics.* It became, in fact, the normal vehicle for expressing in a practical way the overriding concern of most Renaissance Platonists, that poetry serve a moral end. Bernard Weinberg observes:

It will be noted that the Horatian "utile dulci" is inextricably mingled with the thinking of the [Renaissance] Platonists . . . The Platonic ends, as these critics see them, are practically indistinguishable from those that they find in Horace's *Ars Poetica.* Utility and pleasure, equal or unequal, dominant or subordinate. The tendency of the Platonists is to declare that the two are unequal in importance, that utility is dominant, that pleasure is its instrument; and this is true even for those who believe that the art serves desirable ends in a satisfactory way.[27]

The Horatian formula was a household word, accepted practically without question throughout the Middle Ages and the Renaissance. Toward the end of the eighteenth century, when Classical premises were seriously questioned or abandoned, the grip of this formula was weakened.[28]

27. Bernard Weinberg, *A History of Literary Criticism in the Italian Renaissance* (Chicago: University of Chicago Press, 1961), I, 255, 347.

28. The predominance of the Horatian influence on Renaissance critics, despite the veneer of Aristotelian terms and references, is generally accepted by critics of Renaissance poetic and rhetorical theory. See J. W. H. Atkins, *English Literary Criticism: The Renaissance,* 2nd ed. (London: Methuen, 1951), pp. 3 ff.; C. S. Baldwin, *Renaissance Literary Theory and Practice,* ed. D. L. Clark (New York: Columbia University Press, 1939), pp. 187-189; Lane Cooper, *The Poetics of Aristotle: Its Meaning and Influence* (Boston: Marshall Jones, 1923), pp. 103-104; M. T. Herrick, *The Fusion of Horatian and Aristotelian Literary Criticism, 1531-1555* (Urbana:

Horace discussed poetry in a spirit and on a level quite different from those of Plato and Aristotle. His critical interests were not philosophic but practical; his intellectual milieu was not that of the Greek academy, but more that of an urbane, sophisticated Roman poet. Consequently, his noetic, which we shall try to characterize later, had marked differences from the first two reviewed and was actually more akin to that of most Renaissance and eighteenth-century critics discussing the function of poetry. Rome of Horace's day had become through conquest and organizational genius the center of the Empire. Its political and economic stability laid the foundation for a new cultural edifice. Rome had become *the city* and the prototype (though in many ways dependent upon Athens) of the several "Augustan," "classical," city-centered cultures that followed in the West.

While it is true that most classical cultures in the West have been largely derivative (though the Greek considerably less so), Rome showed a special genius for assimilation. During the reign of Augustus (27 B.C. to A.D. 14) the absorption of Greek culture was intensified, in part unconsciously, because of a somewhat germane sense of order and perfection, but also consciously, in order to offset certain erotic and romantic Asiatic influences which were deemed harmful to the moral fiber of the Roman civilization. The memory of a pristine Roman austerity and the vision of an even greater political destiny ahead gave cultural efforts of the time a strong moral dimension. It is natural, then, to expect a Roman view of the arts that would help foster a moral climate helpful to the success of the Empire. Augustus himself, as well as such wealthy Romans as Massala, Maecenas, and Pollio, were willing patrons of the arts, at least in part

---

University of Illinois Press, 1946), *passim*; Joel E. Spingarn, *A History of Literary Criticism in the Renaissance,* 2nd ed. (New York: Columbia University Press, 1924), pp. 19-20; Weinberg, *A History of Literary Criticism in the Italian Renaissance,* II, 798 ff.

for this reason. To a significant extent Horace was the critical spokesman for this patriotic position. And though most of his poetry transcends a didactic stress, much in his *Satires* and his six Inaugural *Odes* (3. 1-6) shows a strong conviction of the need for moral strength, if the Empire is to be healthy. One important ingredient in his view of the function of poetry derives from this politically centered moral concern.

Another ingredient, aesthetic in nature, is significantly analogous to this. We have already said that Horace's approach to poetry was not philosophic but practical. His *Ars Poetica,* his most sustained treatment of poetry and its function, was written in the rhetorical tradition and was appreciably influenced by rhetorical considerations. The fusion, and at times confusion, of the arts of poetry and rhetoric date back to the Alexandrian period of criticism, the Hellenistic third and fourth centuries B.C. Ironically, Aristotle himself was one source of this development. Though by writing his *Rhetoric* and *Poetics* he clearly distinguished between the two arts as comprising different inner movements and different ways of composing, he treated the matter of style in both arts in the *Rhetoric.* We shall discuss this important problem in Chapter 4. Though Horace, in turn, has many valuable observations about what makes for successful poetry, the over-all rhetorical orientation of his treatise has its drawbacks.

It is generally agreed that the *Poetic* of Neoptolemus of Parium, a third-century Hellenistic critic, is the source of the *Ars Poetica.* The following passages from C. O. Brink's *Horace on Poetry* identify its tradition as stemming from Neoptolemus and from Aristotle's *Rhetoric.*

So far as the substance of Horace's critical doctrine is concerned, I find very little in the section on style which does not seem to be derived from Neoptolemus ...

The *Ars Poetica,* considered on its own, bears out both the two-fold division [of style and subject matter] and the precedence of the section on style, with its corollary on "order" . . . It is hard to avoid the suspicion, once Aristotle's *Rhetoric* and *Poetics* are brought into the picture, that Neoptolemus' large headings are the headings of the *Rhetoric* transferred to verse. The application was made possible by the rhetorical character of Aristotle's doctrine on poetic style . . .

Only a small amount of the content [of Neoptolemus' treatment of poetry] may be derived from the *Poetics* . . .

Horace (exceptions apart) has drawn on Neoptolemus' critical doctrine, and in turn, Neoptolemus' treatise was based (directly or indirectly) on Aristotle's rhetorical doctrine, recast so as to apply to the style of poetry.[29]

The fundamental pitfall awaiting the critic who treats poetry in a rhetorical context is that he is led to forget the fact of the essential autonomy of poetry, itself the corollary of the special kind of knowledge poetry is, a knowledge secured as it should be by critical attention to poetry's unique structure. Forgetting this, he is led to turn poetry into an instrument of persuasion in which the final criterion of style and other factors will be the suasive effect upon the audience. This danger is most patent at the theoretical level of criticism. Aristotle avoids it to a great extent because he has already isolated the autonomy of the poem and has stressed the importance of structure, which for him consists mainly in plot. Ideally, of course, style should also be a part of structure. But the danger also exists on the level of practical criticism, if one's approach to poetry is largely pragmatic, as Horace's is in the *Ars Poetica* (including whatever theoretical observations he has to make). This danger can be abetted when aesthetic judgment operates in the practical, politically centered milieu outlined above which stood in significant analogy with it.

29. C. O. Brink, *Horace on Poetry: Prolegomena to the Literary Epistles* (Cambridge: Cambridge University Press, 1963), pp. 99–100.

Brink is less critical than I shall be of Horace's view of the function of poetry. Yet when speaking of the tradition which Horace absorbs from Neoptolemus, he wisely says that, while the new approach of the Alexandrian critic to poetic subjects greatly simplifies Aristotle's procedure in the *Poetics,* a pedagogical advance to be sure, "the didactic gain involves a greater loss: the metaphysics of mimesis no longer disturbs literary criticism—but neither does it stimulate philosophical inquiry." Earlier, Brink says: "Aristotle's reaction to Neoptolemus' mixture of moral instruction and aesthetic enjoyment would doubtless have been sceptical. One thing is common to both, and only one: the defence and justification of poetry. For the rest, Neoptolemus disregards Aristotle's subtle and speculative theory of mimesis and catharsis. Instead he expresses the common Greek conviction that poetry must instruct as well as please."[30]

Brink also observes that Neoptolemus' use of the Aristotelian universal in poetry looks more to literary models to be imitated than to the realism demanded by the *Poetics.* But through Horace, he adds, we get a sense of Neoptolemus explaining "his demand in moralistic fashion as poetic teaching through ethical commonplaces and character drawing. This teaching will make the poet into a *doctus imitator*—the counterpart of the *doctus poeta* of the Alexandrians, whose syllabus presumably dispensed with the *Socraticae chartae.*"[31] The *Ars Poetica,* then, suffered significant limitations from belonging to this rhetorical tradition of discussing poetry. Many of the qualities which Horace rightly and effectively demands of a successful poem—decorum, refinement, good form, urbanity—are ultimately relevant to the Aristotelian view of mimesis, yet we must always understand them as conceived of in this rhetorical context. In the hands of a less gifted critic, this conception could easily degenerate, as it

30. *Ibid.,* pp. 143-144, 129.
31. *Ibid.,* pp. 146-147.

later did, into a formalism mainly concerned with stylistics or a strongly moralistic view of poetry. This latter danger, as we shall see, is present even in Horace to a greater extent than some are willing to admit.

C. S. Baldwin notes the irony of the greater influence of Horace on critics of the Renaissance and the eighteenth century than of the more perceptive Aristotle. He wisely attributes this to Horace's tendency to rhetoricize. His *Ars Poetica,* Baldwin observes, is shrewd, lucid, brilliant, and adaptable enough to the short flights of ordinary thinking on the subject to explain all its popularity. Sententious saws impeccably expressed have a superficial appeal. Together with the recital of types of dramatic character and of speech techniques and patterns to fit their social niche, they are excerpted from rhetorical textbooks. They are good enough, he wryly remarks, for the Pisones, father and sons, for whom the *Ars Poetica* was immediately written, and for the exigencies of the schools of declaiming; but they speak of a world quite apart from Medea, Dido, and Orpheus.[32]

Horace's concept of morality was likewise pragmatically centered, growing out of the milieu already discussed. He favored a blend of such Stoic and Epicurean principles as would insure a moderation equally removed from gross hedonism and dry asceticism. This moderation aimed at a workable social pliancy. Grant Showerman says that while Horace could approve of extramarital dalliance with Chloe (though I personally should be unwilling to engage in the biographical fallacy of so literally interpreting his poetry), he would draw the line at adultery because it wounded family integrity, the basis of national vigor. His religious views had the same focus. While he acquiesced in the religious forms of his day, including the quasi-political emperor worship just beginning, he normally did not frequent the temple.

32. C. S. Baldwin, *Ancient Rhetoric and Poetic Interpreted from Representative Works* (New York: Macmillan, 1924), pp. 242-246.

"For him," continues Showerman, "as for Cicero, religion is one of the social and civic proprieties, a necessary part of the national mechanism."[33] Horace dipped elegantly but lightly into life, and his critical theory reflects this. While both he and Aristotle thought that the supreme good was political, their understanding of what this involved varied in proportion to their respectively empirical and more philosophic noetics. This should be remembered when assessing Horace's view of the function of poetry.

Sprinkled throughout Horace's early work, the *Satires,* we find preparatory statements on the function of poetry, developed later in the *Ars Poetica.* He considered satire an important and unique Roman contribution to the Classical tradition, a development of the "old comedy" of Eupolis, Cratinus, and Aristophanes (1.4 1 ff.). Its main function was to correct those at fault, but never with malicious slander or censure. (It will be remembered that Plato and Aristotle disapproved of personal venom as lacking the universal character demanded of literature.) Horace also recognized the appeal of the intuitive insight over abstract moralizing: "*ridiculum acri / fortius et melius magnas plerumque secat res*" (1. 10. 14-15). A similar remark in the *Epistles* recognizes the educative power of poetry that praises great men and sings of heroic times (2.1 116 ff.). Finally, the moral function of poetry is sanctioned in the Inaugural *Odes.*[34]

But Horace's most explicit, sustained, definitive, and highly influential statement about the function of poetry occurs in lines 333-346 of the *Ars Poetica.* His famous please-and-teach formula with its advice to mix the useful with the pleasing (*utile dulci*) occurs here. For centuries it was to be a primer for both schoolboys and men of learning.

---

33. Grant Showerman, *Horace and His Influence* (Boston: Marshall Jones, 1922), pp. 31, 54 ff.

34. Atkins, *Literary Criticism in Antiquity,* II, 58 ff.

Aut prodesse volunt aut delectare poetae
aut simul et jucunda et idonea dicere vitae.
quidquid praecipies, esto brevis, ut cito dicta
percipiant animi dociles teneantque fideles:
omne supervacuum pleno de pectore manat.
ficta voluptatis causa sint proxima veris:
ne quodcumque velit poscat sibi fabula credi
neu pransae Lamiae vivum puerum extrahat alvo.
centuriae seniorum agitant expertia frugis,
celsi praetereunt austera poemata Ramnes:
omne tulit punctum, qui miscuit utile dulci
lectorem delectando pariterque monendo.
hic meret aera liber Sosiis, hic et mare transit
et longum noto scriptori prorogat aevum.

Fairclough's translation in the Loeb Classical Library is as follows:

Poets aim either to benefit, or to amuse, or to utter words at once both pleasing and helpful to life. Whenever you instruct, be brief, so that what is quickly said the mind may readily grasp and faithfully hold: every word in excess flows away from the full mind. Fictions meant to please should be close to the real, so that your play must not ask for belief in anything it chooses, nor from the Ogress's belly, after dinner, draw a living child. The centuries of the elders chase from the stage what is profitless; the proud Ramnes [standing for typical young aristocrats] disdain poems devoid of charms. He has won every vote who has blended profit and pleasure, at once delighting and instructing the reader. That is the book to make money for the Sosii [famous booksellers]; this the one to cross the sea and extend to a distant day its author's fame.[35]

The meaning of this text seems very clear. Horace simply

35. Horace, *Satires, Epistles and Ars Poetica*, ed. H. Rushton Fairclough (Cambridge: Harvard University Press, 1955), pp. 478-479.

43

says that the poet wishes either to please or to teach, to make his poetry either aesthetically appealing or useful; but he is the most successful when he achieves both these ends. At first sight we recognize something of the Aristotelian concern with the significance of poetry and its pleasure. But the context is not that of the *Poetics* at all. One is given three choices: profit, pleasure, and a blend of the two. The context is that of Neoptolemus, a compromise of Greek extremes which favored either one or the other end exclusively. Brink writes: "Neoptolemus' combination of aesthetic and moral effects can scarcely be compared to Aristotle's. He is much more down-to-earth, even trivial. His attitude is *miscuit utile dulci*."[36] While recognizing the direct influence of Neoptolemus, J. Tate also stresses popular Stoic morality as the root of Horace's double function: "On the moral function of poetry we find in Horace simply his account of the conceptions of recent Greek critics (based on the older traditional views), conceptions which, since they were so largely adopted by the Stoics, come to us mingled with a good deal of more or less popular Stoicism." He also understands this function not as binding the poet with moral obligation but rather as a matter of expediency: "He will give moral counsel because the audience, or an important section of the audience, desires it, and it is therefore the best policy."[37] Further, it is easy to recognize another rhetorical parallel to Horace's notion of the function of the poet and his poetry in the traditional function of rhetoric: *docere, delectare,* and *movere.*

That Horace offers the poet three aims for his art, namely profit, pleasure, or a preferred blend of the two, shows his more or less practical sense of the concrete effects of poetry. But that these functions should be considered separable, and hence capable of an extrinsic combination rather than de-

36. Brink, *Horace on Poetry*, p. 57.
37. J. Tate, "Horace and the Moral Function of Poetry," in *Classical Quarterly*, 22 (1928), 65-72, especially 72, 68.

manding an organic union, shows the theoretical distance between his and Aristotle's ideal, and to some extent at least, the distance between Horace the critic and Horace the poet. Plato had separated the functions of pleasure and profit because of his philosophical premises and his ascetical concerns with education. Horace does the same, but because of a more pragmatic, rhetorical approach to his problem. But it is not at all surprising that many Renaissance critics inextricably mingled Horace's *"utile dulci"* with their Platonist habits of thought, as Weinberg, cited earlier, has reminded us.

Unless the elements of profit and pleasure are thought of as organically interrelated, the function of mimesis is misunderstood. The pleasure coming from the least poetic creation is valuable and is actually constituted as pleasure, precisely because the mind is engaged with the poem as a structured insight. And only for this same reason can there be any profit in a poem. Despite the practical and, to some extent, informal purpose of the *Ars Poetica,* Horace, in offering pleasure and profit as alternatives, shows that he does not consider the two as necessarily related in an organic fashion. Further, it is clear from the lines that immediately follow, that this separation is not an oversight. It is repeated five different ways, and rather tellingly when he speaks of the differing tastes of the old and the young. This, surely, is considering poetry in a rhetorical context. In the light of such an explicit and sustained statement, it does not seem quite accurate to couch his please-and-teach formula in terms of a polarity[38] (though, absolutely speaking, the two values involved may well be thought of in this way).

Tate and Atkins interpret the passage substantially as I do.

38. René Wellek and Austin Warren seem to opt for such a polarity in Horace's passage in their *Theory of Literature,* 3rd ed. (New York: Harcourt, Brace, World, 1962), pp. 30-31, though admitting a need to "give the Horatian terms an extension generous enough to encompass Roman and Renaissance creative practice."

Tate says by way of paraphrase: "Some poets aim merely at giving pleasure (*delectare—A.P.* 333), others at the improvement of their readers (*prodesse—Ibid.*). It is the practice of the most successful poets '*simul et jucunda et idonea dicere vitae*' (*A.P.* 334)."[39] After saying much the same, Atkins adds a word about why Horace chose these three ends: "the utilitarian (*utile*) by reason of its uplifting effects, the hedonistic (*dulce*) by the pleasure it afforded, and the two-fold function by its combination of effects." A few pages earlier Atkins tells why he thinks Horace used Neoptolemus as his source: "His positive purpose and his utilitarian views on literature and life were without doubt the main factors in his choice of material."[40]

Pierre Grimal, the French Horatian, and Brink offer quite a different interpretation of this important passage. Grimal, after saying that pleasing and being useful were traditionally accepted as the poet's functions, states what he never proves and, given Horace's text, seems to me incapable of proof: "*Mais, dit Horace, ces deux fonctions ne doivent pas être separées; leur union constitue l'essentiel du rôle assigné au poète. Horace s'appuie ici sur Néoptolème, qui disait lui aussi que le poète doit à la fois 'servir' et 'charmer les âmes.'*" It is less than convincing for Grimal to assert that Horace viewed as essential to the poet's role the union of the two ends, when Horace himself in the very context in question views them as separable and, in fact, separates them. Further, appealing to the context of Neoptolemus in this matter only serves to weaken the argument, given Neoptolemus' pragmatic rhetorical approach to the problem. Grimal rounds out the discussion with a progressive assertion without proof, that Horace has established this essential unity of the two

39. Tate, "Horace," p. 67.
40. Atkins, *Literary Criticism in Antiquity*, II, 73-76.

ends with the words: *"fonction positive du poète . . . la demonstration ayant précédé."*[41]

Brink's final judgment on the meaning of the passage is much the same, though perhaps more informal. Horace, he claims, "believed that (in the language of the schools) poetry aimed neither at moral benefit alone nor at pleasure alone. To say, poets want *simul et jucunda et idonea dicere vitae,* as Philodemus tells us Neoptolemus had done in his Hellenistic terminology, is adequate for the controversies of the schools. And in these terms Horace restates Neoptolemus' compromise. But the practitioner of the arts wants more than that. He wants to be told *how* to 'mix' moral benefit with poetic delight. But the topic does not detain him. The sequel will show that he has better things to offer when he gets away from the textbook."[42] Brink argues from the larger poetic context of the epistle that Horace resolves the presumed either-or conflict into a both-and harmony, as he does the conflicts between wisdom and craft, form and content, and a poet's native and acquired abilities. Doubtless, Horace preferred such a harmony, but nowhere does he relate the two ends intrinsically; and his five-way split of them should, one would think, detain both Horace and his commentators.

From what has been seen of the practical focus of Horace's attention in matters cultural, moral, and poetic, we may describe his noetic as pragmatic and, compared with both Plato's and Aristotle's, relatively thin and superficial. The rhetorical context of his thinking needs firm stress if we are to appreciate the level of his interest in poetry and especially in its function. (And we should remember that the roots of

---

41. Pierre Grimal, *Horace: Art Poétique; commentaire et étude* (Paris: Centre de documentation Universitaire, 1964), pp. 151-153. Grimal rightly follows Horace in applying the please-and-teach formula to the poet. But there seems to be no essential difference in the formula's import whether it is applied to the poet or to poetry; though the contrary is sometimes suggested.

42. Brink, *Horace on Poetry,* pp. 257-258.

his rhetoric have none of the philosophical depth of either Plato's or Aristotle's.) Form, as we have used the word, meaning the pattern of what is real in life and in the poetry which reflects it, must, in the case of Horace, also be conceived of at a relatively superficial level, as harmonizing with the practical focus of his noetic and the rhetorical context of his thought on poetry. Though he seems to have some inkling of the need of Aristotelian probability, as in *Difficile est proprie communia dicere* (*A.P.*, 128), "imitation" is used only in the rhetorical sense of copying Greek exemplars; and the Hellenistic theory of invention, a blend of fancy and fable with real life for the sake of pleasing, replaces the earlier, philosophically conceived mimetic concept: *"ficta voluptatis causa sit proxima veris"* (*A.P.*, 338). Another aspect of "verisimilitude," again more rhetorical than poetic and not far from what is later called "sincerity," appears in *"si vis me flere, dolendum est/primum ipsi tibi"* (*A.P.*, 102–103).

But most important for our purposes is the claim made earlier, that when poetry is thought of in a rhetorical context, its autonomy of function is easily replaced by something very like the suasive function of rhetoric. Given his basic orientation of discussion, Horace is the empirical Aristotle without Aristotle's underlying realism, and Plato the moralist without Plato's philosophic dimensions. Yet this is not to say that Horace is a rigorist, nor that he lacks intuition and charm when he discusses poetry and its function. But his views are too superficially conceived to buttress critically the minimal demands of the function of a Classical mimesis. Such a rhetorically conceived view of poetry habitually turned in this direction, both among the Hellenists and later when Horace's please-and-teach formula became the household word of Medieval, Renaissance, and eighteenth-century critics. Most critics in this tradition lacked Horace's charm and shrewdness when discussing poetry, and, indeed, the more mechanical among them twisted his formula almost out of recognition. Yet the source of this long tradition extending to the end of the eighteenth century is Horace's rhetorical view expressed in the please-and-teach formula. Eventually the relative autonomy of mimesis conceived by Aristotle split into the dichotomy of formalism and moralism that heralded the decay of the tradition.

FORM IN THREE PHASES

Earlier in this Chapter the Classical mind was characterized as outward-going, predominantly centered on the world of objects in a human context, and dependent on it for its basic life and activity. Form, for this mind, was the substantial and intelligible center of what was real. Because the arts were considered a kind of knowledge, they too clustered about the same magnet. It is natural, then, to expect theory about the humane function of the arts to deal with the problem of how form passes from the world of objects to the human mind, and with what purposes it fills in this passage. Ultimately this is to understand both the operation of mimesis and its worth to its audience.

In the opening chapter of the *Poetics* Aristotle proposes to treat the arts under three headings: their *medium* of imitation, the *objects* they imitate, and the *manner* of this imitation. This division suggests a useful pattern for developing the present study. Without being bound by all his categories and distinctions, but rather by following his basic intuitions about mimesis and the reality it imitates, we may profitably consider these three aspects as *three phases of form in a poem,* conceived in analogy with the form imitated in nature. In this way we may evolve a valid and minimally necessary notion of mimesis and its function and achieve a framework in which to evaluate the views of the eighteenth-century critics being studied.

The three phases I shall discuss are the cognitive element, the structural element, and the element of style, corresponding roughly and in general, but with a change in the order used by Aristotle, to "the objects," "the manner," and "the medium" of imitation respectively. They are not to be taken mechanically, nor do they introduce any false separation of "form" and "content."[43] It is hoped, rather, that distinction will unify. It is hoped, too, that Aristotle's realistic noetic and methodology will emerge as the most suitable guide for understanding the nature of mimesis, native to the Greeks and inherited by the tradition they began. Each of these phases reveals one or more aspects of the analogy between form in nature and form in this kind of art, achieved through transformation, thus underlining the truth in Else's claim that for Aristotle "a poet, then, is an *imitator* in so far as he is a *maker*," and my own claim that the reverse is true as well, when properly understood. Against this background, too, the shortcomings of the Platonic and Horatian approaches to poetry and its function will become clear, when these three early polar critical views are reflected by the critics at the end of the tradition.

One final note. The words *didactic, didacticism, moralistic,* and *moralism* are used in a sense generally inimical to the demands of mimesis; *ethical interest* and *moral concern* are used in a sense more germane to it, that is, as interpreting human values and meanings without violating the autonomy of mimesis.

43. My use of this triple division is purely for convenience. Some see "manner" as referring to the mode of performance rather than as referring specifically to the concept of structure or genre. I see no need to enter such a controversy here, for the concept of structure I develop is clearly Aristotelian. What limitations, with respect to his treatment of style, I have to the claim that Aristotle does not separate "form" and "content" will be discussed in Chapter 4.

2

FORM AS THE PROBABLE:
THE COGNITIVE ELEMENT

It is a truism to speak of Classical art as characteristically intellectual. Although it was in no way limited to the interests and activity of the mind, it was surely dominantly associated with it by metonymy. Clarity, form, balance, correctness, irony: all are readily taken as hallmarks of the Classical. Because the Greeks tended to think of the mind as the pilot of the person, they would naturally think of poetry as involving a special form of mental activity. (Τέχνη, we recall, was a power or activity that directed the knowledge of doing or making from the realm of ordered understanding to actual accomplishment.) And even though Plato feared a lack of intellectual control in the poets and their poems, he assessed poetry precisely as a form of knowledge, and Aristotle answered his misgivings under the same rubric.

Mimesis as Meaning

We begin our more detailed investigation of the problem of this study by discussing poetry as a form of knowledge, as cognitive. This tradition presumed that poetry "meant something," with Plato feeling that it really did not mean enough. Yet this is not to say that the cognitive element is another phrase for the "content" of a poem, especially if this is opposed to its "form," as though form were a box or a container. Where the tradition was reduced to formalism or to thinking of poetry as philosophy "dressed up" or "decorated," this separation was accepted; but in such cases, as we shall see, a true notion of mimesis had been lost. To speak of Classical art as "cognitive," then, is to say that it is object-centered, oriented in its inspiration to the world of nature, and of human nature in particular. The Classical poet's lodestar is reality itself; his sensibility is "objective." Aristotle suggests that poetry satisfies both our appetite for imitation and our appetite for harmony (*Poetics,* 1448b). The cognitive element tends to stress the first of these, but not in a separable or distinct way from the second, which tends to express itself in structure. That is why Aristotle proposes to talk about the arts as imitating "objects" and, more sharply, as imitating "according to probability or necessity." Mimetic art feeds upon nature, upon reality, but in a peculiar way. This chapter, then, is concerned with how Aristotle thought form in nature enters poetry or art as a unique kind of knowledge, how this affects the reader or audience, and how eighteenth-century critics understood and dealt with this factor.

It would be misleading to think of mimesis as a kind of knowledge without implying, at least, that this "kind" peculiarly depends upon structure, itself the work of the mind. (Perhaps we too readily tend to refer all kinds of knowledge to science and/or philosophy as their prime analogue.) We must recall that, as Else says, "a poet, then, is an *imitator* in so far as he is a *maker.*" Yet it is just as inadequate to think of structure independently of something structured. Today, especially when speaking of the plastic arts or music, one can be embarrassed by asking "what is meant." Yet in a very deep and large sense this seems to be a necessary question to ask about all art. And the question should not be caricatured into a demand that all art be "representational." In any case, the orientation of the Classical mind toward reality gives a kind of priority or initiative to the cognitive element, though to make this priority absolute would be to make poetry into philosophy or, with Plato, to measure the value of poetry by its "content," its accuracy and fidelity in copying the ideal forms. Yet there is a priority here which reveals something of the objective sensibility of Classical art. But the imitator is maker, truth is beauty, content is form, each through the other.

THE COGNITIVE ELEMENT AS REALISTIC KNOWLEDGE

The first aspect of this cognitive element which we must stress is its realism, the first clue to understanding Classical sensibility. For Aristotle all kinds of knowledge were realistic. The mind was awakened, called into activity and even, in a sense, into being by the things it knew. Randall describes his view well: "Whatever exists has a 'form' or 'essence' by which it can be understood. Whatever occurs has a set of 'reasons why' by which it can be rationally grasped. Whatever is experienced has a set of *archai,* in terms of which human thinking can find it intelligible. These 'forms,' 'reasons why,' and *archai* are made accessible to *nous* through experience, and man's reflection on it. To find them is the aim of human knowledge: to advance from observation, from sense, to reasons why."[1] The process of knowing, then, is instigated in one very important sense by what is known, though as a living process it is essentially immanent and spontaneous. Randall speaks of the contextual nature of this realism: "Thinking is understood in terms of what is thought. There is some object or objective in the environment, in the situation or context, to which the activity is a

1. John H. Randall, *Aristotle* (New York: Columbia University Press, 1960), pp. 97-98.

response, and toward which it is directed. The activity cannot be understood without reference to such an environment or context and to the objective to be found in it."[2]

For Aristotle all reality was a constant becoming, a dynamic achievement of stature. It was a process rhythmically achieving its goal or entelechy. This goal is hinted at as potential in each thing, in the intelligible form, and made manifest in the dynamic process of achievement. Reality, then, is intelligible in its very make-up and manifests this in its dynamic process of becoming, in its very self-achievement. It is easy to see why he thought of finality as the first and most intelligible of the causes.

A man as a knowing animal manifests this same pattern and process of becoming by imitating nature. His knowing comes about in seeing the intelligibility of nature, of which this process is a part. This interpenetration of knower and known is the very process of imitation, of knowing. According to Randall: "In the act of knowing, the power of *nous* to understand, and the power of the world to be understood, receive a common fulfillment, a common operation. Human knowledge becomes one with what the world really is: the intellect, *nous,* becomes itself the intelligible structure of things."[3]

We have said earlier that Aristotle's noetic and methodology were realistic. We now see that this realism is not merely contextual but actually constitutive of his thought. Though it may seem a bit naive, given some modern forms of epistemology, it is very true to say that, granted Aristotle's analysis of knowledge, mimesis as a poetic theory demands a very realistic ontology if it is to thrive or to occur at all. The first step in achieving poetic form is contact with form in nature. This is one reason why Else can say: "Aristotle is a Greek, for whom creation means *discovery* ($\epsilon\H{\upsilon}\rho\epsilon\sigma\iota\varsigma$), the

2. *Ibid.,* p. 66.
3. *Ibid.,* p. 98.

uncovering of a true relation which already exists somehow in the scheme of things."[4] If we remember that Aristotle treated of mimesis primarily (though not exclusively) as drama, the objectivity of the cognitive element makes sharp sense. From its name, drama imitates action, and in its own deep thematic way, it is symbolic action. The "given" quality of human action is its concern. The entire institution of the theater tends to exploit this objective stress. Yet the philosophic basis of this objectivity is even more ultimate and underlies all theater, even though the theater is its most brilliant and expressive metonym. In passing we may also suggest that there is a sense in which, for all the immense advances since Aristotle's day, every healthy poetic theory must respect this basic realism in a transcendent way. Themes must be humanly valid and, to be achieved, they must derive from the "given" quality involved in all experience. And this is a far cry from asking that all art be imitative in the sense of being "representational." Randall has an interesting comment on the analogous situation of finding a point of departure for philosophy:

For Aristotle, "knowing" is not a problem to be solved, but a natural process to be described and analyzed. In the light of our experience of many other approaches to the construing of the fact of knowledge, the approach of Aristotle, it is here submitted, is the only sensible and intelligible, the only fruitful attitude.

Indeed, any construing of the fact of "knowledge," whether Kantian, Hegelian, Deweyan, Positivistic, or any other, seems to be consistent and fruitful, and to avoid the impasses of barren self-contradiction, and insoluble and meaningless problems, only when it proceeds from the Aristotelian approach, and pushes Aristotle's own analyses farther.[5]

4. Gerald F. Else, *Aristotle's Poetics: The Argument* (Cambridge: Harvard University Press, 1957), p. 320.
5. Randall, *Aristotle*, pp. 105-106.

The world of the Renaissance and the Enlightenment saw the beginnings of the impasses Randall speaks of here both in philosophy and in poetic theory.

THE COGNITIVE ELEMENT AS THE PROBABLE

Today it is a commonplace in criticism to distinguish between the truth of fact or science as knowledge that is reportorial of how things are, and the truth of poetry as a way of responding to things. Despite disagreement about what this truth of poetry intimately is, all are agreed that poetry is not tied to mere fact or its analysis. Its precise creativity is manifest in the free manipulation of fact without distortion of poetic meaning. This process, which we shall call transformation, is the key that opens the door of personal vision and releases the "larger" poetic truths about life.

We should note here a characteristic weakness of much literary criticism in antiquity, as well as in the Renaissance and the eighteenth century, namely, a tendency to confuse these two ways of knowing. Aristotle makes a clear distinction between them when he says that poetry deals precisely not with what is actually real or possible, as history and philosophy properly do, but with what is probable. And yet, one reason why his treatment of style in poetry is limited and at times misleading is that he does not follow through with this distinction by applying it to language. We shall see more of this in Chapter 4. Behind this weakness, where it persists down to the end of the eighteenth century, are the philosophical, and especially the epistemological, limitations involved in the otherwise important stress on universality and objectivity, to the *relative* neglect of what in modern times has been recognized as a greater and valid concern for the individual and subjective elements in all knowledge. We shall see more of this in Chapter 5. Those critics who tended to make faulty judgments about the moral "content" of a poem and who treated poetry as if it were rhetoric did so largely because they confused poetic with reportorial knowledge.

Aristotle says it is false to think that poetry differs from history because the poet uses verses rather than prose. "The true difference is that one relates what has happened, the other what may happen. Poetry, therefore, is a more philosophical and a higher thing than history: for poetry tends to express the universal, history the particular." Now the universal is also the goal of philosophy and of the other sciences, so he must explain further. "By the universal I mean how a person of a certain type will on occasion speak or act, according to the law of probability or necessity" (1541b). It is like philosophy in being concerned with the more substantial and permanent human values and motives, yet it does not report essences the way metaphysics is accustomed to. Else says correctly that while Aristotle is answering Plato's slur on the poets for stopping short at appearances or particulars, his universals are not Plato's ideas. For him, metaphysics, physics, and mathematics have only theoretical objects. Poetry has to do with human life, with contingency and approximation. Human action has principles, says Else, "but they are valid only 'for the most part' (ὡς ἐπὶ τὸ πολύ). That in fact is why Aristotle so carefully uses the double formula 'according to probability or necessity' throughout the *Poetics*; for necessity can never be absolute in the sublunar world." It is the business of ethics and politics to expound these human principles.[6]

Is poetry, then, a kind of science of statistics? Aristotle indirectly answers this by describing poetry's probable as a structure, something made, knowledge constructed. The object of the probable includes: "Things as they were or are, things as they are said or thought to be, or things as they

6. Else, *Aristotle's Poetics*, pp. 304-305.

ought to be" (1460b). In this way human experience, human belief, and human ideals or values are all made available through the poem. The structures of artistry must be the norm of success in dealing with details, as long as probability is safeguarded. In 1461a & b we read that accidental factual error, which in real life or in the truth of science would be a fault, may be defended in art either as an insignificant mistake or as a deliberate artistic effect. But an artistic error is not to be tolerated because then the probable is neither well interpreted nor adequately achieved. Here the creative purpose of the poet is considered paramount in order to give artistic existence to the probable. He adds: "With respect to the requirements of art, a probable impossibility is to be preferred to a thing improbable and yet possible." Else notes well that the paradox of the poet being an imitator inasmuch as he is a maker rises to a climax when Aristotle says: "So even if he should chance to 'compose' things that have happened, he is none the less a maker; for there is nothing to prevent some actual events being such as might happen, i.e., being 'possible'; (which is the principle) by virtue of which *he* is their maker." Else comments: "These events are already there, they have already happened, and yet the poet 'makes' them just as much as if he had invented them himself. What the poet 'makes,' then, is not the actuality of events, but their logical structure, their meaning."[7] Finally, we read what

7. Else claims that these comments on improbability and irrationality have been wrenched out of context by some critics, yet the implication that the poet artfully manipulates details to express what is significant is still valid for mimesis. *Aristotle's Poetics,* pp. 624 ff., 321. A further point here for clarity. In a basic and very important sense, Aristotle's poet does not *make* or *constitute* the probable; he *finds* it in the objective order of things. Aristotle is not Kant. Yet in a very significant sense, because the poetic universal, the probable, is not the universal of philosophy, the poet *does make* the probable. This, at root, is why he is a *maker.* By his shaping activity, deep down at its cognitive center, he *transforms* his "given" material without ceasing to be object-oriented and to be strongly under its influence. Otherwise we would be back with Platonic mimesis

offhand we might think quite improbable of the logical
Aristotle: "To justify the irrational, we appeal to what is
commonly said to be. In addition to which, we urge that
the irrational sometimes does not violate reason; just as 'it
is probable that a thing may happen contrary to probability'"
(1461b)!

The upshot of Aristotle's hints is a stress upon the probable
as an artistically achieved insight which possesses the substance of philosophy without its abstraction, and at the same
time the immediacy of human life, which all his commentators find in his treatment of the arts. Else speaks of this
kind of knowledge as "a view of the *typology of human
nature*, freed from the accidents that encumber our vision
in real life."[8] Mure stresses the implication of coherence in
meaning rather than of generality. He makes the point that
we are not looking for Theophrastian *characters* in Aristotle's kind of tragedy, but that we feel rationally "because
we then recognise the true connections underlying the apparent confusion of actual practical life . . . . We exchange
the bare fact for the reasoned fact, and get a glimpse of what
'real' life really is."[9]

The probable, then, is a realistic yet not a factual view of
human concerns, a heightened and intensified insight. Since
Aristotle's time it has been paraphrased as "the humanly
significant," "truth-to-life," "the universal." Perhaps to call

(in its highest form, of imitating the Ideas), and we would have to admit
that in Aristotelian mimesis "matter" and "form," "form" and "content,"
are actually separable. Else's remark that for Aristotle "creation" is
εὕρεσις, finding, must be understood in the context of my claim here. If
the cognitive element in the *Poetics* is thus understood, a strong case can
be made for a deep continuity in poetic epistemology between Aristotle
and Coleridge and the tradition that stems from him. And what I say
here is involved in, or at least germane to, the theory of such modern
critics as Bate, Brooks, Vivas, Wellek, Wheelwright and Wimsatt.

8. Else, *Aristotle's Poetics*, p. 305.

9. G. R. G. Mure, *Aristotle,* corrected ed. (New York: Oxford University
Press, 1964), p. 227.

it "the thematic" might also be valuable, for this phrase specifies as a highly important inheritance from the *Poetics* the concept of poetry as a cognitive, thematic process. Daiches has judged Aristotle's observations on the probable "perhaps the most germinal sentences in the history of criticism";[10] and J. W. H. Atkins has described the idea as a "new position at which is perhaps his most valuable contribution to literary theory, namely, his conception of poetry as a revelation of the permanent and universal characteristics of human life or thought."[11]

TRANSFORMATION IN THE PROBABLE

Ever since theories of creative imagination have been developed, we have become accustomed to thinking of the creative activity as revealing itself through transformation. But it must also be involved in an adequate view of mimesis, for the poet imitates inasmuch as he is a maker. Although this process of transformation is revealed more precisely in what we call structure, the subject of the following chapter, a brief mention of it is needed here. This need is part of the impossibility of separating form and content in an adequate concept of mimesis.

Transformation in a Classical poet will naturally show a different mode of operation and will result in a different kind of poem than in a poet of more subjective sensibility. The use of nature imagery in Shakespeare's Sonnet 73 ("That time of year thou mayst in me behold") differs noticeably from Yeats' in "The Wild Swans at Coole" or even from Keats' in "Ode to Autumn." Yet it is important to see that

10. David Daiches, *Critical Approaches to Literature* (Englewood Cliffs: Prentice-Hall, 1956), p. 39.
11. J. W. H. Atkins, *Literary Criticism in Antiquity* (London: Methuen, 1952), I, 80.

in all instances the process of transformation is active and is responsible for the poem which emerges.

If we consider what is cognitive in the probable not as a Platonic *idea* but as a *view,* a point of view of an outward-going sensibility, it is easy for us to see that mimetic poetry is intellectual without being philosophical and realistic without being reportorial. Sonnet 73 presupposes an audience which accepts a universal human nature with widely agreed-upon views about death and readily imagined views of the similarities between human kind and physical nature. Yet we have neither a meteorological nor a medical report, but a poem. In Classical science or philosophy the *idea* is completely controlled by the objects dealt with, and hence content exhausts the element of form. But in the poem the *view,* at home with form in nature and filled with conviction of its ultimate value, is in control of what is cognitive, and hence structures all its contours to achieve the probable. The poet imitates inasmuch as he is a maker.

Transformation in mimetic poetry had great variety. Aristotle described the probable as dealing with "things as they were or are, things as they are said or thought to be, or things as they ought to be." The Classical mind, characteristically open to the rich plenitude of nature, sought this richness in the intelligible fruitfulness of form. What was "according to probability or necessity" was open to the active foraging of the mind. Elaborating, heightening, developing, perfecting through the artistry of the mind the implications of form was the central concern of the poet. This has too often simply been called "idealization," as though the poet were expected to show human values in their perfect, Platonic form. Rather we should recall the basic epistemological claim which Randall makes for Aristotle's contextual thinking, if we are to understand the probable correctly: "In the act of knowing, the power of *nous* to understand, and the power of the world to be understood, receive a common fulfillment, a common operation."[12] It is not so much the presenting of ideals, abstractions, or schemes, as it is the rich understanding of form. For this reason I prefer to call this process "ideation," a process which presents intensified understanding through structures entirely aimed at this end. The stress is on the quality of the work of art, measured by its intense coherence and intelligibility, rather than on presenting a perfect copy or an ideal. Ideation is the process involved in forming a *view*.

THE PROBABLE AS REPRESENTATIVE REALITY

It may be of some value at this point to say a word about the mode of existence of the poem in this system. René Wellek's excellent article on the problem in the context of a more complicated modern situation is quite Aristotelian in its basic claims.[13] I bring the subject up at all because of the Platonic tendency to fuse being and thought (a difficulty experienced by extreme idealistic theorists of our own day, but deriving from a reverse Platonic spin that turns philosophy into art, rather than art into philosophy), and because of a tendency some find among the Chicago Critics to treat mimesis as a thing more than as a symbol. Plato's dialectic in judging poetry reflects this tendency where the ontological value of an imitation is judged in direct proportion to how close a copy of the original its content is. John Dennis uses this same norm in judging the pre-eminence of all religious poetry over any other kind. Plato makes the carpenter a better artist than the poet. One difficulty that such critics as Wimsatt have with the Chicago Critics is that for the latter mimesis is given a reality something like that of a chair. This

12. Randall, *Aristotle*, p. 98.
13. René Wellek, "The Mode of Existence of a Literary Work of Art," in *Southern Review,* 7 (1942), 735-754.

second kind of "reification" is also reflected in Dennis' demand for poetic justice in a play, where a culprit must be punished before its end. Otherwise he will surely go Scot-free, since God cannot punish him in the last reckoning![14]

From what has already been said about the probable, it should be clear that it is realistic only inasmuch as it reveals or represents real values, distilled meanings, or the universal as a poetic view: what is seen as meaningful in an existential context, yet transformed, and hence as transcending the particular limits of this context. This existence has been called real in an *intentional way* by St. Thomas, and the concept is used by Maritain in explaining his own view of how emotion enters a poem: "I use the word 'intentional' in the Thomistic sense, reintroduced by Brentano and Husserl into modern philosophy, which refers to the purely tendential existence through which a thing—for instance, the object known—is present, in an immaterial or suprasubjective manner, in an 'instrument'—an idea for instance, which, in so far as it determines the act of knowing, is a mere immaterial tendency or *intentio* towards the object."[15]

The probable, then, is real only as it *represents,* not in any ontological manner, not in the way a chair, a bed, or a building might be real. To be sure, there is a structural thingness about a poem, but this is *for* its meaning, in fact concretely it *is* its meaning. Further, this pattern of meaning leaves a material warranty of its thingness on a printed page, on a stage, disturbs the air waves and the brain cells of its audience. But it remains, in René Wellek's words, a meaningful system of norms to be fulfilled when experienced,

14. See W. K. Wimsatt's discussion of the problem of the Chicago Critics in *The Verbal Icon* (Lexington: University of Kentucky Press, 1954), p. 50. See also John Dennis, *The Critical Works of John Dennis,* ed. E. N. Hooker (Baltimore: Johns Hopkins Press, 1939-1943), I, 183, 7, 19-21.

15. Jacques Maritain, *Creative Intuition in Art and Poetry* (New York: Pantheon, 1953), p. 120.

and this only according to the potential of each reader: "Thus, the real poem must be conceived as a system of norms [meanings, de Rougemont's well-known "calculated trap for meditation"] realized only partially in the actual experience of its many readers. Every single experience (reading, reciting, and so forth) is only an attempt—more or less successful and complete—to grasp this set of norms or standards."[16]

This status helps clarify why mimesis is relatively autonomous, for pleasurable contemplation. A poem tells us about life intensely without being pragmatically ordered to a further rhetorical purpose. Sidney, though not always systematically consistent in this matter, expresses Aristotle's answer to Plato's charge that the poets tell lies and thus highlights the real, contemplative autonomy of mimesis without being in any way escapist: "Now, for the Poet, he nothing affirmes, and therefore never lyeth."[17] This highlights the special detachment generally claimed by the poetic mind in order to be free to transform its materials. Though immersed in nature as the climate and object of poetry, the poet must exercise an independence of movement in order to function properly and, paradoxically, to be able to represent the real. When communicated to the poem, this detachment is the basis of the relative autonomy already claimed for it. Photographic realism and pragmatic moralism are inimical to this view of art. Aristotle was aware of the enmity. Yet his tendency to think too univocally about the "fine" and the "practical" arts, if followed too systematically, could obscure a poem's "reality" and its consequent autonomy. Precisely because the fine arts "make" meaning rather than things, because they are concerned with structuring views and insights and not simply with the production of artifacts in general, they must be distinguished from the practical arts.

16. Wellek, "The Mode of Existence," p. 745.
17. *Elizabethan Critical Essays*, ed. G. Gregory Smith (London: Oxford University Press, 1904), I, 184.

The tendency of the Chicago Critics to apply the Aristotelian philosophic concepts of matter and form to drama and poetry makes them "too Aristotelian." This, I believe, is what Wimsatt has in mind when he criticizes how they deal with language in poetry. But Aristotle's sense of the probable in the *Poetics* secures him from this shortcoming. The probable is realistic only in a representative way, and hence mimesis is autonomous.[18]

NATURE IN THE PROBABLE

The kind of knowledge I have assigned to the probable, and the kind of detachment claimed for the poet in forming it, demand an adequate object. This object is nature, the reality imitated. To be adequate it must consist of more than the surface of life, for the probable deals with the deeper, permanent values which men think important. For the same reason it must be more than what is mechanically derived from a more or less photographic observation. Men's motives and characters, the causality, to use a favorite word of Aristotle, that is the root and principle of human activity, rather than the surface of human life, must comprise what is meant by the probable, if mimesis is to remain vital. Form must be fetched from an adequate depth in the contextual experience already spoken of. It would be theoretically handy and satisfying if we could say that Aristotle based this depth of form on his *Metaphysics*. But this is neither true nor necessary. Randall, among others, has warned against making Aristotle a Thomist. He calls him an empiricist, but his description of what this means surely is not the mechanistic and merely photographic notion we derive from Locke. Deriving intel-

18. Randall, *Aristotle*, p. 278; Wimsatt, *The Verbal Icon*, pp. 62–63. This point will be discussed more fully in Chapter 4. It must be remembered that Aristotle thought of the poet as "making plots," not poems, which partly explains his limits when speaking of the place of language in a play.

lectual knowledge from sensation is not considered a contradiction nor is sensation at best a barrier to such knowledge,
as Locke thought. The word empirical refers largely to the
methodology of contextual knowing, though it also prescribes a limit to grasping Platonic forms in Aristotle's system. "Aristotle is opposed," adds Randall, "to traditional
'Empiricism,' with its assumption of a world completely
without structure. This logical realism of Aristotle places
him at the center of the 'classic tradition.' That tradition
needs criticism and extension, but it is important to know
what is being criticized."[19]

More directly in the context of the *Poetics,* Gerald Else
has some balanced and enlightening things to say about
what is being imitated as "nature" in Aristotle's view of the
probable: "In saying that poetry is 'more philosophical' Aristotle does not say that it *is* philosophy . . . In his scheme,
metaphysics, the science of Being, and its congeners physics
and mathematics . . . are a special group of 'theoretical'
sciences; and the theoretical sciences have theoretical objects
only. Human life and action belong to the practical sphere
and have nothing to do with metaphysics." The principles
of human life have to do with "probability or necessity."
They are not the scientific principles of the theoretical
branches of learning.

Further, with respect both to the ultimate cause of tragedy
in something like Fate and to the ultimate secrets of life,
Aristotle is deliberately silent, as he is when he discusses
politics or ethics. And yet, as Else makes clear, Aristotle's
limitation of tragedy to the hero's reactions and his failure to
deal with what happens to him from outside the realm of
human events, the very thing to which he is reacting, is inadequate theory. "He defines tragedy as an imitation of an
action, but speaks of it only as 'telling of' the universals: the

19. Randall, *Aristotle,* pp. 95-97, 299.

word μίμησις does not appear. What it 'tells of' are the building blocks that fit together to constitute the whole; but what it imitates is the whole, and in this case the whole is more than the sum of its parts."[20] This limitation of Aristotle's system, which is due to his notion of a closed universe in which God's influence cannot be known, does not rob mimesis of its essential need to feed upon a strongly metempirical nature in order to be and to remain viable. Aristotle's notion of the probable, of men's motives and characters, and of human causality demand of the human scene a third dimension of depth well beyond Lockean empiricism. But more important still, the Greek experience of successful tragedies, which regularly took into account the divine motivation on which Aristotle is silent, and the religious element in Greek life both take this depth of focus for granted. Asserting that Aristotle did not completely systematize the whole Greek experience is quite another thing from denying its impact on the actual work of the poets.

Hence, even without the help of a systematic analysis of the ultimate motives of tragedy to bolster the assertion, it is quite necessary to state that mimesis needs the deeper reaches of human nature as the object of its imitation. I may add that the long experiences of the Christian centuries surely fed upon a deeply metempirical sense of what was real, nourished in an atmosphere of vigorous faith and reason. Later in this chapter we shall see that many eighteenth-century critics lost a sense of this need when speaking of mimesis, owing in great part to a radically altered concept of human nature derived from the new sciences and philosophies.

It is a truism to say that in its richest achievements the Classical literary tradition focused attention upon human nature, upon man's thoughts, motives, and ambitions. Other "things" were imitable only in their human context. The

20. Else, *Aristotle's Poetics*, pp. 305-307.

often-quoted *"Homo sum"* of Terence shows this preoccupation in antiquity, and Pope's "proper study" shows the tradition still alive some twenty centuries later. The main concern of the *Poetics* was drama and the epic, genres dealing with the larger problems of human life. Among the other arts, Greek sculpture dealt almost exclusively with the human corporeal form as expressive of the human spirit, while music and the dance sought to embody the ethical themes of myth and legend. This interest in a human subject matter gave the arts a peculiarly humanist stress, and the human skill they manifested, despite the experience of failure in tragedy, made them eminently worthwhile. Man's mind, unique in all the world, was the pilot of his life and made him apex of a world that could destroy him. It made him uniquely capable of self-reflection and of communion with other minds. Its peculiar power of universalizing could distill what was significant and thus nourish and fashion his personal and social life according to the ideal of perfection perceivable in nature. And so he was the endless subject of his own wonder and enquiries and, practically, the exclusive subject of his own art. The Greek idea that virtue was closely associated with knowledge naturally dictated the ethical possibilities of the arts for serious humane education. As a consequence we have the uniquely Greek ideal of *paideia,* centered largely on the humanism of the arts, a system thoroughly human in matter, process, and purpose.

Centuries later Dr. Johnson, foremost of the English humanists, frequently voiced this traditional concern. "A blade of grass is always a blade of grass, whether in one country or another . . . Men and women are my subjects of inquiry; let us see how these differ from those we have left behind." "He who thinks reasonably must think morally." And again, "We are perpetually moralists, but we are geometricians only by chance. Our intercourse with intellectual nature is necessary; our speculations upon matter are voluntary, and at leisure."[21] Even with the changes and importance of modern scientific knowledge, this humane point of view is still the center of our interests, as it was for the mimetic tradition.

THE PROBABLE AS COMMUNION

Such serious humanistic concern postulates an audience. Some feel uneasy when art is related to communication. If this is meant in the often vulgar sense of mass-media publicity, or even as a more polite rhetoric, the concern is understandable. Allen Tate's distinction between communication and communion, the latter applying to the shared insight of poet with audience, fits the tradition of mimesis well.[22] This is precisely what is meant by pleasurable contemplation. A potential audience suffices. Communion closes the circuit begun in nature under the poet's agency.

Most opposition to orienting a poem to an audience tends to derive either from a fear of rhetoricizing poetry or from a dislike of affective criticism. Both these concerns are valid when propaganda or a false psychologism is involved. But romantic talk about the poet speaking to himself in any other sense than that which would secure the intuitive "uselessness" of poetry is not worth considering. Given the social nature of man, it seems idle to split hairs about whether art in its very make-up has an intrinsic orientation to the audience. This seems especially true of mimesis, with its objective character and serious intent and its built-in safeguards against becoming mere propaganda.

For Plato and Aristotle, a sense of purpose or finality was the ultimately intelligible measure of a thing (Aristotle

21. Hester L. Piozzi, *Anecdotes of the Late Samuel Johnson, LL.D.*, ed. S. C. Roberts (Cambridge: Cambridge University Press, 1925), p. 66; Samuel Johnson, *Lives of the English Poets*, ed. George B. Hill (Oxford: Clarendon, 1905), I, 99-100 ("Milton").

22. Allen Tate, "The Man of Letters in the Modern World," in *The Forlorn Demon* (Chicago: Regnery, 1953), pp. 3-17, especially 12-14.

called it the most important of the four causes of his system). This is natural to expect in systems where being and meaning were co-ordinate with each other, each in its own way specifying the other: what was real was intelligible, and vice versa. Further, as we have seen, the method for achieving this finality will take its character and cue from a notion of what is intelligible, form, and from "where" it resides, either in experience or in ultimates. Plato's idealistic method saw only one goal for the various human efforts, the most effective achievement of the eternal forms. Hence his idealistic singleness of purpose, energized by the forms as perfect being, swept the entire human scene along in its own undifferentiated finality. Poetry, then, had value not because of any unique determination or proper finality, but because of what help it could contribute in achieving the forms. It would naturally become a rhetoric for this moral ascent to the forms.

On the other hand, Aristotle's method, deriving from a close sense of context, intent upon the evolving forms in the experienced world of becoming, would recognize and account for many proximate finalities on the way toward the ultimate finality of wisdom. But subordination was not so much a matter of means-to-an-end as of a further fulfillment of things in a reasonable universe. Entelechy, or purpose, is the full stature of a thing, its fulfillment, its fruition, its plenitude. Evolving form becomes its goal, and the goal is recognized in the process of becoming by the contours of its activity, which are intelligible in their dynamism. This, basically, is why autonomy is at the heart of all Aristotelian thought, and especially in Aristotle's view of knowledge.

In all kinds of knowing, for Aristotle, there is a two-fold autonomy. Considering the object orientation of his noetic and the wonder with which it starts both poet and philosopher on their ways, we recognize a prevailing sense of "the given" about things. They are there prior to our knowing them, not only in time but by their very nature. This is why all knowledge is *essentially* imitation. The Judeo-Christian sense of the gratuity of the Creation is a deeper and more religious awareness of the same quality, which is nevertheless a very important element in all Greek thought. The second autonomy is the sheer fruition of knowing, the higher aspect of the life of *nous* or reason, whereby, as Randall puts it, reason is "an end in itself, the supreme 'for what' or *hou heneka*. The best life is the life of sheer knowing . . . This is the satisfaction of the supreme desire with which man is endowed by nature, the desire to know." This two-fold autonomy reveals the world that separates the Greek idea behind liberal learning and the idea of knowledge as power that, in Pieper's phrase, aims to make us "masters and owners of nature," which he claims was the hallmark of the Cartesian revolution. Aristotle, of course, inherited this notion from Plato, though Plato unfortunately forgot it when speaking of poetry.[23]

Aristotle has been accused of being an "affective critic," one who specifies and measures the finality of a poem by its emotional or pleasurable effect upon its audience. Butcher expresses the problem as follows: "To those familiar with modern modes of thinking it may seem a serious defect in the theory of Aristotle that he makes the end of art to reside in a pleasurable emotion, not in the realization of a certain objective character that is necessary to the perfection of the work. An artistic creation, it may be said, is complete in itself; its end is immanent, not transcendental. The effect that it produces, whether that effect be immediate or remote, whether it be pleasure or moral improvement, has nothing

23. Randall, *Aristotle,* pp. 270-271. See also Edwin Muir, *The Estate of Poetry* (Cambridge: Harvard University Press, 1962), pp. 106-107, for a report on Pieper's view.

to do with the object of it in its essence and inmost character."[24]

The same difficulty is implied in the following passage by Richard McKeon: "A poem is 'made,' and it possesses, therefore, a unity and an order which are not dependent on the truth or falsity of any statement it contains or on the moral consequences to which it may lead; for its form, if it is a poem, is self-contained, and its 'likeness' is not a repetition or copy of a natural object, such as the action of a man, but their presentation in the distinct and heightened necessity and probability achieved by the use of the poetic medium."[25]

It is quite true that for Aristotle a thing in the real order has its fulfillment in its own perfection. By this very token, however, one aspect of this perfection, which indeed entirely pervades it, is the thing's intelligibility, because it is intelligible by its being. Now it is in this sense that contemplation is the native end of all things knowable. It may not be intrinsic in the limited sense used in the *Physics* or the *Politics* referred to by Butcher and implied in the passage quoted above, but if it is not metaphysically intrinsic to things to be known, then our only alternatives are idealism or absolute skepticism—hardly Aristotelian choices! But if for Aristotle pleasurable contemplation is the goal of all knowledge, it is peculiarly so in the case of poetry. For a poem is a "thing" only in the sense that it is a meaningful structure. And, it will be recalled, structure is explicitly given as the cause of this pleasure. It does not exist formally in any other order than that of poetic structure. It is a peculiar kind of reality whose entire being is to mean. The self-identity of the structured probable, achieving as it does the larger sense of perma-

24. S. H. Butcher, *Aristotle's Theory of Poetry and Fine Art,* ed. John Gassner, 4th ed. (New York: Dover, 1951), pp. 207 ff.
25. Richard McKeon, *Thought, Action and Passion* (Chicago: University of Chicago Press, 1954), p. 113.

nence by enshrining the individual, concrete, and empirical character of what it imitates, is what we call today the *concrete universal,* equally meaningless for any purposes of propaganda as for any purposeless wasting of its fragrance on the desert air of noncontemplation or noncommunion. Pleasure, then, in the *Poetics* is stressed as an end not in any "affective" sense that would violate the intrinsic finality just discussed, but rather to indicate that it is not didactic or rhetorical in nature. In fact the autonomy of structure is buttressed rather than weakened by this claim for autonomy of function. This solution also emphasizes the weakness Wimsatt has noticed in Chicago Aristotelianism, namely, that of making a poem a "thing," too reified, and of treating it as if it were governed by the laws of physics. The passage I have quoted above from McKeon seems to share the same difficulty, but, paradoxically enough, by making the cognitive element of mimesis much less realistic than it was for Aristotle and consequently overreifying the function of language.[26] At all events, it seems to me that Aristotle basically wishes to stress the mature pleasurable contemplation we have been discussing as the central and characteristic function of poetry. What other "uses" it may have should not violate this autonomy.[27]

By the same token, in spite of the problem connected with katharsis, I find it difficult to think of Aristotle as an "affective critic," or to find "affective" Coleridge's fumbling to define poetry in terms of pleasure, as Wimsatt in another context does. Unlike the more typical and thoroughgoing "affective critics," they both secure the autonomy of structure—and Aristotle most clearly so—without an intrinsic dependence upon its effects; at worst Coleridge seems to be attempting to define structure in terms of its effects.[28]

26. Wimsatt, *The Verbal Icon*, p. 50. See below, p. 149.
27. Butcher, *Aristotle's Theory*, pp. 198 ff.
28. Wimsatt, *The Verbal Icon*, pp. 59–61. I am thinking of Coleridge's

But the Renaissance and eighteenth-century view of the function of mimesis was enshrined in the Horatian formula. What Platonic and Aristotelian elements were funneled into it had lost the philosophic taste of their sources. The rhetorical, moralistic tone of the view was a caricature of Plato's moral idealism, unsatisfactory as this had been; and what traces there were of Aristotle's stress on pleasure centered a good bit upon style. If one must relate the Horatian formula to the function of the probable, one may say that poetry should please by teaching. But the tendency was to reverse the formula, pointing to a rhetorical understanding of poetry. In any shape the formula reveals an unhappy approach to the purer notion of the function of mimesis. Teaching has overtones of indoctrination, whereas what is intended is vision. This vision could and did supply the mind with rich insights into ethical values, but not at the expense of its autonomy, a significant aspect of its peculiar power.

The Changing Concept of "Nature"

We have seen that mimesis must feed upon the form found in nature and that this form must be metempirical and deeply humane. The world imitated is the world of human affairs and motives, reaching well below the appearances on the surface of life, and the world of inanimate nature was important only as context for this humane world. We should expect the twenty-some centuries that intervened between Aristotle and the eighteenth century in England to bring about many changes in this concept of nature to be imitated in mimesis. Lovejoy has distinguished more than sixty uses

famous chapter XIV of the *Biographia* and of his "On Poesy or Art," which, though genetic by modern standards, surely imply, at least, a concern for structure that does not fit truly "affective criticism."

of the word "nature" in eighteenth-century England, a multiplicity which suggests deep change and, conceivably, the confusion we associate with most periods of marked transition. It would be impossible to analyze this multiplicity in detail, but we can perceive a recognizably changed noetic at work in most critical thinking of the time. It derives from a radically altered view of the universe and of man's place in it, developed in the various phases of the new science and its philosophy. The critic's concept of nature and of its poetic imitation undergoes radical alteration. In fact, mimesis as outlined in the previous pages is largely lost sight of, and eventually the idea as a guiding one for understanding poetry and literature is replaced by notions deriving from the Romantic "sensibilities."

While these fresh departures were welcome ingredients in the change, what was lost in the tradition of intellect might well be mourned. It is one of the ironies of cultural history that the Neoclassical decades, often self-styled as the ultimate refinement of the Renaissance Classical revival, should achieve the ultimate collapse of the Classical tradition and that the instrument of this destruction should be the very power thought of as the architect of this edifice, the human reason. It is a paradox that a culture professing so thoroughly the Classical ideal should within the matter of a few decades lose hold of the master Classical idea of reason and objectivity. And it seems the ultimate in the parody of reason that the quest for certainty and clarity should be the source of so much distrust of the human mind.

The many factors at work here are well known and documented in the history of ideas, but a compact summary of them should help us understand the changed concept of "nature" involved in most critical thinking about mimesis and its function at the time. What was considered a Neoclassical age of reason, an age marking the humane triumph of the mind over the world about us, was actually an age dominated by a cosmological view, one which measured man by his context rather than the other way about. Despite its motive of freeing man's mind from the errors of the past, of making understanding instead of authority a norm of true knowledge—both oversimplified statements of the problem and of the answers given—the prevalent climate of mind was that of a cosmological rationalism, one which took its cue from the spirit of the new science. It effectively replaced Classical and Christian humanism as the predominant Western view and was a potent factor in dislodging mimesis as a viable theory of poetry and the arts. What happened to the concept of nature in this climate is of direct interest, then, to our study. I suggest three major manifestations of this cosmological rationalism influencing this critical thinking. These are, first, the development of mathematical and physical sciences as a major directive of philosophic thought; second, the growth of interest in cosmological theodicies; and third, the elaboration of theories of human life issuing directly from this cultural matrix. Together these three currents of thought swept man from his central position in the universe, and with him Classical and Christian humanism as the dominant philosophical and cultural force in the West.

At the risk of oversimplifying a complicated situation, I suggest that the dominant and limiting character of the thinking which shaped this cosmological noetic was its univocal quality, an inability or unwillingness to cope with the analogies everywhere present in human life, both because of man's situation as a creature of God and as a mysterious blend of matter and spirit. It caused men to think of all areas of reality as if in one line, without due consideration of the multiple transcendences involved. Most vital philosophies of the West had produced—and still produce—a dualism of one sort or another, precisely in order to cope with this complexity. Josef Pieper, speaking of the intellectual basis of liberal education in the tradition of the Greeks and of the

Scholastics, to which the eighteenth century was remotely heir, says:

> The Middle Ages drew a distinction between the understanding as *ratio* and the understanding as *intellectus*. *Ratio* is the power of discursive, logical thought, of searching and of examination, of abstraction, of definition and drawing conclusions. *Intellectus,* on the other hand, is the name for the understanding in so far as it is the capacity of *simplex intuitus,* of that simple vision to which truth offers itself like a landscape to the eye. The faculty of mind, man's knowledge, is both of these things in one, according to antiquity [with Plato and Aristotle as its spokesmen] and the Middle Ages, simultaneously *ratio* and *intellectus*; and the process of knowing is the action of the two together. The mode of discursive thought is accompanied and impregnated by an effortless awareness, the contemplative vision of the *intellectus*.[29]

Inside the Christian tradition faith would be more akin to *intellectus* and theology a blend of both. In the noetic formed by the time of our study, *ratio* received overwhelming stress in philosophy, science, and even in discussions of Christian belief and behavior.[30] Analogy found very little favor in such a climate. The various levels of reality, which traditionally had been thought of as different but related, were now literally leveled; and, ironically, for all the tendency to think of them in an univocal way, they were strangers. God, man as body and soul, and the universe were thought of as if in a cosmological continuum, and *ratio* did most of the thinking. This led to an intellectual climate in which knowledge was valued more as power than as vision. As a consequence, methodical skepticism became the ironic pattern for the mind's activity. With mathematical clarity and certainty con-

---

29. Josef Pieper, *Leisure the Basis of Culture* (New York: Pantheon, 1952), pp. 33-34.

30. Walter J. Ong, s.j., has studied this problem at great length in *Ramus, Method, and Decay in Dialogue* (Cambridge: Harvard University Press, 1958).

stituting the practically universal norm of knowledge, the several levels of reality were appraised in a way fit only for scientific investigation. Hence the humane context of both microcosm and macrocosm tended to pale, and the Classical and Christian climates of mystery and finality were replaced by merely cosmological concerns. The mind thus became a tool for the discursive possession of things, not an eye opening upon the landscape. In such a climate it was natural for mimesis to lose its vitality.

Especially since the advent of Christian thought, analogy in being, among beings, and even among the various grades of reality inside a single being (the human body and soul, for example) was deemed necessary in order to avoid contradiction, agnosticism, or a doctrine of "two truths." Even in an expanding universe physics will always remain only physics and hence will need some metempirical insight to keep it humanely meaningful and, indeed, intelligible at all. Yet fascination with mass, gravity, and number elevated physics and mathematics to a realm of absolute science, thus filling the contemporary vacuum created by a decline in adequate philosophy. This substitution gave the new point of view the ascendancy formerly held by Classical and Christian humanism. Secondly, no matter how our knowledge of the physical universe grows, God does not cease to transcend it by his otherness and his constant creativity. Yet we have, for example, the odd conception of space as a divine attribute in the otherwise admirable efforts of Boyle and Henry More to save God's existence in a mechanized world. Finally, human knowledge, if it is to be counted knowledge at all, must in some way transcend its object, no matter how important the object looms in experience. Yet we are faced with the theories of Hobbes and Descartes that imprisoned the soul in a material corner of the brain, incapable of mastering the giant of its own creation, the new science; or which at best gave it a patchwork rescue either of a blind assertion of piety or of mere "common sense." Synthesis was sorely needed to absorb the sudden and invigorating conquest of the geometric and physical aspects of the universe, but it was not forthcoming. The mechanical dialectic of the univocal made it impossible; instead we find the irony of systematic dissolution in the name of scientific unity, surely a parody of analogy, the odd marriage of clarity and skepticism which characterized the Enlightenment mind.

This new scientism had a two-fold current, the one predominantly mathematical, the other experimental and positive in nature and method. The two met in England when God said, "Let Newton be," and all was light! Thereafter, through Locke, Hume, and the Associationists, England became full heir to this two-fold tradition.

THE NEW SCIENCE AND NATURE

(a) *Mathematical Considerations.* It is hard to overestimate the importance of Copernicus' new astronomy. It was figuratively as well as literally world-moving. It found psychological acceptance in the shifting and widening centers of intellectual interest of his day. But in itself it offered a much more simplified geometric figuration of the universe, with the sun at its center, than the older Ptolemaic system. Without denying the physical nature of the heavens, Copernicus enhanced the contemporary tendency to look for mathematical clarity and simplicity in the complexities of the real world. The Aristotelian physics that had held sway in Europe until this time was anthropomorphically naive in its theory of fixed bodies, its overfacile specific finalities, and its tendencies toward a-prioristic and even theological reasonings. We need not be surprised that the learned world should shift to the new system, especially because it was truer, surely, than what it replaced. But the tendency in the wake of these discoveries to substitute astronomy and physics for philosophy poses a cultural problem. Two important implications for the fate of humanism arose from this tendency. First, the newly grasped immense importance of space and of the universe tended to minimize the stature and importance of man. Because the world was no longer the center of the universe, neither, most likely, was man. Secondly, the passion for mathematical clarity began to assert itself outside its proper sphere and to shatter the stubborn mysteries of human life.[31]

Kepler developed the tradition that Copernicus had begun in the three following ways. First, he emphasized an inner mathematical causality consisting in the underlying geometric harmony discoverable in observed facts, as opposed to the previously predominant interest in specific finalities allied to a more physical concept of the nature of things. It was a shift from asking "why" to asking "how." Secondly, he considered the physical world exclusively quantitative. Things differed in number, rather than in quality. He also revived from ancient atomic skepticism the distinction between primary and secondary sensibles. Thirdly, he claimed that the only certain knowledge was that of mathematical relationships.[32] It is clear where this trend of thought was leading despite his personal religious convictions.

Galileo added greater exactness to Kepler's conception of a mathematically ordered universe by exploring anew the problem of motion. Though his method was more experimental than Kepler's, it was still mathematical. It consisted in translating perceived phenomena into their mathematical equivalents with the help of the newly invented algebra, in demonstrating their relative mathematical significance, and in experimenting to find a more complete proof of his math-

31. Edwin A. Burtt, *The Metaphysical Foundations of Modern Physical Science*, 2nd rev. ed. (London: Kegan Paul, Trench, Trübner, 1932), pp. 26–35.

32. *Ibid.*, pp. 53–57.

ematical hypotheses. By exploiting the concepts of figure, weight, motion, and extension in mathematical interrelationships, he could explain the physical universe. The older qualitative and finalistic concepts of Aristotelian physics were explained as deceptive, subjective, and secondary qualities of sensation, not of things sensed. He furthered Kepler's distinction by claiming objective reality only for those qualities called primary. Through these steps, man was moved out of the world of nature because he was mathematically unintelligible. His life of pleasures, colors, and sounds was subjective. His ability to discover the physical world was his only contact with it, and it did not make him in any way superior to its mathematical glories.[33] The problem of knowledge raised here will be discussed later in more detail. Now we should note that man is alienated not only from the universe but from his own mind and that this profoundly affected the Enlightenment noetic. Also, it is too seldom noted that the modern problem of knowledge had its source in the new science, rather than in any strictly philosophic context. Its being posited in mechanical rather than in human and finalistic terms had until relatively recent times prejudiced its effective discussion.

It is interesting to note that these three leaders in the new astronomy and physics were profoundly influenced by Plato's *Timaeus,* the only Platonic text known to the early Middle Ages and one which received renewed attention in the Renaissance revival among the anti-Peripatetics. This document, with a strong Pythagorean cast to it, gives Plato's view of the world as mathematical and geometric, and of the ideality of space. It reveals another aspect of his idealistic methodology and reasserts the estrangement of Plato's climate of thinking from what we have claimed as a necessary environment for mimesis and the traditional humanist view

33. *Ibid.,* pp. 64-65, 70-72, 77-78, 197-198.

of the art.[34] Even the Neoplatonism of the Renaissance with its richer confidence in the concrete, the only viable philosophy at the time this new cosmological noetic was forming, gave little real support to contemporary poetic theory, in need of an ally to rally forces against the new scientism. This will be clear when we discuss certain of the critics who were Platonist in their convictions.

One further step in this tradition was needed to complete the divorce of man from the world. This was supplied by Descartes' opposition of the *res extensa* to the *res cogitans*. Matter and spirit had no inner affinity for him. When they met, either for general activity or more specifically for knowledge, it was accomplished by an extrinsic order prearranged by divine disposition. Descartes' passion for mathematical clarity pervaded his system and prompted his emphasis upon the methodology of thought, often at the expense of its content. More specifically, his stress on the primary qualities of sensation to the neglect of the secondary, and hence his distrust of the vitality of sensation itself, turned his criteria of knowledge inward toward his famed "clear and distinct ideas" to augment his primary certitude of *"cogito ergo sum."* Finally, his localizing the soul in a small portion of the brain literally and figuratively imprisoned it and emphasized rather than solved the problem of knowledge.[35]

(b) *Empirical Considerations.* The second current of this new scientific thought, empiricism, was most pronounced in England. More than a trace of the empirical bent of mind appeared as far back as Roger Bacon, Scotus, and Ockham. But its modern, more mechanistic energy begins with Francis Bacon, whose thought was to change for centuries the face of European education and learning. For our purposes his achievement is two-fold. First, as F. H. Anderson observes

34. *Ibid.,* pp. 43, 47, 197.
35. *Ibid.,* pp. 108-109.

in his *Philosophy of Francis Bacon*, "It is Bacon's avowed intention to merge metaphysics with physics and promulgate a materialistic philosophy." Bacon identifies, Anderson continues, "learning with philosophy and philosophy with empirical science. The substance of learning becomes experimental knowledge, and the instrument of education becomes technical information for the satisfaction of man's need through the invention of 'works.' "[36] His philosophy was "designed to force, once and for all, a definite parting of the ways between philosophical learning, with its maxims, deductive demonstration, ontology and meditation, on the one hand, and, on the other, experimental philosophy, with its inductive observation of facts and things, its assignment of primacy to natural history, its distrust of logical principles, its fruition in useful inventions and great mechanical works, and its search from the beginning to the end for the processes, schematisms, and laws of operation in matter."[37] Secondly, Bacon strove to separate theology from reason and to put the science of God effectively beyond human concern. His own words are: "The singular advantage which the Christian religion hath [over pagan religions] towards the furtherance of true knowledge is that it excludeth and interdicteth human reason, whether by interpretation or anticipation, from examining or discussing of the mysteries and principles of faith." He ascribes the fall of the angels and of Adam and Eve to the union of reason and of religious knowledge![38]

In the interests of natural science the power and limits of reason are distorted into a scientism clearly inimical to the

---

36. F. H. Anderson, *The Philosophy of Francis Bacon* (Chicago: University of Chicago Press, 1948), pp. 48, 13.

37. *Ibid.*, p. 295.

38. *Ibid.*, p. 54. See also Elizabeth Sewell, *The Orphic Voice* (New Haven: Yale University Press, 1960), pp. 62, 100, 109-110, for Bacon's mistrust of poetry, despite her emphasis upon his myth-making powers.

traditional humanism. The odd humility of Bacon's theology against theology helped exile God from the range of the human mind and establish the secularist mentality to cope with the world of experience. Man thus divided from his deeper self, his world, and God is not the man of the Christian humanist tradition.

Bacon's summons to the empirical method was answered with great enthusiasm. No one should quarrel with it as a limited method. The work of Harvey, Boyle, and Priestley witnessed its enlightening and beneficent character. But Bacon's intention to substitute empirical science for a philosophy had culturally dehumanizing effects which paralleled those of the mathematical tradition. It had such direct effects on the work of Hobbes, Locke, and Hume, to be treated later in these pages. With them empiricism became absolute, first in a nominalistic phase and then as skepticism.

Before discussing the role of Newton's fusion of the mathematical and empirical traditions in the formation of the noetic we are describing, we should note the effects of the new scientism on the spiritually minded Platonist, Henry More. Though opposed to Hobbes' materialism, More sought vindication of his spiritual view of matter in certain of Galileo's and Descartes' concepts. It is important to see that the pressure of this noetic was so potent that More was forced to pose his spiritual problem in materialistic terms and, finally, to formulate an answer quite at variance with traditional idealism. He postulated an extended spirit, being led by this scientistic tradition to believe that nothing unextended could exist. Such is the dubiously Platonic World Soul which he suggests as God's plastic agent in the world, calling it the "spirit of nature." Even God himself must be extended, and so space is thought to be the divine presence, a notion which influenced Newton appreciably. And so from a spiritual Platonist More becomes the cosmographer of the nontranscendent, all-but-pantheistic God, an exigency of the new science as theology.[39]

As we have already noted, the two currents of the new scientism met in Newton. By opposing the hypothetical method previously dominant among the mathematicians, he strove to reduce empirical findings to a more mathematically exact formula. His formulation of the law of gravity is an outstanding example of this synthesis. Had he always worked with complete fidelity to his rigorous requirements of method, his scientific contribution to posterity would have been no less distinguished than it is; yet his share in dehumanizing philosophy would not have been so marked. But because he developed into a fuller synthesis many of the philosophic implications of the new scientism, his philosophy was deemed complete and practical. The shift to the new colorless and silent world of mathematical mechanics was complete when Newton's physics was posited as a metaphysics. His followers who lacked his humane and religious sensitivity spelled out the psychological and theological implications of this position. Because he failed to abide by his fundamental dislike of the hypothetical, he ironically substituted his mechanics for philosophy. Randall does not hesitate to say that for a century after Newton all philosophizing, especially in its more technical aspects, was an attempt to come to terms with, to analyze, criticize, and extend Newton's thought.[40] And Burtt concurs that his metaphysical hypotheses held sway with a borrowed and undemonstrated certainty wherever his scientific influence penetrated.[41]

Newton accepted the Cartesian dualism of body and spirit, a mechanistic interpretation of the primary and secondary

39. Burtt, *Metaphysical Foundations,* pp. 134-137.
40. *Newton's Philosophy of Nature,* ed. John H. Randall and H. S. Thayer (New York: Hafner, 1953), pp. xiii-xiv.
41. Burtt, *Metaphysical Foundations,* pp. 20-21.

qualities of sensation, and, finally, the imprisonment of the soul in matter. His tendency to interpret all reality according to his inadequate scientific method managed to hide his positivism even from his disciples. His personal religious convictions show a different bent, but his influence on posterity was not from this source.[42]

Newton made force and mass correlative in formulating the law of gravity; and although he did not reduce bodies to mere geometrically patterned masses, his followers did.[43] But his ability to express mass in motion in purely mathematical terms led him to speculate about the exclusively mathematical nature of time and space, and then of absolute time and space. The next step—aided by fears of appearing, as he did to Berkeley, an atheist—was to associate univocally the omnipresence and eternity of God with infinite time and space. In fact, he conceived of space as the divine *sensorium,* the medium of Providence's influence in the universe. Finally, in his notion the divine operation in the world is not transcendent, but is that of the renewer of cosmic energies and traffic director of the spheres.[44] Newton's thought, as developed by his less religious successors, became a potent means of depriving the world of divine and human meaning. The old world passed with Newton.

THE THEODICIES AND NATURE

This scientism became the predominant climate of theology and of psychology. The concept of a personal and transcendent God elaborated over the centuries owed much both to Christian theology and to humanist philosophy. Although Christian theology and Aristotelian physics and metaphysics were dialectically independent of each other, they shared to

42. *Ibid.,* p. 226.
43. *Ibid.,* pp. 241-242.
44. *Ibid.,* pp. 247, 253-255, 258, 290-293.

some extent a natural affinity in the minds of men who learned all the arts and sciences as part of their Medieval or Renaissance education. Finality made sense to these men in both disciplines, for it is natural to seek purpose in what one studies. Aristotle spoke of it as the first and most significant of the causes. Given the lack of the empirical knowledge later available, the old physics understandably took on a strongly a-prioristic complexion. With empirical evidences exhausted, it was tempting to assign to a thing a likely specific finality. When a stone dropped to the earth, it was natural enough to think of this through an analogy to attraction or love—and it should be remembered this was only analogy. But when the law of gravity made more obvious and concrete sense, the men of the new mentality unfortunately tended to deny the *principle* of purpose while rejecting a specific error made in its application. The new philosophy wanted to throw out the baby with the bath water. It was progressively more interested in how things worked than in why. When this spirit spread to their thought about God and man, the West experienced a profound shock from which it is still trying to recover. A sense of finality secured the needed sense of transcendence spoken of before. A changing universe without a sense of purpose easily became a desert, man a hopeless wanderer in it, and God little more than a processor of sand.

The unparalleled development of theodicies in the seventeenth and eighteenth centuries issued partly from the breakdown of Christian unity as a source of truth about the Revelation and partly from the growing tendency to look to reason as an independent basis for religion and ethics. It was the age of deism. Earlier forms of "natural" theology, though dialectically independent of faith in the Revelation, were usually fostered in an atmosphere of this faith. But Enlightenment deism grew in a largely rationalistic culture, overtly self-confident, yet often enough beset with misgivings about the validity of the Revelation. The mathematical passion for clarity and its peculiar kind of certainty charmed much of its theorizing. And yet it is ironic that this deism, as opposed to the more timeless theism, was largely a Christian offshoot or even, perhaps, heresy. It could hardly have developed apart from the Christian intellectual tradition which it replaced. It sought new underpinnings for the Christian answers to ethical and religious problems, answers which had taken longer to construct than the cathedrals. By comparison it was a self-conscious and vacuum-like structure. The abstract character of its mathematical method lacked the more enduring, humane, and concrete sense of ritual and mystery, and of the older confidence in reason found in earlier "natural" theologies, despite Voltaire's claim that deism was the religion of Adam and Seth and Noah. The classic example of this facile deism is the *De Veritate* of Edward, Lord Herbert of Cherbury, which made him the father of English deists.

Some deists, however, related their thought more intimately to Christian belief. Shaftesbury, though falsely accused of atheism because he was antipuritanical, meant his views as a part of a broad sort of Christian doctrine. Samuel Clarke, a low-church divine during the reigns of Queen Anne and of George I, saw deism as a propaedeutic to Christianity, not as a way of life.[45] But others, like Matthew Tindal in *Christianity as Old as the Creation* (1730), thought too great a stress could not be placed on natural religion, which differed from Christianity only in the manner of its communication. Christianity was but a republication of natural religion.[46] John Toland claimed Christianity was not

45. *Religious Thought in the Eighteenth Century,* ed. John M. Creed and John S. Boys Smith (Cambridge: Cambridge University Press, 1934), p. 26, from *A Discourse concerning the Unchangeable Obligations of Natural Religion, and the Truth and Certainty of the Christian Revelation* (1705).

46. *Ibid.,* pp. 33-34.

mysterious, nor faith an assent to anything above reason. Otherwise it would contradict man's nature and God's wisdom.[47] Charles Blount, writing at the end of the seventeenth century, went as far as rejecting Christianity completely, for Revelation must be universal or be contrary to the nature of man. This odd gloss on "Go, teach ye all nations" did not save Blount from suicide![48] Hume's rejection of the possibility of miracles as a violation of the "laws of nature" and his "demolition" of causality and consequent rejection of theism as a reasonable position should be remembered at this point, too.[49]

Despite the efforts of such churchmen as Law and Butler to keep alive the Christian sense of God's mysteriousness and transcendence, theology in England was swiftly going the way of the new science and deism. And this trend, as Creed and Boys Smith wisely observe, though intended to broaden theological scope by asserting the dignity of reason, ironically had the opposite effect. They say of these theorists: "Their lack of historical knowledge and sympathy, which led them to regard their own Rational Theology as also the original and universal theology of mankind, made it in fact temporary and local. In dispensing with Revelation, or regarding it as merely a republication of this Natural Religion, they were in effect narrowing the content of religion, instead of, as they supposed, rejecting the merely 'mysterious' and insecure. Their narrow use of reason, and their view of the world as the smoothly running handiwork of God, involved an optimism too shallow to reckon adequately with evil and suffering."[50]

Mention of the problem of good and evil naturally brings

47. *Ibid.,* p. 19, from *Christianity not Mysterious* (1696).
48. *Ibid.,* pp. 22-24, from *Oracles of Reason* (1693).
49. *Ibid.,* pp. 130-146, from *Of Miracles* (1748) and *Dialogue concerning Natural Religion* (1779).
50. *Ibid.,* pp. xvii-xviii.

to mind the contemporary popularity of the doctrine of the Great Chain of Being. Based on the principle of plenitude and the Platonist continuum of forms, this doctrine considered all things in the universe, including man, as existing univocally for the totality of it, a wry comment on the previous humanist notion of a man-centered cosmos. Even God, though often granted a nominal transcendence, was governed by the cosmological exigencies of this plenitude and continuum. Plenitude, and not intrinsic value, was the norm of the good. It was more important to God that the species of lion exist than one more individual man.[51] Evil was an inevitable effect of God's infinite goodness. For anything else to be wholly good, it would have to exhaust goodness, hence be another infinite God. Hence, from Bishop King's *De Origine Mali* we hear talk of the "evil of defect" in all things created and "a creature is descended from God, a most perfect Father; but from Nothing as its Mother, which is Imperfection."[52] In such a context of puerile and extremely univocal reasoning Lovejoy speaks well of God as "an embarrassed Creator."[53] Though Soame Jenyns was hardly a great thinker, the intellectual climate of the day was congenial enough to produce him and not reject him out of hand. Of our trouble in understanding individual evil, he writes: "Our difficulties arise from our forgetting how many difficulties Omnipotence has to contend with: in the present instance it is obliged either to afflict innocence or to be the cause of wickedness; it has plainly no other option."[54] Pleasure and pain had to be judged by the same cosmic norm:

51. Arthur O. Lovejoy, *The Great Chain of Being* (Cambridge: Harvard University Press, 1936), pp. 222-225.

52. Arthur O. Lovejoy, "Optimism and Romanticism," in *PMLA*, 42 (1927), 927-928.

53. Lovejoy, *The Great Chain of Being*, p. 210.

54. *Ibid.*, p. 210, quoted from *A Free Inquiry into the Nature and Origin of Evil* (1757).

my pain is the price of pleasure for someone else on the party line of Being.

The Christian view of pain and evil as partly a mystery, partly a punishment for sin, yet redeemable even here below, yields to an irredeemable cosmological determinism. The dichotomy of the flesh and the spirit is now metaphysical, no longer the result of a fall from innocence, something "natural,"[55] which Basil Willey reminds us "meant what is congenial to the mind of an abstract Man."[56] And even the Roman Catholic Alexander Pope saw fit to speak as a cosmological deist in his *Essay on Man*.

THE NEW PSYCHOLOGY AND NATURE

When the new scientism inundated the study of psychology, the cosmological noetic was complete. Man was no longer the ambiguous part of nature that he had been to the Greeks, involved in it contextually as knower and known, yet able to transcend it in this very life of the mind. Now he was a captive of mechanistic nature and by this essentially

55. *Ibid.*, p. 178.

56. Basil Willey, *The Eighteenth-Century Background: Studies in the Idea of Nature in the Thought of the Period* (London: Chatto and Windus, 1940), p. 10. Students of theology tend to concur upon the cosmological quality of much theological opinion of the time. Norman Sykes in his *From Sheldon to Secker: Aspects of English Church History 1660-1768* (London: Macmillan, 1959) sympathetically discusses the essential struggles facing churchmen of the time: see especially "True Religion and Sound Learning." See also his *The English Religious Tradition* (London: Student Christian Movement, 1953), pp. 52-63; S. C. Carpenter, *Eighteenth-Century Church and People* (London: Society for the Promotion of Christian Knowledge, 1959), pp. 271 ff. and ch. iii "The New Divinity," pp. 25-55; Gerald R. Cragg, *The Church and the Age of Reason 1648-1789* (Grand Rapids: Eerdmans, 1964), pp. 71-80. Henri Daniel-Rops, while mainly discussing the situation in Catholic France, is of the same opinion in his *The Church in the Eighteenth Century*, trans. John Warrington (London: Dent, 1964), chs. i and iii.

estranged from nature and himself, surely a strange parody of the fruitful union of the knower and the known. This new mechanistic pattern had two main symptoms, the one epistemological, the other psychological. In their development the lines of communication between nature and man were seriously damaged, the last stroke dealt to the foundations of the essentially outward-going poetic theory of mimesis.

The prevailing passion for mechanical and mathematical clarity was responsible for posing the problem of knowledge in an unanswerable way, in terms of the presuppositions of the new physics, rather than in the larger context of experience, the full scope of reason, and the metempirical. Whether one prefers to recognize an intellectual problem occasioned by the fact of knowledge or to see in its very experience its own guarantee, surely most will agree today that discussing the problem in mechanistic terms will never solve it. Skepticism and serious intellectual commitment will continue to divide men till the day of doom, while perhaps at times enjoying a kind of peaceful coexistence inside the minds of many individuals. The only point I wish to make here is the futility involved in the manner of posing the problem, and its consequences for poetic theory of the time.

We have seen that Kepler's compelling dream of a completely mathematical world revived the ancient atomists' distinction between primary and secondary qualities of sensation, that is, between what was common to the report of some of the senses—shape, for example—and what was proper to each—color, sound, and the like. Galileo attributed this secondary quality to deception. This was partly a reaction to the overeasy anthropomorphic finalities assigned in accordance with the old physics and partly a ready answer to the difficulties raised by the new. It is one thing, however, to say that color is not in the object of sight in a naively formal way and to draw the conclusion that sensation is a confusing and deceitful barrier to intellectual knowledge. It is quite another to say that in seeing, a person is vitally proportioned to what he sees, because he and the object are mutually related as causes, and hence what is reported—that the apple is red—is a vital way of knowing what a thing is. In either supposition color cannot be isolated mechanically, that is, held apart from the person's vital experience of seeing it; hence it is gratuitous to suppose deception for merely mechanical reasons. But this distinction was not made. Descartes withdrew into the mind for the sake of the clarity and the distinction of ideas as normative of their truth.

In England, Hobbes, though rejecting the Cartesian dualism, continued the march away from the humanist understanding of man by opting for an absolute materialism. Sensation and intelligence were but intricate patterns of motion and force. Ideas were corporeal images of corporeal things. The universal idea as traditionally understood was no more than a word, not a meaning, reflecting the complex motions registered in the human organism. The secondary qualities of sensation were mere deceptions, caused by the conflict of motions of the material object and those coming from within the one sensing. All was now the *res extensa*.[57]

Commenting on Hobbes' materialism, and especially on his reduction of finality to one of the many images produced from within, Burtt says: "Aided by the decline of the notion of God as Supreme Good, [his system] set the fashion for almost the whole modern development of psychology. Locke, the next great psychologist, followed Hobbes' method still more explicitly and in greater detail, with the result that after him only an occasional idealist ventured to write a psychology in terms of different main assumptions."[58]

57. Burtt, *Metaphysical Foundations,* pp. 117-123; *Critical Essays of the Seventeenth Century,* ed. Joel E. Spingarn (Bloomington: Indiana University Press, 1957), I, xxvii-xxviii.
58. Burtt, *Metaphysical Foundations,* pp. 126-127.

It is precisely in his detailed analysis and investigation of the psychological processes from a materialistic point of view that Locke was so influential. Like Hobbes before him, he reduced the superficial though minute data of consciousness to mathematically clear order in a thoroughly mechanical way. Thought was only complicated sensation; the universal idea was gone, innate ideas must not be admitted on any score. His influence and praise can be found in practically every major and minor psychologist and author of eighteenth-century England, with the notable and heartening exception of Dr. Johnson. Locke's mechanical concept of the human mind is clear in his disparagement of wit, simile, metaphor, and mystery, much as is Hobbes' in his pedestrian Davenant letters and comments on *Gondibert*.[59] His rather gauche and unimaginative rejection of the Latin and Greek Classics in *Some Thoughts Concerning Education* shows how inhumane the new psychology had become. And yet here was mankind at its proper study.[60] It is interesting to note in passing that, like so many others in England who were developing this new tradition, Locke was a pious moralist. He apparently saw no conflict between being such and his materialization of the human mind and destruction of the human and divine bases of morals and religion.

Closely related to these epistemological developments was

59. John Locke, *An Essay Concerning Human Understanding*, ed. A. C. Fraser (Oxford, 1894); Kenneth MacLean, *John Locke and English Literature of the Eighteenth Century* (New Haven: Yale University Press, 1936), pp. 57 ff. and 104.

60. John Locke, *The Educational Writings of John Locke*, ed. John W. Adamson (London: E. Arnold, 1912), pp. 49-50 and 114. Locke has an ominous warning for fathers whose sons show a tendency to write poetry: "If he have a poetic vein, it is to me the strangest thing in the world, that the father should desire or suffer it to be cherished or improved. Methinks the parents should labour to have it stifled and suppressed as much as may be; and I know not what reason a father can have to wish his son a poet." He continues at some length, warning of the danger to such a young man of earning the reputation as a wit, about the company he will keep, and about the poverty that probably awaits him (p. 141)!

Locke's elaboration of the psychological theory of the association of ideas, commented upon by Hobbes before him and, in fact, based on phenomena observed in antiquity. When this theory was popularized by such men as Hartley and Priestley, the full circle that changed human knowledge from a contextual understanding of reality to a psychological chain of neural vibrations had been completed. The panacean character claimed in contemporary theory for association of ideas seems to suggest the old anomaly of the rationalist mind that fostered it, its simultaneous confidence in and despair of reason. Bate has written: "It may be questioned, indeed, whether any philosophical or psychological doctrine has since permeated critical thought in so great a degree as did that of the association of ideas at this time."[61] Fortunately this led to a more vital and effective development in terms of the sympathetic imagination later in the century.

David Hartley gave Associationism its most notable and detailed development, while Priestley did much to make it popular. Hartley acknowledged his debt to Locke for the psychological elements in the theory, and to Newton for the physiological elements contained in Newton's theory of infinitesimal medullary particles to explain sensation. That his analysis of intellectual assent was epistemologically quite as materialistic as Locke's and Newton's can be seen from the following: "Now the cause that a person affirms the truth of the proposition, *twice two is four,* is the entire coincidence of the visible or tangible idea of twice two with that of four, as impressed upon the mind by various objects. We see everywhere, that twice two and four are only different names for the same impression. And it is mere association which appropriates the word truth, its definition, or its internal feeling, to this coincidence."[62]

61. W. J. Bate, *From Classic to Romantic* (Cambridge: Harvard University Press, 1949), p. 96.
62. David Hartley, *Observations on Man, His Frame, His Duty and His Expectations* (London, 1791), I, 325.

For Hartley, ideas, then, are not ways of penetrating to the form of a thing. They are only complex sensations and are to be explained as clusters of sensations awakened by any of the sense stimuli, which originally awakened the simple sensations which by association first formed the cluster. The main sources of association were considered to be cause and effect, similarity of phantasm, and contiguity of the impressions in time or place. How mechanically he conceived the process is clear from a proposition taken at random from his *Observations*: *"To deduce Rules for the Assertainment of Truth, and Advancement of Knowledge, from the mathematical methods of considering Quantity."*[63] His observations and theorizing are a blend of superficial reporting of empirical physiology and facile reasoning, yet his influence was immense. One has only to think of the early Coleridge.

Joseph Priestley enthusiastically forwarded Hartley's work, presenting an edition of the *Observations* in 1775, along with several essays of his own explaining the doctrine to the uninitiated. The express point of one of these essays was to "deduce all the phenomena of thinking from the single principle of *association.*"[64] A few pages later he reminds the reader that Hartley has reduced all psychological activity to association, and for this one needs but a single principle, a sensory one.[65] From this point he later concludes there is no need to predicate a spirit in man. Though a devoutly Christian man, he is sure one is annihilated at death and that immortality has nothing to do with man's intrinsic constitution. Its hope is completely dependent upon Christ's promise of it.[66] He hoped this would be a good apologetic for Christianity with the French materialists! Such views of

63. *Ibid.*, I, 335.
64. Joseph Priestley, *Hartley's Theory of the Human Mind on the Principle of the Association of Ideas,* 2nd ed. (London, 1790), p. xxv.
65. *Ibid.*, p. xxvii.
66. *Ibid.*, pp. xxii-xxiv.

the religious nature of things can well expect analogies in the area of poetry and imagination.

If such allegiance to materialistic Associationism was to be found in green wood, we should not be surprised to find it in David Hume's dry bark of dogmatic agnosticism. Associationism for him accounted for the origin of such stable ideas as substance and causation, which in the older philosophies were derived from experience through penetrating understanding and reasoned argument. Ideas for him were "bundles" of impressions, best accounted for by sheer subjective assemblage and not by a similarity of meaning.[67]

The noetic here evolved, added to the mechanical notion of nature, physical, human, and divine, formed the predominant intellectual backdrop for the area of our study. Now all one can be sure of is that he is not sure, and one must be content with his subjective bundles of associated impulses. Ironically, his emancipated reason, moving exclusively in its univocal orbit, has been the instrument of suicide. Demands for clarity have been answered with agnosticism. A mathematico-physical realism has smothered the human mind which sought to impose itself on nature.

But England has had a long and stubborn tradition of moral interest and common sense. It was the England of Pope, Swift, Fielding, and Johnson, the England of coffee houses and social satire. But poetic theory which tried to follow the framework of mimesis was doomed. Notions of common sense, of taste, and of sense or intuition began to be noticed. But, with the almost single exception of Johnson, there was no critic substantial enough to reassert effectively the Classical premises at the deeper level needed for a vital mimesis, and so they died. They were revived in a different form by Coleridge under quite another set of intellectual principles.

67. David Hume, *The Philosophic Works of David Hume* (Boston and Edinburgh, 1854), I, 25-29; II, 215 ff. and 353 ff.

The Critics and the Concept
of Imitation

The decline of Neoclassicism was intimately bound up with the fate of mimesis both in theory and in practice; and we have seen that a decay in the critical understanding of mimesis was to be expected with the passing of a humane and metempirical view of nature. We should expect, as a consequence, to find proportionate disarray in the critical appraisal of the function of mimesis, its fruition in pleasurable contemplation. Four major trends in this changing concept of mimetic poetry can be found among the critics we are studying.

The first of these was the attenuation or thinning out of the concept of imitation. This means that form in the cognitive element was thought of as derived from a very superficial level of nature, and hence could hardly be called the probable. The visible and audible aspects of life drew more critical attention as the fit object of poetic imitation. Secondly, as a result, we find attention drawn to formalistic elements rather than to a viable sense of form. The surface aspects of a poem rather than the inner source of its life concerned too many of the critics. An isolated sense of style, style as a rhetorical rather than a poetic concern, a rhetorical sense of imitation (copying the ways and manners of authors), idle discussion of the unities, and the dispute about the relative merits of the ancients and the moderns are various aspects of this trend. (Because they center upon the concept of style, we shall discuss them in Chapter 4.) A third tendency was to deny that the arts, especially painting and music, were imitative at all; or if they were, they were so only in a superficial way. This, finally, parallels the fourth tendency, that of thinking of the arts as subjectively oriented, as self-expressive, rather than as imitative, or if still considered imitative, as a kind of transfer of an emotive state from author to audience rather than as the intelligible structuring of emotion's meaning which Aristotle, for example, had in mind in the *Politics* (1341a-1342b) and in the *Poetics* (1447a). Part of this stress comes from the influence of Associationism, and part from such reactions to its mechanical barrenness as the Platonist interest in beauty and sublimity of Shaftesbury and the schools of "taste" and "common sense." But it is interesting to see that the first stable English subjective theorist, Coleridge, depended heavily upon a concept of mimesis, both in the *Biographia* and especially in his too little appreciated essay, "On Poesy or Art," in giving substantial contour to his theories of imagination.

Though it is difficult to draw hard and fast lines in so complicated a milieu, a notable shift in contemporary theory about the function of poetry parallels this shift in the understanding of the cognitive element in mimesis. The incorporation of the Horatian formula into the *Poetics* from the time of the Renaissance, much like the rhetoricizing of poetic theory that concurred with it, was possible only because the philosophic implications of the probable were either unknown or ignored. How misplaced the formula was in the Aristotelian context could not be appreciated where the rationalistic noetic predominated. In the last few decades of the eighteenth century we find modification, change, and even rejection of the formula, but rarely for organic reasons. These variants were usually prompted by an instinctive reaction to formalism or by the new interest in a subjective aesthetics. For the most part, where art was still considered mimetic, this notion was conceived of more and more superficially. Form became a surface quality. Hence the pleasurable contemplation, so substantial to the Aristotelian concept of mimesis, found less and less theoretical understanding; and mimesis itself went the way of formalism and finally was largely rejected as a viable concept of art.

Alongside this tradition of empirical rationalism, and frequently making odd bedfellows with it in the minds of the critics, was the appeal to the Platonic and Neoplatonic ideal. We have already seen that the epistemology of the Platonic tradition was unable to cope with the realistic demands of mimesis. Yet many critics of the Italian Renaissance built their theory of mimesis upon the Platonic ideal, substituting idealization for Aristotelian ideation, and regularly ended, logically enough, with a didactic view of its function. Bredvold has written of how this tradition was absorbed in Neoclassical England.[68]

I have not thought it necessary to spell out the noetic implications of Neoplatonism, because for our purposes they were essentially the same as the Platonic. Although through Plotinian and Christian influences Neoplatonism had a greater interest in art and respect for it as an imitation of the work of the Divine Creator, it still lacked an adequate epistemology to deal with mimesis. Surely the critics who tried to fill the vacuum created by the new empiricism with an appeal to the Neoplatonic ideal were inadequate to the task. Dryden comes to mind immediately. A viable theory of mimesis needed as foundation a sense both of the metempirical and of the immediate. While Neoplatonism, unlike empirical rationalism, had the first of these, it lacked an adequate sense of the second. Hence, though the two joined hands in much of the critical writing of the time, the union was unfruitful in appreciating the demands of poetic structure and in its consequent demand for autonomous contemplation. Neoplatonism, then, if anything, fostered a didactic attitude toward poetry, even though its otherwise inspiring idealism had fostered much creativity in the Renaissance both in England and in Italy.

Another form of Platonic influence was felt through

68. Louis I. Bredvold, "The Tendency towards Platonism in Neo-classical Esthetics," in *ELH*, 1 (1934), 91-119.

interest in "the beautiful." Shaftesbury's writings were important in this connection, though influential only many decades after his death. But he lacked the vigor of mind of his master. His misty writings read more like wish-fulfillment than philosophic argument. Virtue is tied to an emotive experience of the beautiful, and his views blend well with interest in a rhetoric of the emotions (as we shall see in the fifth chapter).

ATTENUATION OF THE CONCEPT OF IMITATION

As the "Father of English Criticism," John Dryden initiated the Neoclassic tradition. He had a penetrating grasp of the Latin heritage in criticism, strongly colored by the Italian and French thought of the Renaissance. There have been few better practical critics in our tradition, but he was not a distinguished theorist. The contemporary philosophic skepticism for which his questioning mind found ready affinity helps explain the limits of his theoretical judgments about poetry, much as it is reflected in his political pragmatism and religious fideism. It shows him to be an odd amalgam of such strange opposites as Hobbes and Plato.[69] He is an interesting example of the conflict of the new scientistic temper with the traditional humanistic heritage.

The artist, he tells us, "should form to himself an idea of perfect nature. This image he is to set before his mind in all his undertakings, and to draw from thence, as from a storehouse, the beauties which are to enter into his work; thereby correcting Nature from what actually she is in individuals, to what she ought to be, and what she was created." On the face of it this passage might be suggestive of Aristotle, had not Dryden insisted that it fits only an epic poet who is the ideal poet. "All his undertakings" lead in this direction,

69. Clarence D. Thorpe, *The Aesthetic Theory of Thomas Hobbes* (Ann Arbor: University of Michigan Press, 1940), pp. 189-220.

for the "transcendental hero" brings poetry to its best in the epic. "The heroes of the poets are to be drawn according to this rule. There is scarcely a frailty to be left in the best of them, any more than it is to be found in a divine nature; and if Aeneas sometimes weeps, it is not in bemoaning his own miseries, but those which his people undergo." We see here the prevailing reason why from the Renaissance on critics preferred the idealistic epic to the emerging and contextual genre of tragedy, and the more idealized Aeneas to the more truly mimetic warriors of Homer. Dryden explicitly points to the reason in saying that comedy and tragedy do not fit this ideal conception of poetry because they deal with individuals and their defects, surely an echo of the toleration of the poets in the *Laws*.[70]

Dryden then takes issue with Aristotle by saying that the pleasure one finds in an imitation comes not from seeing its likeness with the individual but with general, universal nature.[71] His conceptualist understanding of the probable prevents him from seeing that the two are identified in Aristotle's view of the emerging real. Here we have a mixture of the scientistic noetic and a static view of the ideal, from which issues a diluted view of the probable.

Analogous to this judgment is one which prefers painting to tragedy for its external or empirical advantages. In painting, the manners, action, and passions of many characters can be discerned at once, "in the twinkling of an eye; at least they would be so, if the sight could travel over so many different objects all at once, or the mind could digest them all at the same instant or point of time."[72] A time-place context of meaning replaces the deeper Classical sense of intui-

---

70. John Dryden, *The Essays of John Dryden*, ed. W. P. Ker (Oxford: Clarendon, 1926), II, 125, 127-129. Much of what is cited in this chapter comes from "A Parallel of Poetry and Painting."

71. *Ibid.*, II, 137.

72. *Ibid.*, II, 131.

tion in judging what is involved in the probable. An easy confidence in the power of sensation is hardly a substitute for the concentrated intelligibility of human motive originally spoken of by Aristotle. It is Hobbes' psychology translated into aesthetic criticism. Dryden's approval of the unities derives from the same kind of thinking. In the same vein he espouses the widespread Renaissance notion of drama as deceit rather than revelation, a far cry indeed from Aristotle's notion of the universal emerging from symbolic action, which, in turn, reflects the Greek dramatic achievement.[73]

Dryden's theoretical instability is intimately related to the philosophic instability of his time. His editor Ker aptly sums up the situation which explains many of the passages quoted above: " 'Nature' means whatever the author thinks right; sometimes it is the reality that is copied by the artist; sometimes, and much more commonly, it is the principles of sound reason in poetry; and sometimes it is the Ideal."[74] How satisfactory this sound reason was in dealing with what is cognitive and creative in poetry should be evident when we compare these passages with the prevailing noetic on which his skepticism was nourished.

John Dennis, though seriously intent on establishing a new classicism, reveals a narrow view of the tradition he is imitating. He is praiseworthy in his effort to instill a responsible attitude toward the office of critic, with wise emphases on the principles of order, tradition, balance, and reason as guides. Poetry derives from an outward-going mind, not from whim. "If poetry instructs tis by them alone [these principles] it instructs, and if it pleases tis by them partly that it pleases. If poetry instructs to virtue tis by the aid of moral philosophy, and if it gives any other Instruction tis by the assistance of some other Branch of Learning."[75]

73. *Ibid.*, II, 128.
74. *Ibid.*, I, xxiv-xxv.
75. John Dennis, *The Critical Works of John Dennis*, II, 297, from "The

But Dennis' mind was fashioned in the image of Hobbes, Locke, Descartes, and the French Neoclassical critics of the narrower sort. The Cartesian world picture and the mathematical concept of reason were frequently reflected in his judgments.[76] His picture of the nature of the mind and of the world it dealt with is very revealing: "Now Nature, taken in a stricter Sense, is nothing but that Rule and Order, and Harmony, which we find in the visible Creation. The Universe owes its admirable Beauty, to the Proportion, Situation and Dependence of its Parts. And the little World, which we call Man, owes not only its Health and Ease, and Pleasure, nay, the continuance of its very Being, to the Regularity of the Mechanical Motion, but even the Strength too of its boasted Reason, and the piercing Force of those aspiring thoughts, which are able to pass the Bounds that circumscribe the Universe." "For Reason is Order, and the Result of Order. And nothing that is Irregular, as far as it is Irregular, ever was, or ever can be either Natural or Reasonable."[77] This mathematically pat formula of mind equaling reason and reason equaling order and clarity is at once a familiar Enlightenment refinement and a caricature of the better Classical concept of reason.

It is difficult to judge the place in this study of Alexander Pope's spirited manifesto of Neoclassicism, *An Essay on Criticism*. On the one hand, Pope asserts the importance of following nature and tradition, of balance and good taste, and stresses the structural demands of good art. Yet much of the vitality of the piece comes from its poetic conception. Similarly his enthusiastic appreciation of Homer and Shakespeare in his prefaces, while intuitively right and genuine,

---

Causes of the Decay and Defects of Dramatick Poetry, and of the Degeneracy of the Public Tast."

76. *Ibid.*, II, xcii, n. 87; xcviii.

77. *Ibid.*, I, 202.

does not derive from any consistent philosophy of poetry. In fact it contrasts notably with his philosophic *Essay on Man*.

The passage advising the critic to follow Nature has "oft [been] thought" of in the context of imitation, but technically it is not "so well expressed" as to indicate clearly what Pope meant by Nature.

> First follow NATURE, and your Judgment frame
> By her just Standard, which is still the same:
> *Unerring Nature,* still divinely bright,
> One *clear, unchang'd,* and *Universal* Light,
> Life, Force, and Beauty, must to all impart,
> At once the *Source,* and *End,* and *Test* of *Art.*[78]

Lovejoy simply identifies the spirit of this passage with contemporaneous deism: "Pope's rule for literary criticism is the same as the deist's rule for religion."[79] Such a view reflects what he says elsewhere about Pope's cosmological deism and is reinforced by Macklem's study of Pope's view of evil in *The Anatomy of the World*.[80] Herrick observes: "Pope doubtless owed more to Horace than to Aristotle, but if he was not familiar with the *Poetics* itself, he had studied Rapin and Le Bossu."[81]

Pope's most recent editors of his *Essay on Criticism,* Audra and Williams, speculate that he would take for granted the meaning of nature as being something like "that which is permanent and universal in human experience." They

78. Alexander Pope, *Pastoral Poetry and An Essay on Criticism,* ed. E. Audra and Aubrey Williams (London and New Haven: Methuen and Yale University Press, 1961), pp. 246-247.

79. Arthur O. Lovejoy, *Essays in the History of Ideas* (Baltimore: Johns Hopkins Press, 1948), p. 90.

80. Michael Macklem, *The Anatomy of the World* (Minneapolis: University of Minnesota Press, 1958), p. 4.

81. M. T. Herrick, *The Poetics of Aristotle in England* (New Haven: Yale University Press, 1930), p. 95.

rightly deny that his view would be Hobbesian, yet they liken Pope's idea of nature to Dennis' rather mechanically conceived demands for rule and order quoted above: "these assumptions suggest, moreover, a body of thought which conforms closely to Dennis's own thinking about Nature as it is revealed in that critic's work." They also say: "Whatever influence Descartes may have had on this view of Nature [Pope's, that is], and however it may have been appropriated to Deism, its roots lie deep in the pagan and Christian past, nourished by the Stoic doctrine of Logos and by traditional Christian contemplation of God as mirrored in His creation."[82]

These roots are admittedly deep, but the important question is how substantially they nourished Pope's theoretical idea of Nature in the shallow soil of his day. It is hard to tell how rich the analogy is which is drawn between nature and God in "divinely bright." When Pope chose to be a philosopher, he was not above espousing cosmological Deism, despite its inconsistencies with his faith and, by analogy, with a viable Classicism. We should not look to Pope as a theorist, no more than to Dryden, but more to Pope as the intuitive commentator who was clearly aware of the vitality of true poetry, his own brilliant work included, for a thought on the nature to be imitated. Tillotson's *Pope and Human Nature* cannot carry us much beyond this conclusion.[83] As a poet, then, Pope rallied to a relatively substantial awareness of "that which is permanent and universal in human experience"; but as a theorist he is likely to be disappointing, and closer to the notions of his contemporaries than to those of Classical antiquity.

It would be quite unfair to claim Thomas Rymer and Jeremy Collier as representative Neoclassical critics, yet their

82. Pope, *Pastoral Poetry and An Essay on Criticism,* pp. 219-221.
83. Geoffrey Tillotson, *Pope and Human Nature* (Oxford: Clarendon, 1958).

extremes heighten the basic noetic more moderately at work in so many others of the time. In Collier's ironically titled *Short View . . . of the English Stage,* we find an acute ignorance of what imitation means when he objects to the dramatic representation of nobles in embarrassing roles. "What necessity is there to kick the *Coronets* about the *Stage,* and to make a Man a Lord, only in order to provoke him a Coxcomb? I hope the *Poets* don't intend to revive the old Project of Levelling, and *Vote* down the House of *Peers.*"[84] Despite the snobbery involved, the critical obtuseness and moralistic bias should not be minimized in these lines. Imitation is entirely missed, as it is frequently in this essay, while he discusses immorality and the drama. For example: "Profaneness, tho' never so well corrected, is not to be endured. It ought to be banish'd without *Proviso,* or Limitation. No pretence of Character or Punishment, can excuse it; or any *Stage-Discipline* make it tolerable. 'Tis grating to *Christian* Ears, dishonourable to the Majesty of God, and dangerous in the Example."[85] He is equally humorless and uncritical in his objections to anticlerical satire.[86]

Rymer, more directly a "Rules" critic than a moralist, is as imperceptive. Aristotle must be obeyed as the "rule giver" who has methodized poetic practice. Though one might find a reasonable place for this kind of sentiment, Rymer's real motivation emerges a few sentences later: "Nor would the *modern Poets* blindly resign to this practice of the *Ancients,* were not the Reasons convincing and clear as any demonstration in *Mathematicks.*"[87]

Even a critic as representative and responsible as Joseph

84. Jeremy Collier, *A Short View of the Immorality and Profaneness of the English Stage,* 3rd ed. (London, 1698), pp. 175-176.

85. *Ibid.,* p. 96.

86. *Ibid.,* pp. 97 ff.

87. [Thomas] Rymer, "The Preface of the Translator," in R. Rapin, *Monsieur Rapin's Reflections of Aristotle's Treatise of Poesie,* trans. [Thomas] Rymer (London, 1694), [p. 4].

Addison betrays the pressure of the Enlightenment empiricism in the way he understands mimesis. It is blended in his thought without cohesion with an earnest allegiance to the Classical tradition. We think of his Milton papers, his disapproval of current interest in spectacle rather than the creative core of drama, of the decorative as opposed to the functional—"as though a man was great if he were tall!" He likewise derided the fashion of *"deus ex machina"* and excluded poetic justice from intelligent poetic theory.[88]

But Addison's well-known essays on the pleasures of the imagination are Hobbesian and Lockean in conception. The faculty is a mechanical one, a rearranging of sensory impressions, mainly those of sight.[89] Bosker is in error in equating this passive, unintellectual power with the Aristotelian creative power of making.[90] Lane Cooper has long since shown this power as an implicit notion of intellectual imagination later to evolve in Coleridge, and I have frequently referred to Else's fuller discussion of the same idea.[91] With Addison, imaginative synthesis is visual and mechanical, not intellectual and vital. Its primary pleasures "entirely proceed from such objects as are before our eyes," whereas secondary pleasures "flow from the ideas of visible objects, when the objects are not actually before the eye, but are called up into our memories, or formed into agreeable visions of things that are either absent or fictitious."[92] "Ideas of visible objects" are Lockean sensations, and the images of objects "not

88. Joseph Addison and Richard Steele, *The Spectator,* ed. George A. Aitken (London, 1898), I, 226 (No. 44).

89. *Ibid.,* VI, 72-76 (No. 411).

90. Aisso Bosker, *Literary Criticism in the Age of Johnson,* 2nd rev. ed. (Groningen: J. B. Wolters, 1954), pp. 42-44.

91. Lane Cooper, *The Poetics of Aristotle: Its Meaning and Influence* (Boston: Marshall Jones, 1923), pp. 75-76; Else, *Aristotle's Poetics,* pp. 320-322.

92. Addison, *Spectator,* VI, 73 (No. 411). See John Wilkinson, "Some Aspects of Addison's Philosophy of Art," in *Huntington Library Quarterly,* 28 (1964), 31-44, especially 42-44.

actually before the eye" is an old description of the work of
the inner sense of the Scholastics, the phantasm. In this pro-
longed discussion he tried to combine the Neoclassical sense
of decorum or good form with the emergent associationist
psychology. His method is mechanical. Kames and Gerard
were to make similar efforts later in the century, when a
more subjective vitality had asserted itself in poetic theory.[93]
In *Spectator* 421 Addison explicitly accounts for the pleasures
of imagination, "the very life and highest perfection of
poetry," by the theory of association; and in *Spectator* 416
he speculates about the increased poetic intensity and value
as due to Lockean associationism. This is to miss the central
intelligible interplay of cause and effect or of meanings at the
heart of the probable.

Finally we see in Addison a budding tendency to seek the
moral motivation of poetry not in meanings but in sentiment
and rhetorical use of emotion. *Spectator* 70 and 74 are examples. *Spectator* 85 is well known for his praise of the
simple, moral, Gothic qualities of "The Ballad of Chevy
Chase" and "Two Children in the Wood." Of the latter he
says: "The song is a plain simple copy of nature, destitute of
all the helps and ornaments of art. The tale of it is a pretty
tragical story, and pleases for no other reason but because it
is a copy of nature. There is even a despicable simplicity in
the verse, and yet, because the sentiments appear genuine
and unaffected, they are able to move the mind of the most
polite reader with meltings of humanity and compassion."
This is far removed from a Classical sense of mimesis.

IMITATION IN POETRY AND PAINTING

We can observe in another way how critics misunderstood the mimetic concept of poetry by seeing how they

---

93. Martin Kallich, "The Association of Ideas and Critical Theory:
Hobbes, Locke and Addison," in *ELH*, 12 (1945), 310-312.

understood painting and music as mimesis. Critical theories of both these arts grew out of a close dependence upon critical theories of poetry, of painting during the Italian Renaissance, and of music during the eighteenth century. The attenuated notion of poetic imitation and an overemphasis on stylistic elements led to many unfruitful observations about the sister arts. It was not clear to many that the various arts are only analogous to each other. They not only comprise different media, but these very media occasion different modes of perception in widely differing structures. What likenesses exist among them must be sought in their metempirical reaches. But, unfortunately, for much the same reasons that we have already noted, the concept of mimesis as seen in music and painting or in their relationship with poetry, although nominally referring to the essence or inner center of art, was actually empirical in meaning. The precisely imitative in painting was identified with what we call today the representative aspect of art, and musical imitation was sought in the descriptive copying of such accidental elements as the trill of a bird call in flute music. As a result we find either more misunderstanding of the true meaning of mimesis or an entire abandonment of it.

The dominance of poetic theory in the shaping of theories of painting and music was also the occasion, when critics spoke of the humane function of the arts, for revealing a fundamental misconception of mimesis itself. We have seen that, when properly understood, form, to minister to a pleasurable contemplation, must lie deep in the probable, having been transformed and derived from its deeper reaches in nature. When these depths are neglected, form tends to be replaced by a formalism, for the metempirical roots of this kind of art are either obscured or forgotten. Because poetry, in contrast with painting and music, is "conceptual," a critic can still look to an intelligible "content," usually rhetorically formed, to bolster his didactic claims to imitation, and thus formalism can help the false claims of moralism, for no met-empirical norm of judgment need be called upon. In such a critical situation the theoretical incompatibility of rhetorical moralism and mimesis can pass comparatively unnoticed. And in the eighteenth century this was largely so.

But in the case of painting and music, and especially the latter, the analogy of meaning—we cannot speak of concept or intellectualized statement—is much more recessive, incapable of being falsely isolated for rhetorical or didactic purposes. Hence when any function beyond the mere pleasure of experiencing the art is postulated, it is usually conceived of as emotively affecting the audience. Talk about a mimetic "content" becomes less and less meaningful, and these arts, music in particular, tend to be thought of in other than mimetic terms. Where a moral concern remains, it is usually emotive in character: for example, the power of beauty to dispose an audience to moral value, rather than the assertion of a didactic content which teaches a lesson.

For our present purposes it will be sufficient to say that theories of painting at the time were basically those formed in sixteenth-century Italy to explain the massive artistic output of the time. The Horatian *"ut pictura poesis,"* long misinterpreted, was used as a kind of charter for bridging the theories of the two arts. For Horace the phrase merely pointed to the need, when judging poetry, of something comparable to perspective and proper lighting when viewing a picture. But it had long since been used to mark the similarity of descriptive poetry and the visual nature of painting. Because of this stress, the phrase was used to further the empirical and superficial notion of mimesis. Vida, for example, specified the likeness between the two arts as consisting in the visual factors of dramatic spectacle and the obviously visual aspect of painting.[94] Walter Ong, in his study of Ramus, sees a deep connection between the analogies of

94. W. G. Howard, *"Ut Pictura Poesis,"* in *PMLA,* 24 (1909), 85.

the visual in the empirical and schematic aspects of contemporary thought and the death of personal and metempirical appreciation of nature and human life.[95]

But the Horatian phrase was also given a more philosophic coloring by some. Howard observes that it might well have read *"ut poesis pictura,"* because it was used to transfer the critical presuppositions of poetic theory to those of painting. This transfer was most frequently made in giving a Neoplatonic ideal basis to the art of painting. Giovanni Pietro Bellori's *Idea del pittore* (1664) explains in this way the Classical adage that art perfects nature. Dolce, Alberti, and Leonardo explain in the same connection the Neoplatonic notion of art as the *imago Dei* by describing art as a composite of the most beautiful details assembled through accretion rather than through an organic development, which would reflect the emerging of form to its perfection in the order of nature.[96] Dryden's "Parallels" quoted above reflects this mechanical and rhetorical approach to idealization rather than the more intuitive concept of ideation. This tendency to think of forming the Neoplatonic ideal through accretion rather than of forming a significant intuition through organic development is analogous to the notion of imagery as a decoration of an idea in a poem, much like details in a picture, rather than as part of the substance of the insight. This stress was rhetorical in method and in spirit and had the same source as the explicit notion in this Italian tradition of art theory, that a painting was intended to please, teach, and move its audience.[97] Irving Babbitt, who scored the excessive emphasis at the time on the sensory and merely

95. Ong, *Ramus, Method, and Decay in Dialogue,* pp. 92 ff. Alexandre Maurocordato lists several examples of this visual analogy when treating the eighteenth-century concept of imitation in *La Critique classique en Angleterre* (Paris: Didier, 1964), pp. 72 ff.

96. Howard, *"Ut Pictura Poesis,"* pp. 64-67.

97. Joel E. Spingarn, *A History of Literary Criticism in the Renaissance,* 2nd ed. (New York: Columbia University Press, 1924), p. 317.

empirical elements of the arts to the neglect of their intellectual core, has also drawn attention to a rhetoricizing tendency in contemporary art theory, an overemphasis on the rhetorical meaning of imitation, that of copying the models of the ancients. Once again style, with its elements atomized, receives disproportionate emphasis at the expense of the intuition which gives their raison d'être. Vividness masks as vitality. He blames this tendency on antiquarianism and on the Italian cult of the virtuosi.[98]

IMITATION IN POETRY AND MUSIC

The tendency to understand mimesis in a merely empirical way is even more pronounced in contemporary theories of music. A serious aesthetic of music did not develop until the eighteenth century, when it was stimulated by the considerable advances made in absolute music, by the development of new musical instruments, which called for more expanded orchestral composition, and by the works of such giants as Handel, Haydn, and Mozart. Again poetic theory gave the cue for statements about the nature of music. The empirical and thinly rationalistic noetic of the Enlightenment might be expected to have exerted an even greater influence here than upon theories of painting, where the effects were more adaptive than formative. And this was the case. The attenuated understanding of mimesis is again clear, and toward the middle of the century it is rejected in favor of one or another Romantic approach.

Some found it hard to see how music was imitative save in a superficial, onomatopoetic way. Yet for Aristotle it was the most mimetic of the arts. Μουσική, it is true, for him included the dance; yet the more specific elements such as rhythm and melody were singled out as significantly imi-

---

98. Irving Babbitt, *The New Laokoon: An Essay in the Confusion of the Arts* (Boston: Houghton Mifflin, 1910), pp. 10, 13, 15, 23, 33-34, 62.

tative. He considered music as the image of character. "Rhythm and melody supply imitations of anger and gentleness, and also of courage, temperance and of all the qualities contrary to those" (*Politics*, 1340a). Butcher remarks: "Music in reflecting character moulds and influences it." The motions of the soul were thought of as musically rhythmic.[99] Behind this concept, of course, was a stable and universal human nature, seeking an intelligible good. This, ultimately, rather than mere surface manifestations of feelings was what the musician imitated, though ever so intuitively, much as the tragic poet caught deep human motivation in his dramatic action. Feelings ran deep for him without losing their objectivity and intelligibility. The growing cult of "genius" in the eighteenth century was quite a different thing.

John Draper, who has studied the history of the *Poetics* at some length, says of the fate of the mimetic concept of music in the eighteenth century in England: "Commonly ... even those writers who might have insisted on poetry and painting as 'imitative,' were inclined to make an exception [with regard to music]." Among them he lists James Harris, Sir William Jones, Charles Burney, Hawkins, Beattie, and others. When Thomas Twining returned the discussion to an Aristotelian context, he emphasized sentiment as the object of imitation.[100]

Though James Beattie was willing to admit some vague sort of affinity between music and imitation, he could not see in what it consisted. He was rightly unwilling to settle for an onomatopoetic process, for example, in Handel's *Water Music*. Rather, "music . . . is pleasing not because it is imitative, but because certain melodies and harmonies have *an*

99. Butcher, *Aristotle's Theory*, p. 130.

100. John W. Draper, "Aristotelian Mimesis in Eighteenth-Century England," in *PMLA*, 36 (1921), 391-394. H. M. Schueller, in "Literature and Music as Sister Arts," in *PQ*, 26 (1947), 193-205, says that the comparisons "had nothing to do with spirituality or with metaphysical realities in human experience" (p. 196).

aptitude to raise certain passions, affections, and sentiments in the soul. And, consequently, the pleasures we derive from melody and harmony are seldom or never resolvable into that delight which the human mind receives from the imitation of nature." Beattie here seems to misunderstand the integrity of person involved in artistic intuition and to think of imitation in too conceptual terms. The sensory quality of music is given an undue autonomy. In another passage he finds a symphony as meaningless and vague as a song without words. "Can the human mind be rationally gratified with that which it does not perceive, or which, if it did perceive, it would not understand?"[101] He conceives of mind as conceptual clarity and neglects its power of intuition and affinity for mystery.

Henry Home, Lord Kames, like Beattie a Scot, observes in a similar vein: "Of all the fine arts, painting only and sculpture are in their nature imitative." The other arts are original. Imitation for him is visual and empirical in emphasis; he tells us that beauty is properly speaking only visual and visual objects can best be described.[102]

Sir William Jones in the course of his "Essay on the Arts Commonly Called Imitative" disapproved of calling the arts imitative as an empty adulation of Aristotle. Whatever be said of painting, he says, limiting the concept of imitation to the visual and the empirical, poetry and music are of a much more noble origin. Poetry was originally religious, coming from the depths of the human spirit. It was perverted into tragedy and epic, which alone can be called imitative. He clearly understands imitation here as slavish copying. Love poetry to be sincere must not "*imitate* the passions of others" or deal in conceits, but must come from

101. James Beattie, *Essays: On Poetry and Music,* 3rd cor. ed. (London, 1779), pp. 136, 149-152.
102. Henry Home, Lord Kames, *The Elements of Criticism,* 6th ed. (Edinburgh, 1785), II, 3, 518-520.

the heart. Despite this Romantic turn of thought, he thinks of poetry as morally persuasive. Vice turned poetry, originally religious, into indignant moral and satiric verse, which in the course of time turned to more tempered precepts of didactic verse.[103]

He writes in the same vein more directly of music: "It is clear, that words and sounds have no kind of resemblance to visible objects: and what is an imitation but a resemblance of some other thing?" Fugues, counterfugues, and divisions have not the slightest resemblance to objects. In fact, he finds such adornments a "disgrace." Even the onomatopoetic imitations of birds or of brooks can be perceived only by an audience forewarned of their presence! His final warning is against the very idea of imitation. Rather the artist should strive to create an effect on the imagination analogous to the effect on the senses. His intuition is true enough, but his theoretical basis for it is again the same as Beattie's.[104]

After reviewing similar evidence, Draper concludes, as I have, that theorists who gave lip service to a mimetic theory of music tended to have a mechanical understanding of the meaning of the word imitation, mainly stressing the empirically visual demands that we have already seen, and to think of the art as didactic in intent. But "the development, on the other hand, of a sentimental attitude toward the arts gave to music a clearer aesthetic justification. The raising of the emotions was more and more considered an end worthy in itself; and the late eighteenth and early nineteenth centuries saw music and poetry both growing more and more emotional, and the philosophic theories of each stressing more and more the similarities consequent upon this common purpose." He then cites Du Bos, Jacob, Avison, Beattie,

103. Sir William Jones, *The Works of Sir William Jones* (London, 1807), X, 362-365, 374.
104. *Ibid.*, X, 375-378.

Robertson, Twining, John Brown the "minister," Eastcott, and Jackson as substantiating this tendency.[105]

Later in the same study he observes significantly: "Allied to this emotionalism and perhaps also to the harmonious symmetry of Neo-classicism and to its moral didacticism, is the notion, implicit in the philosophy of Shaftesbury and Hutcheson, of a moral harmony that elevates and improves the mind; and in the current sentimental confusion between ethics and aesthetics, this 'harmony' was made more or less a criterion for all the Good and Beautiful." He quotes several remarks of Brown, Algoretti, Mitford, Beattie, and others to found this impression.[106]

In a thoughtful unpublished study, Norman Rabkin has suggested that the gradual substitution among musical theorists of the concept of self-expression for that of imitation gave musical theory the lead in the development of Romantic aesthetics. With a conceptualized moral meaning unavailable, its place was supplied by a Shaftesburian notion of the moral harmony in things. This harmony was seen as existing between man and beast, revealed, for example, in Wordsworth's "natural piety," and even in Coleridge's beloved donkey! In this way another approach was taken to the older scheme of the macrocosm and the microcosm.

IMITATION AND THE SUBJECTIVE

With musical theory thus leading the way, art was no longer mimetic; or if it was, it was such as would engage the emotions of the reader either by association of experiences or by a rhetorical suasion to virtue; or it might express the emotive states of the artist, as distinguished from his mental

105. John W. Draper, "Poetry and Music in Eighteenth-Century Aesthetics," in *Englische Studien*, 67 (1932), 75-77.
106. *Ibid.*, p. 77.

states. This aesthetic was at best transitional. The intellectual sense of form was quickly vanishing and the more substantial theories of intuitive imagination had not yet been described. Some comments were promising, some were vague attempts to express vaguer impressions.

Mark Akenside speaks of the "imagination" as a mediating faculty between sense and mind, representing matter and motion, but in such fashion as to imply moral approbation or displeasure independently of the objects represented. In the same vein, when he speaks of imitation, the word has an emotive primacy unknown to the Classical tradition. What truths the mind represents in the mimetic act must appear "above all the rest, with circumstances proper to awaken and engage the passions." The older notion of intelligible form is quite secondary and in the context imitation receives a visual and empirical stress.[107]

Similar in stress is Edward Young's writing on genius and originality. For him they are more important than invention and imitation. Imitation is limited to copying models, worthy of "the Rules mentality." "Copy nature rather than authors," in itself open to a Classical interpretation, is advice linked by Young to his belief in the perfectibility of genius, "the power of accomplishing great things without the means generally reputed necessary to that end." His description of this quality is expressed as a mathematical proportion: genius is to good understanding as a magician is to a good architect.[108]

Beattie, in the same tradition, stresses emotional sympathy involved and demanded for poetic truth. "Truth to nature" and art perfecting nature must be accomplished through the

107. Mark Akenside, *The Pleasures of the Imagination: A Poem* (London, 1744), "Introduction," pp. 5-7. A similar observation is found in Hugh Blair, *Lectures on Rhetoric and Belles Lettres*, 7th ed. (London, 1798), I, 107.

108. Edward Young, *Conjectures on Original Composition,* ed. Edith J. Morley (Manchester: Manchester University Press, 1918), p. 13.

artist's emotive sympathy with his subject and audience. He must experience and possess the emotion at least as long as he is describing it.[109]

John Brown, in his *Essays on the Characteristics of the Earl of Shaftesbury* (1751), thinks of instruction in poetry as a necessary evil, for man is, alas, reasonable. At all events, it should be kept subordinate to pleasure: "*Instruction* makes a necessary, though *adventitious* Part of its Character." Here we have Horace's separation of profit and pleasure. Further, he finds descriptive poetry the most pleasurable, hence the purest; but it is weakest in instruction. It is perfect when it satisfies the imagination without offending reason or the passions, when "nothing further with regard to these Faculties is expected."

Brown then classifies the genres, a Classical practice here conducted without Classical norms, not according to structure or to the intuitive function and pleasure proper to each, but according to their effect upon the passions and the "Heart of Man." He assigns as Aristotle's reason for preferring tragedy to the epic the advantage of "visible representation," rather than probability or necessity, missing Aristotle's stress on concentration through structure. Finally, he characterizes some poetry as a rhetoric of the emotions. "ELOQUENCE then is no other than a Species of Poetry applied to the particular End of Persuasion. For Persuasion can only be effected by rowzing the Passions of the Soul; and these, we have seen, are only to be moved by a Force impressed on the Imagination, assuming the Appearance of Truth; which is the essential Nature of poetical Composition."[110]

The *Letters on Chivalry and Romance* of Bishop Hurd have long been considered a focal point in the shift from

109. Beattie, *Essays: On Music and Poetry*, pp. 52-53.
110. John Brown, *Essays on the Characteristics of the Earl of Shaftesbury* (London, 1751), pp. 18-19, 21.

Neoclassicism to Romanticism in critical theory.[111] In some ways it is a case of new wine in old bottles. Nature is still the subject matter of poetry, but poetry now includes elements long proscribed, such as popular superstitions, the chivalric social code, and the Gothic. The unity stressed is of an imaginative kind, like the twelve days of chivalric feasting found in the *Faerie Queene,* rather than a more intellectually organic unity. Hurd's "Discourse on Poetical Imitation" reflects much the same spirit. The poet's parish, says the Bishop, is all reality, but invention rather than imitation should be his Bible. He limits the meaning of imitation to the copying of authors and to the visual picturing of things. Invention has lost its older meaning in now being the subjective synthesizing by genius of selected details of reality. Consequently he stresses as the prime object of poetry the representation of feelings and passions and the growing awareness of something like the Shaftesburian moral sense.[112]

Among those who wrote commentaries in English on the *Poetics* up to this time (1789), Thomas Twining had no equal. In fact, his work had to be reckoned with until it was replaced by Butcher's and Bywater's. He knew Greek professionally and was more than ordinarily perceptive of the spirit of the treatise. And, most important for our purposes, he saw that Horace's please-and-teach formula had nothing to do with the *Poetics.*[113]

Twining recognizes two kinds of imitation. The first, which he characterizes as imitation in the most usual, most important, most obvious, and strictest sense, resembles what many of his contemporaries recognized as the only kind.

111. Audley L. Smith, "Richard Hurd's Letters on Chivalry and Romance," in *ELH,* 6 (1939), 58-81.

112. Richard Hurd, *The Works of Richard Hurd, D.D., Lord Bishop of Worcester* (London, 1811), II, 111-115, 118, 128.

113. Thomas Twining, *Aristotle's "Treatise on Poetry," Translated: with Notes on the Translation and on the Original; and Two Dissertations, on Poetical, and Musical, Imitation* (London, 1789), p. 561.

This he calls imitation of "illusive perception"; it includes description, which raises a "strong and clear idea of the object," onomatopoeia, or imitation of "sounds *significant*," and something that interestingly enough resembles Eliot's "objective correlative," the imitation of emotional states through a description of their objects. For Twining this imitation of "illusive perception" has a stronger semantic claim to the word "imitation" largely because of English usage and connotations.[114]

But he also speaks of a second kind, which he calls imitation of "illusive belief." "The word *imitation* is also, in a more particular, but well-known, sense, applied to Poetry when considered as FICTION—to stories, actions, incidents, and characters, as far as they are *feigned* or *invented* by the Poet *in imitation,* as we find it commonly, and obviously enough, expressed, of nature, of real life, of truth, in general, as opposed to that individual reality of things which is the province of the historian. Of this imitation the epic and dramatic poems are the principal examples." This account is thoroughly Aristotelian, as is a further comment on the empirical origins of this imitation: "that general stock of ideas, collected from experience, observation, and reading, and reposited in the Poet's mind." He also sees Aristotle's view of music as significant sound structures analogous to the structure of plot in a drama. But in claiming that the two kinds of imitation are entirely distinct from each other, Twining does not recognize the probable as implicit in his notion of the first kind and an important link with its clear presence in the second. In this he was a child of his times.[115]

Before I conclude this chapter it may be well to recall that Earl Wasserman's study of the bases of imagery, "Nature Moralized: The Divine Analogy in the Eighteenth Century," obliquely corroborates our findings about how the critics

114. *Ibid.,* pp. 8-9, 19.
115. *Ibid.,* pp. 19-26, 48, 54-56.

dealt with the cognitive element in mimesis. He begins with Miss Nicolson's brilliant study, *The Breaking of the Circle,* which maintains that the new science had fractured the bases of a sense of divine analogy in the universe, and traces the career of the progressively vanishing natural sources of an imagery expressive of human value. Correspondences had become less and less mimetic, until by the end of the century they were "a phase of psychology, not ontology." The whole bent of the eighteenth-century aesthetic, he says, was "to root the relationship of image and value in an emotive act instead of an outward perception." The forces behind the change were the new science, and, filling the gap it created, a hesitant Platonism and the philosophy of Shaftesbury. Two passages fitting what has been said here of the Enlightenment noetic are worth quoting:

When Bacon wrote that poetry subjects the shows of things to the desires of the mind, whereas reason doth buckle and bow the mind unto the nature of things, he was assenting to that divorce of head and heart, of object and value, that accompanied the approaching end of the Renaissance; the same divorce that the Romantics would later struggle to repair by once again wedding outward thing and inward meaning. The shows of things belong to the domain of science, where the materials of experience exist in themselves, stripped of values; where a primrose by a river's brim is only a yellow primrose. . . .

*   *   *

The new science, bent upon absorbing all aspects of thought and feeling and upon examining them with the same instruments it was using upon the physical world, at least implied a similarity of inner and outer reality, but only by reducing all to a materialism.[116]

116. Earl R. Wasserman, "Nature Moralized: The Divine Analogy of the Eighteenth Century," in *ELH,* 20 (1953), 39-76, especially 39, 41, 68, 75.

Draper sums up his study of the fate of the critical concept of mimesis in the eighteenth century in the following fashion. In the early decades "'imitation' received the simplest—and most mistaken—interpretation: in poetry it meant primarily the copying of models; in painting, the copying of old masters or of natural objects; in music, it was interpreted in any way that the ignorance or the ingenuity of the writer might suggest." The discussion of the middle decades was largely in terms of rationalism and sentimentalism, and toward the end of the century interest in the concept waned: "More and more of the writers ignored 'imitation' entirely; and the interpretation of Twining, even had it been less timid, would probably have had little actual effect upon either the poets or the aesthetic philosophers. The semantic history of *mimesis* reflects the period of authority during the first third of the century, and the period, during the middle decades, of scientific inquiry and of sentimental reaction, which later passed into the age of Romantic revolt."[117]

Lovejoy makes much more explicit the noetic roots of the rationalism operative in the aesthetic discussion of *nature* earlier in the century, and the phenomenon Wasserman discusses was a natural enough reaction to this. Lovejoy is writing of the parallel of deism and aesthetic theory at the time:

Now substitute "poetry," or "art in general," for "religion" in the foregoing propositions, and you have an outline, not of all, but of the more general and fundamental part, of the neo-classical aesthetics, the actual subjective *motivation* of neo-classicism was, no doubt, a complex affair; and in it the force of tradition and a habit of deference to ancient authority undeniably had a large part. But

117. Draper, "Aristotelian Mimesis in Eighteenth-Century England," p. 400.

the "rationalization" of these motives is what here concerns us. As a theory, resting upon a coherent, or supposedly coherent, body of principles, neo-classicism was, at bottom, neither traditionalist nor authoritarian; it was an expression of the same rationalism of the Enlightenment which was manifesting itself in deism; and in taking "nature" as *its* sacred word also, it was, in the main, using the word in the same primary sense which it had for the deist.

That neo-classicism in theory—though happily not quite always in practice—was fundamentally an aesthetic uniformitarianism can hardly need argument.[118]

CONCLUSION

In discussing the cognitive element in mimesis and its function, we have surveyed important ground for this study. In this kind of poetry, knowledge has a value that is hard to overemphasize yet very easy to misconstrue. Western Classical art was certainly intellectually realistic, produced by an outward-going sensibility that was piloted by a mind eager to find its way into the deeper reaches of nature, its own human nature most of all. In trying to characterize this basic gesture of the Greek mind Randall says well:

Nous meant to the Greek "intellectual vision," and the verbs associated with it, like *theōrein,* or *eidenei,* are sight words, conveying the flavor of "seeing" something. The function of *nous* is to lead to *theōria,* the kind of aesthetic spectacle properly upheld in a "theatre," the natural abode of *theōria.* Ultimately, when Greek culture became very much aware of its central aims, as in Plato, the function of *nous* was seen as leading to a beholding of human life in the world as a transparently intelligible dramatic spectacle. It is such an aesthetic *nous* that Aristotle is trying to bend to his own purposes, more scientific if in the end no less ultimately aesthetic.[119]

It is only natural, then, to expect that, where knowing is

118. Lovejoy, *Essays in the History of Ideas,* p. 88.
119. Randall, *Aristotle,* p. 90, n. 13.

thought of as "seeing," the mere seeing is considered its own adequate reward, and contemplation is considered its proximate fulfillment. This notion of θεωρία is at the heart of the Greek view of education, and is in a special way the goal of Aristotle's view of mimesis.

If this value is hard to overemphasize, it is easy to mis-construe. This happened in the case of poetry as early as Plato and Horace, and in quite a different yet related way among eighteenth-century critics. The autonomy of *nous* which Randall ascribes to Plato's view of the mind must be understood with two reservations, and in the case of poetry they tend to debilitate this autonomy. By focusing his attention on nature in its ideal perfection of the forms, Plato tended to underestimate the value of emerging reality, of *becoming,* and consequently of its rich revelation in ex-perience. Poetry always begins here, and the concrete quality of the emerging real is the basic analogue for poetic structure. Structure, in turn, is the guarantee of its own value and autonomy, and of the autonomy of contemplation attendant upon it. The second reservation results from this tendency to idealize, namely, the Platonic demand for an ascetical ascent to the forms as a direct result of their contemplation. Even though this moral demand was not grossly pragmatic— for with Plato knowledge rather than voluntary action was the center of ethical concern—still this orientation worked against poetry's proper and autonomous value. With Horace, and especially in the tradition that followed his please-and-teach formula, a more pragmatic and rhetorical kind of moralism prevailed. This was especially true where the Enlightenment cosmological view of God, man, and the world weakened the cognitive center of mimesis. In Pieper's words, the aim of having knowledge make men "masters and owners of nature" replaced the more characteristic, con-templative Greek quest of that "simple vision to which truth offers itself like a landscape to the eye." The mind was thus strangely mechanized in the interests of moralism, and poetry was unwittingly made its rhetorical instrument. This phenomenon lay at the opposite end of the spectrum from Platonic moralism.

This cognitive element was not a concept or an idea, but a structured *thing of meaning*. Mimetic structure drew form from nature into the poem to present it to the audience, with due respect for the autonomy it deserved in all three states: in nature as "the given," in the poem as what was significant, and in the mind of the audience as what was pleasurable contemplation. Only an intellectual realism, capable of both immersing itself in nature and yet transcending it, could achieve this autonomy, and this through the transforming power of the Classical imagination. The eighteenth-century critics did not regularly understand poetry in this way, and hence drifted farther from the center of the tradition.

When one sees what the cognitive element in mimesis rightly involves, one can understand why the Enlightenment noetic tended to frustrate the mimetic tradition. This particular artistic tradition, as well as poetry in any tradition, must be nourished by a lively sense of the "given" quality of things. Without this it is hard to see how poetry can truly have a human theme; and to this extent all art is at core mimetic. Though centuries have intervened between Aristotle's time and our own, Bate points to this important consideration in criticizing T. E. Hulme's gesture of withdrawal from life as a formula for modern art: "It leaves unanswered some of the most central concerns of critical theory. The foremost is that involved in the classical belief that form of any sort is nothing except as it is objectively *real*—except as it is found working through nature itself—and that art is of value to the degree that it reveals this form, conveying or recasting it through its own medium."[120]

120. *Criticism: The Major Texts,* ed. W. J. Bate (New York: Harcourt, Brace, 1952), p. 561.

In a more complex context, dealing with "form" in art as developed through several postclassical theorists, Wimsatt says that, though literature is more concerned with the subjective interpretation of experience than with the objects of experience as such, "nevertheless our final view, implicit in our whole narrative and in whatever moments of argument we may have allowed ourselves, has been that 'form' in fact embraces and penetrates 'message' in a way that constitutes a deeper and more substantial meaning than either abstract message or separable ornament. . . . The poetic dimension [unlike the scientific and rhetorical] is just that dramatically unified meaning which is coterminous with form."[121] He expresses a similar idea in a different context, where he sees the poetic metaphor most successful where it obliquely imitates nature (and there is no questioning here of "copying"). "Poetry is that type of verbal structure where truth of reference or correspondence reaches a maximum degree of fusion with truth of coherence—or where external and internal relation are intimately mutual reflections."[122] As if to prove that this is so, in the first of these two contexts he describes quite well the unity of structure and cognition in poetry, when he says: "A refraction of light through a crystal tells something about the light, something about the crystal; the refraction itself is a kind of reality, interesting to observe. Let us say that poetry is a kind of reality refracted through subjective responses."[123]

Following both the Enlightenment's mechanizing and thinning out of the concept of nature, its "given" and humanly nourishing quality, and the understandable idealistic reaction to this, our culture since this time has experienced a serious dislocation of what is deemed "objective" and what

121. William Wimsatt and Cleanth Brooks, *Literary Criticism: A Short History* (New York: Knopf, 1957), p. 748.
122. Wimsatt, *The Verbal Icon*, p. 149.
123. Wimsatt and Brooks, *Literary Criticism*, pp. 737-738.

"subjective." The phenomenon of the "two cultures" shows this cogently. Somehow man and nature must be at odds. Too often only what is scientifically provable, empirical in the narrow sense of the word, is considered "objective," and individual experience must be thought of as "subjective" in the sense of being private and unavailable to any "objective" meaning. The world of the arts reflects this split in some aspects of the Theatre of the Absurd and in the dull litany of the "anti-" and the "non-" commodities that have entered contemporary discussions of the arts. A feeble but perhaps meaningful reaction can be seen, to some extent at least, in the phenomena of "Op Art" and "Pop Art," and in the popularity of folk music. Hulme's criticism of withdrawal and some of the extreme forms of myth criticism reflect two extremes of this estrangement of man from nature in twentieth-century critical theory. "Nature," wherever it is —and it is everywhere inside and outside of us—needs reassertion at a deeply human level. This, perhaps, is one of the major perennial legacies of the mimetic tradition, which will never—or at least should never—go out of style.

Two random examples that seem to miss this subtle but all-important mimetic thrust of all art, if it is to be truly cognitive, are of interest. Rebecca West once said: "A copy of the universe is not what is required of art; one of the damned thing is ample."[124] Introducing Hugh Kenner's *The Paradox in Chesterton*, Marshall McLuhan observes that Chesterton was not a poet but a "metaphysical moralist," because his mind was outward-going. "The artist offers us not a system but a world. An inner world is explored and developed and then projected as an object. But that was never Chesterton's way. 'All my mental doors open outwards into a world I have not made,' he said in a basic formulation. And this distinction must always remain between the artist

124. Quoted in M. H. Abrams, *The Mirror and the Lamp* (New York: Norton, 1958), p. 100.

who is engaged in making a world and the metaphysician who is occupied in contemplating a world."[125] The dichotomy is extreme and would nullify all Classical theory and practice. Chesterton's claim about his mental doors is an apt description of the needfully mimetic gesture of all art, the root of the cognitive which we have been discussing. Else's formula, which makes the poet an imitator inasmuch as he is a maker, is true of all art, but only if it is convertible: that he is a maker only by being an imitator as well.

The double autonomy of all knowing demanded by Aristotle is especially meaningful in poetic contemplation. These two autonomies are a sense of "the given" with its priority in what is known, and the spontaneous fruition of the act of knowing as its own goal. In the sheer fruition of meaning the mind can see the "unselfish" quality of nature that is known, and the open process of knowing it. If "the given" in things demands uncompromising loyalty, fruition is its automatic reward. Art and love are alike in this.

125. Marshall McLuhan, "Introduction" in Hugh Kenner, *The Paradox in Chesterton* (New York: Sheed and Ward, 1947), pp. xxi-xxii.

3

FORM AS THE PROBABLE: THE STRUCTURAL ELEMENT

The Classical notion of art as peculiarly intellectual was not exhausted in speaking of it as cognitive. It was just as essentially patterned. If the poet was a seer, a man of special insight and wisdom, he was a maker as well. This best renders the Greek word for poet, ποιητής, the one who makes, shapes, forms his insight and wisdom. We have already seen Else's basic claim that Aristotelian imitation differed radically from Plato's notion of a "copy" precisely through this peculiar activity of the artist: "a poet, then, is an *imitator* in so far as he is a *maker*." We have been unable to speak of what is cognitive in poetry without involving at every turn the notion of structure, the pattern of what is said. The probable comprises both, not separably, but each through the other. Our word "playwright," as distinguished from its pale homophone, "playwrite," brings this idea to the fore. "Form" in most modern art theory does as well, though at times to the neglect of form as cognitive. This neglect has been occasioned by understandable reaction to the separation of "form" and "content" in earlier theories, as well as by the old bias of thinking that knowledge is primarily or even exclusively measured by science or philosophy. But Keats' commonplace, though an outgrowth of Romantic awareness in part, is quite valid for expressing the Aristotelian conviction: "Beauty is Truth,—Truth Beauty." Both then and now, a poet cannot be exclusively a seer or a maker, but must be each in being the other.

THE STRUCTURAL ELEMENT DESCRIBED

"Structure" is a common word that has many meanings in criticism. It can refer to the physical arrangement and interrelationship of the parts of a play or a poem, such as scenes or episodes. It can also refer to one of the many elements which intrinsically constitute the composition as a *thing made,* such as a rhyme, or, more significantly, a metaphor or symbol. In this sense Aristotle centered his attention on plot in the drama. By metonymy this stress can lead to a more inclusive and absolute sense of the word, the pervasive principle in a composition, which makes structure the product of the playwright's art of making, and whereby it is self-sustaining, self-sufficient, self-consistent and autonomous in its own order, the order of being a *thing made.* This is the ultimate meaning of structure in this study, though as a principle it is concretized in various ways as the discussion develops.

Needless to say, plot and the larger principle of structure which it involves are inseparable from the cognitive element. *What is made* can be coherent only in being a *thing of meaning.* Both in principle and in fact they are two sides of the one coin. Only with difficulty can they be spoken of in relative isolation. Attempts to speak of them by categorical application of Aristotle's hylomorphism, as "matter" and "form," as what is determined and what determines the other, tend to confuse a complicated situation. In some instances this has led to the fallacy that separates "form" and "content" in different ways, reflecting on the one hand the Platonic concept of imitation as "copying," and on the other the formalism of T. E. Hulme and the formalism which some find in the Chicago Aristotelians. If one does wish to speak of matter and form in a poem or play, it can only be by way of analogy. The cognitive and structural elements of mimesis both determine and are determined by one another; this is not a one-way street. Mimesis is both realistic and artful at the same time, each element in and through the other. The poet's work of shaping is intimately one of finding ($ε\check{υ}ρεσις$), in which the paradox that he is an imitator in being a maker works in both directions. This act of finding Else describes, we recall, as "the uncovering of a true relation which already exists somehow in the scheme of things." In a later, perhaps more sophisticated context in the same tradition of Aristotelian realism, Maritain explains why poetry is more philosophic than history "with respect to the very thing grasped, which is not a contingent thing in the mere fact of its existence, but in its infinite openness to the riches of being, and as a sign of it."[1] What is shaped must be significant in its realistic roots, else there could be no shape; yet ultimate significance could not come about without its being shaped. Despite this mutual dependence, structure has the ultimate priority, since mimesis is art. Man and wife are both needed for familial unity, yet ultimately the man is the head of the house!

We have already seen that for Aristotle the cognitive element gives mimesis a special status as a *thing of meaning*. It is concrete without being merely factual, richly philosophic without becoming abstract. A comment by Else indirectly highlights the special status that structure also has for Aristotle. The difference between Plato's and Aristotle's view of mimesis, he says, does not stop at the contrast between "copying" and the cognitive element in the poetic

1. Jacques Maritain, *Creative Intuition in Art and Poetry* (New York: Pantheon, 1953), p. 126; Gerald F. Else, *Aristotle's Poetics: The Argument* (Cambridge: Harvard University Press, 1957), p. 320.

universal. Even the way each conceives of the poet's activity in making his poem reveals completely different views of poetic structure. Plato treats the process of making as if it were part of the continuum of life, an act of man *qua* man; for Aristotle it is an act of the man *qua* artist. Hence the play or poem he produces must be judged differently by each. The context, more particularly, deals with the worth of drama:

This drastic revision is in the concept of imitation itself. For both Plato and Aristotle the dramatic mode is imitation *par excellence*. For Plato it is so because imitation means to him a personal experience and a direct relationship. The poet "is" his characters—that is, he pretends or appears to be them, for the drama remains indefeasibly a mode of Appearance. But he who is or pretends to be another cannot be himself. Hence 'imitation,' in the special sense of impersonation, must be *verboten* or very heavily safeguarded in an ideal commonwealth. The dramatic mode is the worst and most dangerous.

Aristotle is not legislating for a commonwealth, and he is not talking about psychic states in the poet. Plato had unconsciously and inevitably thought of the *actor* and his effect on an audience (for him the poet also was an actor); Aristotle is thinking of the *dramatic character* and his direct relation to the things that are being 'imitated.' Hence Aristotle puts highest what Plato puts lowest.[2]

Structure, then, ultimately achieves this unique kind of reality which a poem or play is—neither a physical thing nor an idea, but a *thing of meaning* in being a *thing made*. Aristotle's somewhat arch comment about how structure ultimately deals with fact is worth remembering: "And even if he [the poet] chances to take an historical subject, he is none the less a poet; for there is no reason why some events

2. *Ibid.*, pp. 97-98. Else is dealing with chapter III of the *Poetics* and Bk. III of the *Republic*.

that have actually happened should not conform to the law of the probable and possible, and in virtue of that quality in them he is their poet or maker" (1451b).

A further point. Aristotle said that art satisfies the human instinct for rhythm and harmony, as well as the instinct for imitation (1448b). The structural element tends to exploit this characteristic of art by being responsible for the sense of wholeness and development involved. Through structure a poem or play has a large and pervasive unity, achieved by a coherent relationship of its parts, by spelling out all the contours of the intuition. Aristotle speaks of a tragedy as being "an imitation of an action that is complete, and whole, and of a certain magnitude" (1450b). It is whole, he says, when it has a beginning, a middle, and an end. This famous comment, often misjudged as tautology, really prescribes a need of development, of organic growth of plot from within its own motivation, from its own set of premises to its own conclusions. Hence the plot comprehends a complete activity that makes sense in itself. But beyond this, the beauty of art demands "magnitude" in a tragedy, a substantial swath of human experience, such as will satisfy our appetite for significance. The function of structure is to achieve the full potential of this magnitude, to spell out the heightened meaning in its round, full contours. This is the structural or shaping aspect of the process of ideation discussed in the previous chapter.

This harmony is also dynamic. Aristotle spoke of the plot as being the soul of a tragedy (1450a), a vital principle that is at work everywhere, entire in the whole play, and metonymously entire in each of its parts. To change the metaphor slightly, the intuition looks out through the plot the way one's personality is revealed in his significant action.

In fact structure is a less dynamic, if conceptually more manageable notion of the poem as an action. For Aristotle it was precisely in action that the substance of nature became at once more real and meaningful, since for him being was becoming. A man was most himself when in action. If the poet (as Else would stress) and, in turn, his poem imitate nature, they do so in action. What is nature's action which they imitate? It is the concrete process whereby nature attains its fulfillment, its meaningful entelechy, whether in individual things or in nature's entirety, with special emphasis, of course, on human achievement. This meaning or significance is the basis of the philosophical universal spoken of above. Hence through concrete action nature is fulfilled, and meaning and reality are one. The poet's activity of "making," and through it the action of the poem, mirror the action of nature, not in the real order, but in the order of ποίησις, of "making." If the poetic universal transcends the limits of mere fact yet shines forth concretely, it does so precisely through this action of the poem, concretely in the structure of the poem dynamically looked at, seen best in the plot of a play. This poetic universal is not the abstract philosophic universal concept, but the poem's concrete counterpart of nature's dramatic achievement, shaped by the response of the poet's "objective sensibility." Here, then, is the ultimate realism of mimesis, which achieves in its own order, as nature does, the unity of universal meaning with the concrete. For this reason it is meaningless to separate "form" and "content" in mimesis, or to think of its universal as an idea, a concept, or an abstraction. Here, finally, is the reason for its autonomy: its shaped, meaningful action is its own end, correlatively intended for pleasurable contemplation. Structures in rhetoric are suasive instruments to make ideas transitively effective, hence not one with the ideas, but separable and capable of variation. But the poet is an imitator precisely in being a maker, and vice versa. Nature's way of being meaningful is dramatic; and so is the poem's.[3]

3. Paralleling the evolution in the cognitive element between the mimetic and the later, imaginative traditions (as opposed to a sharp break between

STRUCTURE AND THE GENRES

The concept of structure in mimesis comes to a more particular focus in the idea of genre or kind. It is familiar to one reading the *Poetics,* and the Classical and Neoclassical tradition respected it with more or less serious attention down to its demise. Johnson rejected too formalistic a notion of the kinds, looking rather to their evolution in the practice of the poets. And even today critics speak of genres, though more loosely and flexibly, with a certain amount of respect for some permanent critical value in the concept. To Aristotle the kinds were specific forms of poetry, such as tragedy, comedy, and epic, somewhat resembling the variety of the "species" of being in the real order of nature. More particularly they were conceived of as having their own structures or activities, required by both subject matter and point of

them), discussed in the Conclusion and in Chapter 2 (n. 2, pp. 58–59), one can see an evolution in the structural element as well. Aristotle habitually thought more in terms of nature than of person, more of essence than of existence. The later tradition recognized the poet's shaping activity in more personal terms, and Maritain could more readily think of the poetic universal as transcending the contingency of mere fact by making the fact a sign of its openness to the richness of existence (see p. 132, above). Both are distinct advances, but they are both evolutionary. Though the mimetic tradition beginning in the *Poetics* had good reason for stressing structure and its autonomy, its later treatment of structure was more and more rhetorically conceived of, and the poetic universal was confused with the philosophical, either abstractly or ideally understood. With the development of lyric poetry in the nineteenth century and in our own, the essentially dramatic character of structure has rightly received more personal and varied interpretations. Yet too biographical and psychological a conception of the poet's shaping power in such interpretations has often led to a neglect of structure; and the merely subjective fact of a poet's having and speaking of an idea or experience has often masked as the poetic universal, which can be secured in a poem only through structure. In this way, Aristotle's distinguishing of poetry from philosophy and rhetoric through his concept of structure has been lost sight of by a later confusion of poetry with psychology and biography. Philosophic idealism, whether of the Platonic or the more subjective modern sort, is frequently the cause of the confusion.

view, for their own peculiar purpose, the "proper" pleasure each offered. The analogy to species of things in the order of nature showed the intrinsic relationship between form and finality, a favorite Aristotelian approach to any discussion. The growth and progress of a play or an epic depended on its peculiar inner make-up, and this, in turn, revealed an inner goal to be achieved, the full shape of the particular type of poem. This shape, finally, determined the kind of pleasure to be afforded the audience. It should be clear from this that Aristotle does not ascribe to what is pejoratively called affective criticism, because pleasure follows very closely the structure of each genre or kind. Each has its proper pleasure ἡδονὴ οἰκεία, the latter word suggesting a pleasure that *is at home*, belongs).

The concept of genre is itself an aspect of mimesis, of the orientation of Classical art theory to nature. Different subject matter demands different treatment. Also different kinds of people and their differing motives and activity will be presented differently, though, of course, under the pressure of the poet's point of view in imitating. The concept is based on the validity of the philosophic universal idea and its structures in nature, with a confidence that is perhaps a bit naive, as the later history of genre criticism was to show. But it reflects the importance of experience as the basis of a healthy mimesis. The Platonic tradition in criticism, oriented toward the transcendent forms of the Good and the Beautiful, did not develop the genre type criticism. The tendency of the nineteenth-century Romantics to reject the idea of genre is an interesting case in point. They have also in recent years been criticized for lacking a sense of structure in a larger sense.[4] But because structure is the foundation of function to be studied in this chapter, we shall review the evidence of the eighteenth-century critics under the heading of the

4. Paul Goodman, "Neo-Classicism, Platonism, Romanticism," in *Journal of Philosophy*, 31 (1934), 160-161.

genres, where the Classical idea of structure comes to a special focus. Each of the genres should have its own proper pleasure.

STRUCTURE AND FUNCTION

The shape of the probable, the shape of a plot, the shape of a genre determines its peculiar character, and in doing this determines the relative autonomy of mimesis, its function in pleasurable contemplation. Unlike the shape of factual or philosophic knowledge, the shape of poetic knowledge is "useless," in that it does not directly serve to report or describe the world of objects. Poetic knowledge, again, does not look to an end beyond itself, its own shape, structure, or activity, in the way rhetoric does, but its structure is its own end, correlative with the pleasure the audience is afforded by seeing it. Perhaps this salutary "uselessness" of poetry comes most to the fore when we think of its structure, its shape that is its own end. The shape of the probable also shows how the separation of teaching and pleasing in most views of the Horatian formula cannot consistently reveal a true notion of mimesis. For the shape is itself cognitive and its pleasure is as much involved in the cognitive as is shape itself. Sidney's view of poetic pleasure as honey on the cup of bitter doctrine is for this reason a rather low rhetorical conception of the art of poetry, even though elsewhere in the same *Apologie* he seems to divine the autonomy which shape or structure gives to the poet's statements. The poets do not tell lies because they are not trying to tell the historical or scientific truth: "Now, for the Poet, he nothing affirmes, and therefore never lyeth." For the remainder of this chapter we shall review how the eighteenth-century critics dealt with structure, especially in their treatment of the genres, as a way of seeing how they understood the function of mimesis. We shall find how wide most of them were of the mark set by Aristotle as intrinsically demanded by the structure of mimesis, when properly understood: "we must not demand of Tragedy any and every kind of pleasure, but only that which is proper to it" (1453b), a notion applicable by metonymy to all the genres.[5]

STRUCTURE AND TRAGEDY

Aristotle elaborated his concept of structure most of all when treating of drama, its plot, and, especially in the case of tragedy, the various details that constituted a complex tragic plot. He saw in such a plot the most intense effects of the poet's shaping power, and for this reason preferred the tragic genre to all others, despite his liking for Homer. Hence what is said in this context about structure and its concern with the audience applies, *mutatis mutandis,* to all the kinds.

All tragedy was a progress from happiness to unhappiness for a moderately good man, but the complex plot stressed the paradoxical thrust associated with Greek tragedy at its best, that is, tragic irony. The unexpected is not irrational. Rather it is written deeply in the "terrible thing" (τί δεινόν) being unfolded to the audience; irony is its innermost logic. The early development of the plot (δέσις) overtly seems to forward the tragic hero's interests, but actually is preparing ironically for his destruction. The turning point (περιπέτεια) suddenly brings this about, and the downward cascade of his fortunes sweeps him from life in the unraveling of the action (λύσις). The complex plot was best when the hero saw the turning point's meaning immediately, when his recognition (ἀναγνώρισις) coincided with it. The effect of this ironic development and revelation constituted the unique

5. *Elizabethan Critical Essays,* ed. G. Gregory Smith (London: Oxford University Press, 1904), I, 184; S. H. Butcher, *Aristotle's Theory of Poetry and Fine Art,* ed. John Gassner, 4th ed. (New York: Dover, 1951), pp. 198 ff., 212 ff. See also *Metaphysics* 981b and *Politics* 1334a and 1339b.

pleasure of tragedy for the audience, a pleasure somehow involving the emotions of pity and fear. Something terrible had happened which somehow involved a fault (ἁμαρτία), and when these were spelled out fully, a humane identification of audience with the action was the result: *homo sum.* I shall deal with the concept of flaw and especially with the audience factor in a moment. Here it is important to see the concept of structure at its best and to understand how it is responsible for the audience's pleasure.[6]

The tragic flaw or fault is one of the several enigmatic words in the scholarship of the *Poetics.* Was it a moral fault in the sense of sin? Most Neoclassical critics understood it this way, and some scholars still defend this view. Butcher suggests that it is a moral frailty, while Bywater and Lane Cooper opt for an error of judgment or ignorance of fact or circumstance, and Roger Pack thinks of it as an external slip. All of them put the element of error or mistake in the psychology of the hero. Else claims that it is a quality of an incident in the plot structure. It is part of his larger interpretation, elaborately developed, of how the complex plot structure intimately controls the response of the audience. For Else the complex plot is at its best in Aristotle's view when it deals with the killing of a blood kinsman. The play then becomes an aesthetic analogy to a court trial. The plot structure reveals a basic innocence through ignorance in the hero's action which elicits the emotional fear and pity of the audience. In this interpretation, "the discovery is then the counterpart and reverse of the mistake. Here the emotional charge which is inherent in the mistake (not in the ignorance *per se,* but in the horrible deed to which it stands in causal relation) finds its discharge. The ἁμαρτία represents the reservoir of emotional potential, the recognition is the lightning-flash through which it passes off."[7] Whatever

6. See *Poetics* 10–14.
7. Butcher, *Aristotle's Theory,* p. 317; Ἀριστοτέλους Περὶ ποιητικῆς. *Aris-*

the word means, it helps to relate Aristotle's notion of tragedy to its pleasurable function for the audience. This is the next problem, that of κάθαρσις.

KATHARSIS

One of the best known and most problematic controversies occasioned by the *Poetics* is that centering upon the meaning of the word κάθαρσις, which Aristotle uses when speaking of the function of tragedy. "No passage, probably, in ancient literature," says Butcher, "has been so frequently handled by commentators, critics, and poets, by men who knew Greek and by men who knew no Greek." It would be foolish to pretend to solve the problem here. I shall mainly outline a few positions which have been taken, as a background for understanding the critics we are studying. These various interpretations are usually expressed in various translations of a key passage in the sixth chapter. Hence any English version tends to prejudice the meaning of the word and the function to which it refers. For practical purposes, however, I shall supply Bywater's and Else's, since they tend

---

totle, On the Art of Poetry, ed. Ingram Bywater (Oxford: Clarendon, 1909), pp. 35, 215; Lane Cooper, *The Poetics of Aristotle: Its Meaning and Influence* (Boston: Marshall Jones, 1923), p. 48; Roger A. Pack, "On Guilt and Error in Senecan Tragedy," in *Transactions and Proceedings of the American Philological Association*, 71 (1940), 360-371; Else, *Aristotle's Poetics*, pp. 378-385. Else reminds us in another section of his argument (p. 306) that Aristotle ignored any causality beyond the human when treating of tragedy, even though Fate loomed large in the actual plays he dealt with. "God or Fate do not break into the charmed circle. The ultimate never confronts us in the *Poetics*, any more than it does in the *Ethics* or the *Politics*—except in the form of Chance or the marvelous, τὸ θαυμαστόν." This would make Else's view of ἁμαρτία seem more cogent since it intensifies Aristotle's notion of structure as self-sufficient. Cedric H. Whitman in his *Sophocles: A Study of Heroic Humanism* (Cambridge: Harvard University Press, 1951), sees the flaw as a moral one, but with a difference. In Aeschylus the hero is morally responsible to God, while in Sophocles he is responsible only to himself (pp. 33-40).

to express two poles in the discussion, the first a psychological interpretation, the second a structural one.

Bywater sees the tragic imitation attaining its end "with incidents arousing pity and fear, wherewith to accomplish its catharsis of such emotions." Else sees it "carrying to completion, through a course of events involving pity and fear, the purification of those painful or fatal acts which have that quality." Bywater's version can stand generically for all those who think of the katharsis as going on in the psyches of the audience. Else would have it that katharsis takes place, not in the audience but in the sequence of events in the plot, so that the dramatic structure is the center of attention, where this mysterious process takes place, and pleasurable experience of the audience is correlative to its aesthetic achievement.[8]

It is even difficult to give an English equivalent of the word κάθαρσις in more or less isolation, without prejudicing the larger meaning of the passage. Some see in it a metaphor of *ritual purification,* others one of *medical purgation.* Further, each of these metaphors has been pressed into the service of a moral meaning and of one that is more aesthetic. Again, some look to passages in the *Politics* or the *Rhetoric* to throw light on the word, others deny the validity of the analogies. Since we cannot hope to solve the original problem here, we shall merely look at two accounts which have been given as offering a plausible background for understanding the critics of our study. These two views seem germane to the larger premises of mimesis and its function as outlined by Aristotle.

No matter which interpretation is actually the one Aristotle had in mind, two facts should be kept in mind for our purposes. The first is that Aristotle conceived of the function of tragedy, like that of any other kind of art, as pleasurable contemplation deriving from the peculiar structure which

8. Butcher, *Aristotle's Theory,* pp. 23, 243; Else, *Aristotle's Poetics,* p. 221; Bywater, Ἀριστοτέλους Περὶ ποιητικῆς, pp. 17, 151–161.

it achieved—ἡδονὴ οἰκεία. This should be remembered when judging the worth of some of the psychological interpretations that tend to bend the notion of katharsis to rhetorical purposes, whether religious, moral, or psychotherapeutic. The second is the Platonic context in which the problem was posed. Having secured the autonomy of tragedy, he may well have sought to show how to allay the scruples of his master about the disturbing emotional character of the art. If this brought him to a logical impasse with his first conviction about the autonomy of tragedy without his seeing it, we may chide him for poor logical thinking. But we should not destroy his allegiance to this autonomy, which, we have seen, has a broader and more lasting character in his notion of mimesis itself. In any case, then, it seems fair to say that one should not readily label his theory of katharsis as affective in the sense rightly rejected by Wimsatt, as that which values art exclusively by measuring the psychological effects of art upon an audience rather than by inspecting the structural element of the art itself.[9]

The following is the Greek of the passage in question. Both Bywater and Else agree on the text: δι ἐλέου καὶ φόβου περαίνουσα τὴν τῶν τοιούτων παθημάτων κάθαρσιν (1449b).

1) The first of the interpretations is Bywater's, with an added suggestion or two of my own. He points out what has been largely forgotten over the years, that there are two steps spoken of in the text, the pleasurable experience of the play, and then—and only then—what has received practically exclusive attention, the subsequent katharsis. "This excitement of pity and fear is, as far as the poet is concerned,

---

9. A review of various interpretations of κάθαρσις may be found in Butcher, *Aristotle's Theory*, pp. 240 ff., and in Else, *Aristotle's Poetics*, pp. 225-226, n. 14. See also W. K. Wimsatt and Monroe C. Beardsley, "The Affective Fallacy," in *The Verbal Icon* (Lexington: University of Kentucky Press, 1954), pp. 21-39.

the end of Tragedy, but it is in truth only a means to its ultimate end, its κάθαρσις of such emotions."[10] Allan Gilbert, who interprets katharsis in an aesthetic way, as Bywater does not, suggests the same distinction, substituting a semicolon for a comma after φόβου, thus separating "pity and fear" from exclusive reference to "κάθαρσις," and linking them with the object of imitation. Hence he renders the passage in this way: "with incidents arousing pity and fear; and accomplishing its [the drama's] catharsis of such emotions."[11] This reading as well as Bywater's see iteration in τοιούτων.

If this separation of the experience of the emotions and their katharsis is valid, what, then, is the experience? Is it proper to speak of *exciting* these emotions, a more rhetorical term that fails to account for the essentially pleasurable experience which Bywater wishes to stress? For surely the excitement of real pity and fear is not a pleasurable experience. Might the emotions be better spoken of as *engaged,* that is, linked meaningfully with their objects and thus through *poetic representation* understood rather than realistically exercised? Bywater does not make this suggestion, but it seems required both by the nature of mimesis as well as by its pleasurable experience.[12]

In our earlier analysis of Aristotle's view of mimesis, we saw that the pleasure attendant upon experiencing poetry centered upon *seeing a representation* and appreciating its *harmonious structure.* Pity and fear can hardly enter the question save *in being known and appreciated.* The actual

10. Bywater, Ἀριστοτέλους Περὶ ποιητικῆς, p. 151.

11. Allan Gilbert, "The Aristotelian Catharsis," in *Philosophical Review*, 35 (1926), 301–302.

12. Butcher, *Aristotle's Theory*, pp. 240–241, n. 3, refers to Reinken's interpretation of τῶν τοιούτων as implying an imaginative transformation of the emotional element, so that pity and fear are imaginatively not realistically experienced.

emotion experienced is more like the joy involved in any rich knowledge.

In turning to the second element, the katharsis proper, Bywater reminds us that the article τήν with κάθαρσιν has possessive implications and should be rendered as "its" to show that other art forms have their own katharses. The *Politics* (8.7), for example, speaks of music as having a kathartic value, among others.

We accept the division of melodies proposed by certain philosophers into ethical melodies, melodies of action, and passionate or inspiring melodies, each having, as they say, a mode corresponding to it. But we maintain further that music should be studied, not for the sake of one, but of many benefits, that is to say, with a view to (1) education, (2) purgation (the word 'purgation' we use at present without explanation, but when hereafter we speak of poetry, we will treat the subject with more precision): music may also serve (3) for intellectual enjoyment, for relaxation and for recreation after exertion . . . In education the most ethical modes are to be preferred, but in listening to the performances of others we may admit the modes of action and passion also. For feelings such as pity and fear, or, again, enthusiasm, exist very strongly in some souls, and have more or less influence over all. Some persons fall into a religious frenzy, whom we see as a result of the sacred melodies—when they have used the melodies that excite the soul to mystic frenzy —restored as though they had found healing and purgation. Those who are influenced by pity or fear, and every emotional nature, must have a like experience, and others in so far as each is susceptible to such emotions, and all are in a manner purged, and their souls lightened and delighted. The purgative melodies likewise give an innocent pleasure to mankind.[13]

The passage, more descriptive than expository and analytic,

13. Politics (1341b–1342a); see also Bywater, 'Αριστοτέλους Περὶ ποιητικῆς, p. 152.

seems to deal with the actual emotions of the audience after the experience of art. There is no indication of how this state derives from the first element, just treated, or how Aristotle understands the metaphor. He seems to be concerned with a practical effect on emotions potentially harmful or at least troublesome to the commonwealth. One is reminded of current psychiatric practice of using drama or something like it to help patients to integrate their distraught minds and clarify their outlook.[14] But it is not clear in this passage how the first element contributes to this effect, or indeed, whether the first process is conceived of as more rhetorical than aesthetic. Again, are we to think of the Athenian audiences as coming to the theater for therapeutic treatment; and if they needed this, would their relatively rare attendance be a sufficient cure for their neuroses? Bywater thinks that the entire theory of katharsis was propounded for the sociopolitical reason of justifying tragedy as good for the commonwealth. Further, he denies any directly moral significance for the term. "The primary error, however, in this [the purification theory of Lessing] and similar interpretations of παθημάτων κάθαρσιν is that it reads a directly moral meaning into the term, as though the theatre were a school, and the tragic poet a teacher of morality."[15] This will be important to remember when we come to consider the opinion of the eighteenth-century critics.

2) Else thinks of the problem in radically different terms. Though κάθαρσις is important for the emotional impact of the tragedy upon the audience, it does not take place directly in the audience but in the structure of the play itself. He thinks of the process as one of purification, not, however, of a subjective state but in the sequence of events that comprise the plot. He translates the key words in this way: "carrying

14. F. L. Lucas, *Literature and Psychology*, rev. American ed. (Ann Arbor: University of Michigan Press, 1957), pp. 275–279.

15. Bywater, Ἀριστοτέλους Περὶ ποιητικῆς, p. 161.

to completion, through a course of events involving pity and fear, the purification of those painful or fatal acts which have that quality."

Else insists that the katharsis is something built into the plot rather than something occurring directly in the audience's experience—in fact, it is available outside the theater, when the play is read rather than experienced, he says. His argument derives from the larger context of the study, namely from the consistent development of the meaning of mimesis and of tragedy which he finds in the *Poetics*. The best material for the complex tragic plot ($\pi\acute{a}\theta$os), according to Aristotle, is the dread slaying of a kinsman. Both in real life and in its tragic imitation this carried with it a special pollution ($\mu\iota\alpha\rho\acute{o}\nu$) calling for expiation and purification. But when this crime was committed in ignorance ($\acute{a}\mu\alpha\rho\tau\acute{\iota}\alpha$), there was place for expiation by exculpation in the law courts. This was the practice in antiquity and is provided for in Plato's suggested code. Hence the complex plot involving $\acute{a}\mu\alpha\rho\tau\acute{\iota}\alpha$ provided an analogy to this trial by spelling out the tragic irony of the pitiful and fearful acts step by step. The ironic conflict between $\acute{a}\mu\alpha\rho\tau\acute{\iota}\alpha$ and $\acute{a}\nu\alpha\gamma\nu\acute{\omega}\rho\iota\sigma\iota$s thus brings about a cleansing of the crime in and through its dramatic structure in the plot. Because this situation is charged with emotion, the audience is deeply engaged in both mind and heart. This constitutes the unique mimetic pleasure of tragedy.

In this way, Else says, Aristotle answered Plato's troubled objections to the emotional impact of tragedy. Plato thought of emotions as irrational, but Aristotle thought of them as rational, in that they depended upon good judgment. With the judgment well made in the play, the obvious benefit to the audience was manifest in this peculiar pleasure. The $\pi\alpha\theta\eta\mu\acute{a}\tau\omega\nu$ of the formula refers to the dread deeds, not to the emotions in the audience. Else sums up his view with reference to Sophocles' *Oedipus Tyrannus* thus: "the sequence would be: (πάθος, i.e., deed of horror, inherently μιαρόν but performed in ignorance →) steady augmentation of the horror as the climax approaches → recognition, undoing (reversing) the ignorance → grief and remorse of the doer, certifying the ignorance as cause of the deed and the deed therefore as οὐ μιαρόν → pity (→ tragic pleasure)."

He admits that his solution does not deal with the passage from the *Politics* quoted above. He rightly says that he is concerned with the coherence of the *Poetics,* not with the *Politics,* that it need not have reference to this part of the *Poetics* in any way. Part of the *Poetics* is presumed lost, or perhaps a promised part may not have been written. At all events, Else's position commands favor, and both positions outlined here supply a valuable background for reading the critics of the eighteenth century.[16]

16. Else, *Aristotle's Poetics,* pp. 438-439. The problem is treated more fully on pp. 224-232 and 423-447. Else's discussion of katharsis strengthens the importance of the autonomy of structure and consequently of its function in pleasurable contemplation, as leading ideas in the *Poetics.* His refusal, then, to determine the meaning of the term in the *Poetics* directly by its meaning in the *Politics* need not be taken as cavalier. His study aims at seeing the argument of the *Poetics* as a whole, as offering a coherent view of the poetic art. Besides, years ago Butcher showed that Aristotle was willing to allow further possible "uses" of mimesis beyond the direct confines of autonomous contemplation (Butcher, *Aristotle's Theory,* pp. 198 ff.), much as it is clear that drama can be of value to psychotherapy and religious art can be a source of piety to those who worship. But in any case the proximate autonomy of both structure and contemplation should not be sacrificed. For a strong rejection of Else's view of κάθαρσις, ἀναγνώρισις, and ἁμαρτία see W. K. Wimsatt's "Aristotle and Oedipus or Else," in *Hateful Contraries: Studies in Literature and Criticism* (Lexington: University of Kentucky Press, 1965), pp. 72-89.

At this point it is also worth stressing what is often forgotten regarding the *Poetics.* It is much less formal than Aristotle's other treatises. It is more descriptive and empirical than systematic, despite its basically philosophic concern. Though certain Aristotelian patterns of thought are recognizable throughout the treatise, they are not applied with the kind of categorical precision one is used to in the treatises dealing with scientific knowledge. Aristotle seems mainly concerned with exploring the

NEOCLASSICAL OPINION OF KATHARSIS

Wellek and Warren suggest that critical discussion of the genres in Neoclassical France tended to blend rationalism and authoritarianism. A sense of propriety and tradition, rather than any close attention to the peculiar constitution of structure, commonly predominate most critical treatment of the genres. And Horace is the authority most quoted. English Neoclassical critics, usually more pragmatic than their cousins across the channel, reflect this tendency strongly.[17] One searches them in vain for an original treatment of the genres or an awareness of how function grows out of structure. In fact, the process is usually reversed. A moralistic katharsis must be effected, and the matter and its treatment must take a cue from this. And the probable is replaced by a narrowly conceived moral lesson. Though Aristotle's framework of the *Poetics* is schematically repeated, the spirit of this document is effectively replaced by Horatian ideas and formulae. This is especially true with respect to the please-and-teach formula which practically everywhere has replaced the Aristotelian notion of functional pleasure following upon structure. Again, as we saw in Chapter 2, Neoplatonic idealism tends to usurp the function of the probable by offering a moral ideal instead of a significant insight into life. The importance of structure is lessened or ignored, the difference between moral doctrine and poetic knowledge vanishes, and a strong didacticism replaces the theory of katharsis as we have been discussing it.

Sir William Temple, in his essay "Of Poetry," states what even the most liberal Neoclassical critics would subscribe to

---

structural and cognitive implications of mimesis together with the historical experience the Greeks have had of the arts.

17. René Wellek and Austin Warren, *Theory of Literature,* 3rd ed. (New York: Harcourt, Brace, World, 1962), pp. 260 ff.

about the purpose of tragedy. "The chief end seems to have been instruction, and under the disguise of fables, or the pleasure of a story, to show the beauties and the rewards of virtue, the difformities and misfortunes or punishment of vice; by examples of both to encourage one, and deter men from the other; to reform ill customs, correct ill manners, and moderate all violent passions."[18] Blackmore and Rymer bolster this view in claiming a religious origin for tragedy, and they see in the chorus the mission of rectifying ideas of morality and divinity, of moderating the passions, and of purging the mind of the audience from vice and corruption.[19]

It is difficult to know precisely what Dryden thought of the matter. At times he takes a didactic pose, at times he seems to seek only pleasure as the function of poetry. One has only to recall his plays to know he was not a Puritan, yet his remarks on comedy, for example, which we shall soon discuss, are hard to understand in any other context. In a "Prologue To the University of Oxon . . ." he ascribes a noble purpose to the stage:

> Here they who long have known the usefull Stage,
> Come to be taught themselves to teach the Age.
> As your Commissioners our Poets goe,
> To Cultivate the Virtue which you sow:
> In your *Lycaeum*, first themselves refind,
> And Delegated thence to Humane kind.[20]

Katharsis has for him a clearly moral function. While explaining the superiority of poetry to philosophy in the moralistic fashion introduced into England by Sidney, he says of

18. Sir William Temple, *The Works of Sir William Temple, Bart.* (London, 1814), III, 423.

19. T[homas] R[ymer], *A Short View of Tragedy* (London, 1693), p. 19; *The Tragedies of the Last Age* (London, 1678), pp. 11-12.

20. John Dryden, *The Prologues and Epilogues of John Dryden*, ed. William B. Gardner (New York: Columbia University Press, 1951), p. 56.

tragedy in particular: "to purge the passions by example, is therefore the particular instruction which belongs to Tragedy." For there we see persons of highest quality fall because of their pride and want of commiseration, "to cure us of these two [vices]."[21] Further, he extends to tragedy Bossu's directive for writing an epic, saying that the moral should be pointed first, so that it "directs the whole action of the play to one centre; and that action or fable is the example built upon the moral, which confirms the truth of it to our experience."[22] Here structure and function are related, but inversely, compared with Aristotle's view.

Charles Gildon sees the same relationship as Dryden. Katharsis is taken in the medical sense but with a moral purpose: to remove "that Violence which [the passions] may have on a Mind too much possess'd by them." In this way the Greeks tried to refine the soul's perturbation and to teach a lesson. Gildon is one of the very few who considered tragedy superior as a kind to epic. He held this opinion because the object of tragedy is more excellent and extensive and "the lessons taught by it [are] of more general use and importance." We witness a tragedy, he tells us, first with floods of tears and later more coldly, all passion spent![23] Such a mixture of mechanics and morals is familiar. Clarence Green shows Gildon contradicting himself when he speaks of the function of poetry, which should not surprise us, given Gildon's critical milieu.[24]

John Dennis, who was also a spirited defender of poetic justice in drama, looked to the arts to remedy original sin.

21. John Dryden, *Essays of John Dryden,* ed. W. P. Ker (Oxford: Clarendon, 1926), I, 209-210.

22. *Ibid.,* I, 213.

23. Charles Gildon, *The Complete Art of Poetry* (London, 1718), I, 197; *The Laws of Poetry* (London, 1721), pp. 149-150.

24. Clarence Green, *The Neo-classic Theory of Tragedy in England during the Eighteenth Century* (Cambridge: Harvard University Press, 1934), p. 131.

"The great Design of Arts is to restore the Decays that happen'd to human Nature by the Fall, by restoring Order." He spoke of the drama in particular as a "philosophical and moral Lecture, in which the Poet is Teacher, and the Spectators are his Disciples."[25] Green quotes several others with similar views of the function of the stage, including Vicesimus Knox, J. P. Kemble, and Horace Walpole.[26]

The problem of morality and the stage occupied several numbers of Addison's and Steele's *Spectator* papers. Though Addison is more intelligent and tolerant than Steele in his appreciation of literature and drama, he shares much of the keen but shallow turn of the Enlightenment mind. Steele is more obviously sentimental and moralistic. Addison would have his readers seek the pleasures of the stage for moral purposes only. He complains that the accomplished gentleman of the English stage is one familiar with other men's wives but indifferent to his own; and he suggests that someone write a *Stage Morality*, a sort of ethics book in novel form depicting the typical man created by the contemporary stage.[27] Steele wrote: "I will answer for the poets, that no one ever wrote baudry for any other reason but dearth of invention."[28]

Critics of the latter part of the century retained much of the point of view of the earlier Neoclassical critics, but this was fused with some of the new subjective elements, as we saw in the previous chapter. Beattie, for example, while recognizing that art perfects nature through the expression of genius and his sentiments, still speaks of poetry as a kind of rhetoric of the emotions, katharsis giving us a pain that

25. John Dennis, *The Critical Works of John Dennis*, ed. E. N. Hooker (Baltimore: Johns Hopkins University Press, 1939–1943), I, 336; II, 308.

26. Green, *Neo-classic Theory*, p. 134.

27. Joseph Addison and Richard Steele, *The Spectator,* ed. George A. Aitken (London, 1898), I, 199 (No. 39); VI, 235 ff. (No. 446).

28. Quoted in Joseph W. Krutch, *Comedy and Conscience after the Restoration* (New York: Columbia University Press, 1924), p. 1.

we would not miss for the world![29] Hugh Blair, whose lectures were for decades the pabulum of Oxford, had a much more organic view of poetry and especially of drama. Yet his orientation is still moralistic and tends to make poetry a rhetoric of the emotions. Through katharsis, tragedy aims "to improve our virtuous sensibility." The errors in the conduct of the tragic hero are to guard us against similar errors in ourselves, and the chorus is meant to praise virtue. The pleasure in witnessing a tragedy results from the conflict of pleasure and pain, where pleasure predominates because of the humanity and kindness awakened in us.[30] Edward Young, the lover of melancholy and night thoughts, says that we enjoy a tragedy because we love to be miserable and yet unhurt.[31] Surely nothing could be further from mimetic tragedy in its original understanding.

Bishop Hurd thought that tragedy should awaken other emotions besides pity and fear. The tragic passions are nothing but "indignation at prosperous vice, or the commiseration of suffering virtue." The poet is supposed to give us pain, but "nature and reflection fly to our relief and though they do not convert our pain into joy—they have an equivalent effect in producing an exquisite joy out of our preceding sorrows."[32]

George Walker makes emotional claims for tragedy quite at variance with the claims we have seen demanded by mimesis: "Tragedy exercises her utmost power on even the unlearned and untutored, if there be found a feeling and benevolent heart." "No one ever conceived the intention of

29. James Beattie, *Essays: On Poetry and Music*, 3rd cor. ed. (London, 1779), pp. 114-118.

30. Hugh Blair, *Lectures on Rhetoric and Belles Lettres*, 7th ed. (London, 1798), III, 275, 293-295.

31. Edward Young, *Conjectures on Original Composition*, ed. Edith J. Morley (Manchester: Manchester University Press, 1918), p. 41.

32. Richard Hurd, *The Works of Richard Hurd, D. D., Lord Bishop of Worcester* (London, 1811), II, 30; I, 121, 177.

the tragic poet to be, to comfort his audience; he means to distress them."[33]

Green makes "honorable mention" of "very few" among contemporary critics who denied the Horatian formula when speaking of the function of tragedy. "The most vigorous and authoritative expression of this point of view was that of Thomas Twining (1789), who apparently agreed with what he was sure Aristotle had meant—that pleasure was the end of poetry."[34] With respect to tragedy in particular he is unique in his day in holding a theory of katharsis quite close to that of Bywater. While allowing that Aristotle saw a potential in tragedy for refining the passions, "he no where, either in his definition," says Twining, "where we might surely have expected him to be explicit, or in any part of his book, calls that effect the *end* of Tragedy. All his expressions prove, that *his* end, both of Tragic and of Epic Poetry, was *pleasure*."[35] His knowledge of Greek and his genuine sense of the large lines of the *Poetics* made him almost unique in opposing the Horatianized version of the document.

The bulk of evidence, then, shows that the dominant critical view of the time saw tragic katharsis as a moralistic function, whether emotive or rationalistic in stress. Granted: the critics spoke without philosophic intention and were often in practical controversy with irate divines who held dim, unreasonable views of the theater; nevertheless their way of expressing their opinions made clear that they had little idea of what tragic mimesis entailed or was meant to achieve. The Aristotelian probable had become confused with the Neoplatonic ideal, and Horace's pragmatic formula spoke for the deep moralism involved in this ideal as well

33. George Walker, *Essays on Various Subjects* (London, 1809), I, 58, 66.
34. Green, *Neo-classic Theory*, p. 137.
35. Thomas Twining, *Aristotle's "Treatise on Poetry"* (London, 1789), pp. 561-562.

as in the vacuum caused by the more materialistic noetic of the Enlightenment. In such an impasse, the older demands made for structure and its autonomous function were forgotten.[36] Behind this defect was the fairly common notion that a stage presentation was meant to deceive the audience into thinking that what was presented actually was happening before them. "The function of dramatic art both tragic and comic," says Green, "was in the opinion of a large body of neo-classicists and in their own phrase, to delude the audience into a belief in the reality of the action represented upon the stage."[37] This stage deception theory was a direct denial of mimesis and the probable, as Johnson so masterfully showed when he demolished the demand for the unities of time and place.

Perhaps nowhere more tellingly than in the discussion of katharsis does the mimetic critical tradition show how far it had strayed in theory from its origins in the *Poetics*. This reveals two basic and far-reaching facts. Because of noetic limitations—either Neoplatonic or rationalistic—the distinctions between art and life are not clearly recognized. The moralism which derives from these inadequacies then asserts itself. Secondly, the sense of the autonomy of structure, and hence of the autonomy of contemplation, becomes minimal. Now knowledge, in its most autonomous form, in mimesis, is much more an instrument of power, albeit of a pious sort. The theater is no longer the most brilliant and expressive metonym of this contemplative view of the mind.

G. Giovannini has observed that "the large meaning which Renaissance critics failed to grasp in the *Poetics* is: given material potentially pitiful and fearful, it should be exploited in a structure so well ordered according to the law of internal

36. Joel E. Spingarn, *A History of Literary Criticism in the Renaissance*, 2nd ed. (New York: Columbia University Press, 1924), p. 64.
37. Green, *Neo-classic Theory*, p. 128.

consistency that the tragic emotions themselves shape into a well-ordered design."[38] M. K. Danziger, speaking of eighteenth-century critical views of the heroic villain, says: "Fundamentally, they do not show an adequate awareness of the differences between art and life. Except in those cases in which the doctrine of imitation is used to explain the appeal of a Satan, hardly any distinction is drawn between the response to historical figures and the response to the characters in an epic or a tragedy."[39] Gordon McKenzie, speaking of Edmund Burke, wrote: "The fallacy that morality is the same in art and life comes from the identification of judgment as the faculty which governs the subject no matter how or where it appears."[40] Finally, we find a confirmation of this confusion of art and life as a result of a moralistic motive in the materials Earl Wasserman has studied in his interesting article, "The Pleasures of Tragedy." Even though the reasons offered for our enjoyment of tragedy change from a materialistic and mechanistic Cartesian bias in the beginning of the century to a more emotive one later on, they are psychological rather than aesthetic throughout. Even though "the end of tragedy then [later] becomes, not the purgation of pity and fear, nor the inculcation of specific moral and ethical doctrines through pity and fear, but rather the exercise and strengthening of the spectator's general faculty for sympathy," this is still a matter of rhetoric, here a rhetoric of the emotions.[41] It is easy to see how poetic

38. G. Giovannini, "Historical Realism and the Tragic Emotions in Renaissance Criticism," in *PQ*, 25 (1953), 304-320, especially 319.

39. Marlies K. Danziger, "Heroic Villains in Eighteenth-Century Criticism," in *Comparative Literature*, 11 (1959), 35-46, especially 46.

40. Gordon McKenzie, *Critical Responsiveness* (Berkeley: University of California Press, 1949), p. 88.

41. Earl R. Wasserman, "The Pleasures of Tragedy," in *ELH*, 14 (1947), 285-307, especially 288-289, 305. Robert Marsh finds Hartley urging an imitation that is "historical" in its closeness to actual moral situations, motivated by the odd blend of Platonistic and mechanico-associationist

justice would flourish, where aesthetic and structural concerns were largely ignored in determining the function of tragedy for the audience.

POETIC JUSTICE

Poetic justice usually means that the good are rewarded and the evil punished, in a play or in some other art form. Aristotle thought tragedies that observed this demand very weak, as well as catering to an illegitimate demand of the audience. Of course, it detracts from the universal quality of the probable in favor of the particular moralistic ending, just as it also does not reflect life as it is. Comedy was a different matter, for its essential thrust is redemptive and renewing.[42]

Rymer and Dennis were the two best known abettors of poetic justice among eighteenth-century English critics. "In former times," says Rymer, "*Poetry* was another thing than *History*, or than the *Law* of the Land. *Poetry* discover'd crimes, the *Law* could never find out; and punish'd those the *Law* had acquitted . . . what a wretch made they [the poets] of *Oedipus* when the *Casuist* excus'd his *invincible* ignorance?" More punishment and justice must be meted out by the poet than by the historian. The malefactor must not leave the stage unpunished, "nothing left to God Almighty, and another world." He will not survive the play, hence how can God deal with him? Rymer claims the poet is responsible for all the evil effects of his characters' deeds, and this replacement of Providence is demanded if the play is to please! In his *Short View of Tragedy* he suggests that Desdemona should have feigned death, then Othello would have cut his own throat in remorse, and the audience would

---

values we associate with him, in "Hartley's Theory of Poetry," in *Journal of Aesthetics and Art Criticism*, 17 (1959), 473-485, especially 476, 485.

42. *Poetics* (1453a), and see Butcher, *Aristotle's Theory*, pp. 224-225, 305 ff.

have gone home admiring the beauty of God's Providence![43]

John Dennis, a more reasonable critic than the irascible Rymer, also urged the doctrine of poetic justice, and did so in his usual over-logical fashion that missed the logic of the probable. "I conceive," he said, "that every Tragedy ought to be a very solemn lecture, inculcating a particular Providence, and showing it plainly protecting the good, and chastening the bad, or at least the violent: and that if it is otherwise, it is either an empty amusement, or a scandalous and pernicious Libel upon the government of the world." He is shocked by the promiscuous perishing of good and bad in Shakespeare, which calls Divine Providence into question. Nature and tradition call for poetic justice: "For what Tragedy can there be without a Fable? or what Fable without a Moral? or what Moral without Poetical Justice?" He has consummate skill with the sorites. He stretches his argument to the limit. Many faults committed in a tragedy issue from passion, and since God cannot punish them eternally, the poet must, so that other men will not yield too easily to their passions![44]

Addison opposed this doctrine as contrary to nature and reason both. He engaged in controversy with Dennis. Life, he said, does not operate in this way; hence, it demands a false kind of imitation. Secondly, to dominate a theme by poetic justice robbed the play of a katharsis of pity and fear. The sight of suffering in a man largely though not entirely virtuous helps achieve moral instruction and tragic katharsis.[45] Dennis countered with the sorites quoted above, adding

43. Rymer, *Tragedies of the Last Age,* pp. 25, 26, 37, 14; *Short View,* pp. 135 ff.

44. Dennis, *Critical Works,* I, 183; II, 7, 19-21. A. N. Wilkins has ironically shown that Dennis himself wrote a better play, *Appius and Virginia,* for having violated poetic justice, in "John Dennis and Poetic Justice," in *N & Q,* n.s., 4 (1957), 421-424.

45. Addison and Steele, *Spectator* (Nos. 5, 40, 48), summarized in Green, *Neo-classic Theory,* p. 140.

that if poetic justice is contrary to the way life goes in our experience, the poet as creator must be like God, the first Creator; he must be all-knowing and all-just. And finally he added the above-quoted need to settle justice before the characters ceased to exist.[46]

The doctrine of poetic justice exposes the essential weakness of the noetic of the age, its inability to see the complexity involved both in human experience and, in a different manner, in the probable, with consequent confusion of art and life. Poetic truth rather than poetic justice (or meaning rather than brute fact) is the poet's concern. If he achieves this truth, the meaning of morality will come clear without any need to turn his poem or play into a law court or confessional. The really great poets achieve this sense of balance without usurping a role that is not theirs, and the perceptive critic sees this. Coleridge did in the case of Shakespeare, of whom he wrote: "With him there are no interesting adulteries; he never rendered that amiable which religion and reason taught us to detest; he never clothes vice in the garb of virtue."[47] This view is inimical to both poetic justice and artistic irresponsibility. Mortimer Adler has shown that poetic justice lacks a sense of verisimilitude and probability: "No more immoral lesson could be taught. The doctrine of poetic justice is the teaching of Satan and the friends of Job. If

46. Dennis, *Critical Works*, II, 21. For a later survey of the controversy see Amrick Singh, "The Argument on Poetic Justice," in *Indian Journal of English Studies*, 3 (1962), 61–77.

47. Samuel T. Coleridge, *Coleridge's Shakespearean Criticism,* ed. T. M. Raysor (Cambridge: Harvard University Press, 1930), II, 266. Dryden held regularly for poetic justice in tragedy though not in comedy; suggesting, perhaps, in the first case an imperfect grasp of probability in the face of real life, but in the second a shrewd awareness that comic distance and its essential optimism deal with "real life" quite differently from their tragic counterparts. See John M. Aden, ed., *The Critical Opinions of John Dryden* (Nashville: Vanderbilt University Press, 1963), pp. 187 ff.; also Maynard Mack, "Introduction," in Henry Fielding, *Joseph Andrews* (New York: Holt, Rinehart and Winston, 1948), pp. xiii-xvi.

there is any basic insight which both Greek and Christian share, it is that virtue is a condition of happiness, and not of material success."[48] F. L. Lucas says much the same of the Book of Job's meaning: "The whole burden of that great book is a passionate protest against this facile notion that virtue is sure of being rewarded with worldly prosperity."[49] And François Mauriac points to the philistine essence of the concept: "One can readily reach a living soul behind the saddest of faults and failings; but vulgarity is unsurmountable."[50] If a poet resembles God as creator, he can only achieve this dignity by acting as a man. When he tries to play God, he can only destroy.

COMEDY

Comic theory, both in the *Poetics* and among eighteenth-century critics, was much more sketchy and elusive than tragic theory. Aristotle saw that comedy dealt with the laughable (τὸ γέλοιον), but of a special kind. The fifth chapter of the *Poetics* begins: "Comedy is, as we said, an imitation of relatively worthless characters; not, however, covering the full range of villainy, but merely the ugly and unseemly, one branch of which is the laughable. Namely, the laughable is some mistake or piece of ugliness which is not painful or destructive to life: as for example, to go no farther, the laughable (comic) mask is one that is ugly and distorted but does not cause pain" (1449a—Else). He thought of comedy at its best as a dramatic form, largely influenced by Homer, and as a salutary replacement of invective which the earlier writers of iambics practiced. Laughter in comedy

48. Mortimer Adler, *Art and Prudence: A Study in Practical Philosophy* (New York: Longmans, Green, 1937), p. 67.
49. F. L. Lucas, *Literature and Psychology*, p. 265.
50. François Mauriac, *The Viper's Tangle*, trans. W. B. Wells (New York: Sheed and Ward, 1947), p. 226.

was more meaningful and universal than satire, which easily verged on the lampoon and drew sub-human delight from the defects of others. Else says that he agreed with Plato in seeing the danger in unreasonable laughter, but advanced beyond his master in seeing comedy as a more impersonal and artful depicting of rather than an immersion in the defects of others. Hence in his view the laughable of comedy is not merely subject matter but dramatic form and structure as well.

But Aristotle did not develop notions of comic structure, at least in what we have of the *Poetics.* A proposed second part dealing with comedy is now missing. Only conjectures paralleling what he said of tragedy can be made. The *Tractatus Coislinianus* is precisely this, once thought of as Aristotelian in composition or at least by descent. This document of unknown origin and date speaks of a comic katharsis: "through pleasure and laughter effecting purgation of [comic] emotions. [Comedy] has laughter for its mother."[51] From what Aristotle has said in the *Poetics,* we can safely presume comedy was thought of as drama with some kind of peculiar pleasure deriving from what is significantly laughable. As one may expect, the eighteenth-century critics looked to this genre for a moral katharsis, partly because of their general moralistic orientation, partly because of the parallels with tragedy, and partly because of the subject matter often treated in comedy, which might offend the sterner moral sensibilities of the time.

The history of comedy has long been marked by conflicts between dramatist and moralist, especially during the Restoration and the generation that followed. This should be remembered when we read what the critics had to say about

---

51. Else, *Aristotle's Poetics,* pp. 143–145, 184–189, 309–314; Lane Cooper, *An Aristotelian Theory of Comedy with an Adaptation of the Poetics and a Translation of the "Tractatus Coislinianus"* (New York: Harcourt, Brace, 1922), pp. 69–70, 228.

the function of the comic. They assume a tone too pious to be taken very seriously, yet they also manifest the unsubtle quality of their minds in dealing with this perennial problem. Krutch rather cynically says that the comic dramatists of the Restoration, mainly interested in entertaining, taught, if they meant to teach, the obvious lesson of the cuckold. Yet one need not take an either/or attitude toward comedy that deals with sexual infidelity. The genre had a long and humane history, but the eighteenth-century critical mind lacked the flexibility needed to appreciate its worth. Collier and Rymer are perhaps extreme examples of the Puritan response to the theater, but they accentuate a solidly imperceptive critical acumen that discussed the function of comedy.[52]

Hobbes' idea of laughter attracted several critics, especially in the early part of the century. "The passion of laughter is nothing else but a sudden glory, arising from a sudden conception of some eminency in ourselves, by comparison with the infirmity of others or with our own formerly."[53] This is the unaesthetic laughter of which both Plato and Aristotle disapproved, but which Aristotle thought under control in comedy, because drama depicts rather than berates. Drama achieves aesthetic distance to objectivize the situation. Yet this was rarely clear to the critics. Hobbes' theory found approval with many of those who spoke of comedy. Addison espoused it. William Whitehead took a cue from it in saying pride was the basis of the comic artist's attitude. Morris said the same of satire. Brown, seeing ridicule as deriving from contempt, maintained that the comedian made the audience laugh at and despise the comic object at the same time. And Knight, toward the century's end, echoes Hobbes quite faithfully in saying that comic laughter arises from a sense of

52. Krutch, *Comedy and Conscience*, pp. 40–41.

53. Thomas Hobbes, *Leviathan, or the Matter, Forme, & Power of a Commonwealth Ecclesiasticall and Civill* (Oxford, 1881), p. 40.

triumph over the object of laughter. It is reassuring to find Hutcheson, Beattie, and Campbell rejecting such inhumane views of the comic tradition.[54]

Dryden seemed to find comedy an embarrassing country cousin in the gathering of the loftier genres. Laughter indeed distinguishes man from the four-legged beasts, but just barely so. Comedy is inferior to tragedy because it deals with low characters; farce is worse because it deals with the monstrous and chimerical. Tragedy owes its superiority to the higher quality of the people being instructed. And besides, comedy wakens malicious laughter.[55] This social stress represented a common misunderstanding of the *Poetics* from the Renaissance on. While Aristotle did speak of the high and the low as characteristically involved in tragedy and comedy, his stress was not on social quality or snobbery but on a de facto situation obtaining at the time. Significance was the ultimate concern.

Draper explains some of the moral defense of comedy at the time by the rising social status of the Puritans. "As the Puritan bourgeois returned more and more to the forbidden pleasures of the theatre, criticism rationalized the change and justified it on the basis of the supposed ethical teaching of the stage, and of literature in general." In this connection he cites Akenside, Brown, and the *Gray's-Inn Journal,* and he quotes John Newbery's *Art of Poetry* as claiming: "As the Church is the School of Religion and Piety, so the Theatre, under due encouragement and proper inspection, becomes a School for Morality and Virtue."[56] The rise of the novel at this time owes much to the same situation.

Another source of moralistic comic theory was Locke's

54. John W. Draper, "The Theory of the Comic in Eighteenth-Century England," in *JEGP,* 37 (1938), 212; Addison and Steele, *Spectator,* III, 178-181 (No. 205).

55. Dryden, *Essays,* II, 132-136; I, 85-86.

56. Draper, "Theory of the Comic," p. 214.

opposition to Shaftesbury's claim that ridicule was the test of truth. Addison sided with Locke in seeing a danger in "laugh[ing] men out of virtue." Steele saw difficulty in not being able to reclaim those laughed at. Brown, Whitehead, Blackmore, and Knight were of like opinion.[57] Collier was as humorless in another direction. He found most comic characters evil, though painted attractively and rewarded by the playwright. "A fine Gentleman, is a fine Whoring, Swearing, Smutty, Atheistical Man." Playwrights should be like Sophocles and Aeschylus, writers of homilies.[58]

John Dennis is surprisingly broad when treating comedy. Despite his usually dry and thin logical approach to the problem, he tends to see comedy as an imaginative view of human foibles. He thinks that modern comedy surpasses that of the ancients in awakening laughter and giving the audience true enjoyment. His reason is Aristotelian: the comic structure spread throughout the play affects the audience. He praises Wycherley for centering the *ridiculum* in the plot, which is the very life and soul of the theater. Yet the moralistic end of comedy is sought: to "amend the follies of mankind by exposing them." Wit is valuable in satire and even in burlesque insofar as it reveals a kind of truth or verisimilitude. Though admittedly closer to the idea of comedy than others, he still tends to think of its function in rhetorical terms.[59]

"A Discourse on Comedy in Reference to the English Stage" shows George Farquhar to be one of the most perceptive critics of his own art. His shrewd judgment peers through the theoretical limits he betrays. He suggests that comedy would be in a healthier state if critics knew something of it before presuming to judge, and if audiences

57. *Ibid.,* pp. 215-216.
58. Jeremy Collier, *A Short View of the Immorality and Profaneness of the English Stage,* 3rd ed. (London, 1698), pp. 123, 141-143.
59. Dennis, *Critical Works,* I, 157, 282-285, 7; II, 160.

knew what to look for. Critics of mathematics or logic never approach their tasks with the same ignorance critics of the arts show. Again, the courtier looks to the comic writer for wit and purity of style, the citizen for honor and ridicule, the divine for modesty, and the ladies for intrigue. Yet the fact remains that if one is to find the end of a comedy, he must look to the art form for what it is. With most of his contemporaries, Farquhar speaks of comic pleasure as a means of teaching, but when he speaks wisely about verisimilitude, he seems very close to a notion of the autonomy of mimesis. The same seems clear when he discusses the place of the fable as a "symbolical way of moralizing." Finally, he echoes Sidney's wise saw when he states the poet does not lie because he is not telling the factual truth.[60]

Fielding's prefaces and interchapters in *Tom Jones* and *Joseph Andrews* are familiar sources for contemporary comic theory. Fielding sought the benevolence and good humor of his readers, under the theoretical influence of Shaftesbury as well as the more pervasive impact of contemporary latitudinarian Christianity and the new religious enthusiasm. Both these forms of Christianity played a role in making sentimental benevolence desirable. Though the framework of Fielding's critical remarks is Classical, his stress on benevolence shows one of the many forces at work that turned art theory from mimesis toward the new interests in emotional persuasion.

Hurd, for example, shows a renewed interest in the "humors." The different types of character which they isolate are more important for our edification than is plot, for instead of viewing their disordered passions we are moved to correct our lives. Again, the farce, though meant to awaken laughter, should mainly instruct, for the vulgar must

60. George Farquhar, *The Complete Works of George Farquhar*, ed. Charles Stonehill (London: Nonesuch, 1930), II, 335-338, 341.

be exposed before they amend![61] Hugh Blair is disturbed by the Restoration drama because the Rake as hero can easily corrupt young men.[62] And James Beattie urges that, because of the same danger, comic dramatists make the vices of their characters not only laughable but clearly ridiculous. The bawdy play engages laughter while leaving the moral judgment inactive. He finds it hard to see how the audience can laugh at a crime and retain a sense of its enormity. This, surely, misses the point of the probable.[63]

Once again, as in the case of tragedy, Twining restores balance to the discussion. Contradicting Beattie's claim, he denies that the laughable is moralistic in Aristotle's concept of comedy. He insists that imitation looks to the complexity of life as experienced, not to a moralistic abstraction from it. Again, when speaking of the object of laughter in a comedy, he insists that the author present the whole human situation for intellectual and pleasurable contemplation, rather than offering an isolated moral aspect of it in order to teach a lesson. "We translate the words of ancient authors," he complains, "by words to which we annex different ideas, and then raise objections and difficulties from our own mistakes. The consequence of taking αἰσχρόν [base] here in the restrained sense of *moral* turpitude, has been, that those writers, who had so taken it, have been obliged to deny, that γέλοιον means *laughable*, because the laughable in general could not truly be defined, 'a species of *moral* turpitude.' "[64] We have here from a contemporary scholar as fine an arraignment of eighteenth-century moralism as one could wish.

It is interesting, finally, to see this moralism reflected in popular taste of the time. By the middle of the century, interest in the Classical tragedies had gradually yielded to

61. Hurd, *Works,* II, 30, 37-39, 99.
62. Blair, *Lectures on Rhetoric,* III, 350-351.
63. Beattie, *Essays,* pp. 391-394.
64. Twining, *Aristotle's "Treatise,"* pp. 213-218.

interest in the heroic plays, and the sentimental comedy had replaced the comedy of wit. The heroic drama appealed to admiration and the ideal, and the new kind of comedy to emotional escape. Both neglected the intellectual realism underlying mimesis as essentially dramatic. The heroic plays were too unreal for pity and fear, but not for admiration.[65] The writers of sentimental comedy, not content with making virtue attractive, in great part in a maudlin sort of way, made it necessarily successful as well. Krutch says: "Since everyone recognized the *non-sequitur* of this relationship which the dramatist had established between uprightness and success, no one was edified."[66] Mimesis, as peculiarly dramatic, yields to an idealistic, moralistic phenomenon; and it is easy to see why the preference of epic over drama, a complete reversal of Aristotle's opinion, organically founded on the nature of mimesis itself, should have common acceptance at this time.

EPIC

Aristotle characteristically thought of epic as a genre approaching the perfection of tragedy in two senses. Tragedy had reached maturity, historically speaking, while epic was still on its way. Secondly, the goal toward which it was striving resembled the precisely dramatic and structural achievement of tragedy, with its plot as organic center of the poem, and this was symptomatic of a sure sense of structural unity. Else remarks: "Thus the concepts of 'drama,' aesthetic excellence (unity, etc.), and perfection (complete *energeia*) of poetry form a constellation of ideas for which 'dramatic' can serve as a label. Dramatic method and dramatic form go hand in hand." This central insight of drama as the prime analogue of poetic form controls all his discussion of the

65. Green, *Neo-classic Theory*, pp. 27-28.
66. Krutch, *Comedy and Conscience*, p. 239.

perfection of the epic and of his preference for tragedy over epic, despite his clear love for the *Iliad*.[67] At all events, his critical judgments follow structural, not moralistic or didactic, considerations. The practice of eighteenth-century critics could not have been more different.

H. T. Swedenberg observes in his exhaustive study of the theory of epic in Neoclassical England: "Most of the English critics of the first two-thirds of our period again and again stated the general theory of the epic moral as it had been elaborated by Le Bossu . . . [He] had asserted that the first step in the making of an epic poem is the choice of some general moral maxim." The selection of action, characters, and other structural elements follows this lead. Dryden, Dennis, Pope, Goldsmith, Newbery, and writers in the *Athenian Mercury* and the *Gentleman's Magazine* were all of this opinion. Homer saw dissension among the Greeks, and so composed the *Iliad*! Addison, Bentley, Blackmore, Pemberton, Wood, Belsham, and Blair opposed this opinion, however.[68] And Blair archly adds that an epic so composed "would be such as would find few Readers."[69] And yet all of this last group of critics maintained the primary importance of a moral orientation for the epic. Some critics, Pope for example, also claimed that epics should be interpreted allegorically.

These critics generally agreed that an epic poem should awaken admiration in the audience. This view was basically moral or didactic in its orientation. Ramsey, Willkie, Dryden, and others claimed that by hearing of morally virtuous acts the audience was moved to admire them. Others, such as Trapp and Blackmore, thought that the audience was moved

67. Else, *Aristotle's Poetics*, pp. 203-204, 571-572.
68. H. T. Swedenberg, *The Theory of Epic in England 1650-1800* (Berkeley and Los Angeles: University of California Press, 1944), pp. 193-194.
69. Blair, *Lectures on Rhetoric*, III, 193.

by the novelty of what was marvelous or terrifying, an opinion dependent upon Shaftesbury's cult of the Sublime, for the epic was thought to be the most sublime form of poetry.[70] It is interesting to note that Aristotle's approval of the tale of wonder in the epic centered on the skill and charm in the telling, which, for example, he found in Homer's treatment of Achilles' pursuit of Hector. "It is Homer who has chiefly taught other poets the art of telling lies skilfully" (1560a). This was the irrational kind of wonder (τὸ θαυμαστόν, τὸ ἄλογον), the unlikely episode made acceptable through the storyteller's art. It was of relatively minor import for him, apart from its charm, and was called "irrational" to distinguish it from the basic sense of wonder which he saw behind all the arts and philosophy.[71] By the eighteenth century, however, the wonder or admiration attendant upon the epic had centered upon the Platonic ideal and its ethical or moral import for the audience. Even the Sublime had strong overtones of this sort.

Wonder or admiration, which Aristotle saw as the beginning of all the arts and philosophy, was quite foreign to the Neoclassical mind. An interesting example of this lack comes to the fore in the various discussions of "epic machinery." Else has reminded us that Aristotle thought of the lover of stories as a philosopher, "for 'myth' is made up of marvels." "Poetry too is a manifestation of the desire to know and to communicate knowledge . . . Such learning brings as many wonders and paradoxes before us as any Marco Polo, but it is aimed at the typical and significant—the καθόλου—rather than the merely peculiar." But it is interesting that when the Neoclassical critics thought of "epic machinery" it was less as a mythic voice of probability than as a threat to "verisimilitude" and was often as not understood in a limited, univocal way. Further, when dealing with it as part of the

70. Swedenberg, *Theory of Epic*, pp. 194-195.
71. Else, *Aristotle's Poetics*, pp. 621-626.

structural element of the poem, it was regularly looked at as an ornament or decoration in the manner of imagery.[72] Maurocordato gives a schematic synopsis of the variety of opinions extant in the early half of the century, opinions which run the gamut from utter rejection of machinery of all sorts, through a refusal of pagan and superstitious types, a rejection or an acceptance of Christian types, with careful distinctions made between the virtual world of pagan machinery and the efficacious world of Christian, to a preference for abstract allegory and Addison's liking for machinery, though always with the proviso that the strong charm of the irrational in the supernatural must not offend rational probability of verisimilitude.[73]

As with the other genres, consideration of the structural element suffers in the case of the epic because of the primacy accorded the didactic function. Swedenberg remarks: "The constant emphasis laid upon the didactic element in the epic led to the conclusion that the poem must end fortunately for the hero, if the reader is to be properly edified and moved by the admiration which the epic should engender." Dryden, for example, censured Milton for failing to conform to this norm.[74]

Blair offered the most satisfactory conception, at this time, of the function of epic. He not only rejected Le Bossu's apriority and Pope's call for allegorical interpretation, but also thought that it would be idle to read an epic "that, at the end, we shall be able to gather from it some commonplace morality. Its effect arises, from the impression which the parts of the Poem separately, as well as the whole taken together, make upon the mind of the Reader: from the great examples which it sets before us, and the high sentiments

72. *Ibid.,* pp. 624-625. His reference is to the *Metaphysics* 982b.

73. Alexandre Maurocordato, *La Critique classique en Angleterre* (Paris: Didier, 1964), p. 338.

74. Swedenberg, *Theory of Epic,* pp. 169-170.

with which it warms our hearts. The end which it proposes, is to extend our ideas of human perfection; or in other words, to excite admiration."[75] This can be done, he adds, only by showing great virtue to purge the mind of selfish, sensual, and mean pursuits in favor of public-spirited affections. This process must be grounded firmly upon moral sentiments and impressions. If, for example, the skeptical philosophers could weaken the reasoned distinction between virtue and vice, the epic poet should be equal to refuting such false reasonings by his constant appeal to his audience's emotional assurance that virtue is deeply rooted in human nature.

The critical preference at this time of the epic over tragedy as the noblest and most perfect genre is highly significant. Though most critics from the Renaissance on claimed to be following Aristotle's lead, they quite universally deserted him in his preference for tragedy in the last chapter of the *Poetics* (26). Aristotle's argument here turns characteristically on the concept of structure. He first disposes of an argument against tragedy then current, which Else believes originated with Plato. Fourth-century Athens saw a dearth of good tragedians, so that the leadership and dominance in the theater fell to the actors and their not unwonted excesses. But, Aristotle replies, the temporary lack of competent practitioners of the art does not argue the inferiority of the art itself. A private reading of the older plays will show the superiority of the tragedian's sense of structure. But, more positively, a good tragedy brings to flower in its structure the intensive unity characteristic of the poet's art, in which everything is shaped for the sake of the plot. While he approves of the *Iliad*—"the poem as a whole"—it does not enjoy this kind of unity. For one thing, the many episodes preclude it. But more to the point, given its length, its plot development is much less economic and tidy than the plot

75. Blair, *Lectures on Rhetoric*, III, 195-197.

of the *Oedipus*. Length here is not a mechanical consideration but metonymy for achieved imaginative structure centered in plot, which, it will be remembered, for Aristotle
was the most intense artistic analogue of human action being
imitated. He is back to the argument of the fifth chapter,
that an epic's best recommendation is in how well it approxi-
mates a tragedy in being successfully structured.[76]

In discussing this problem most eighteenth-century critics,
again, used moral rather than structural norms. Following
the Renaissance Neoplatonic tradition, they looked to the
epic for ethical ideals. Such Puritanism as was involved in
contemporary Christian ethical ideas was also a contributing
factor. In the epic one ran no risk of the immoral stage, and
proper rewards and punishments were usually meted out.
On the other hand, the more pragmatic side of the Enlightenment mind needed solutions to ethical problems, and it could
be at least partially satisfied with those solutions the epic
offered. Further, some critics thought of tragedy as a study
not only of human limitations but also of the pathological,
the sinful, and the warped, while the epic presented something closer to an image of the ideal human existence.[77]

76. Else, *Aristotle's Poetics,* pp. 634-653. E. M. W. Tillyard in his *The
English Epic and Its Backgrounds* (London: Chatto and Windus, 1954),
p. 6, shows a petulant impatience with Aristotle's preference for tragedy
over epic. He scores his "flagrant failure to perceive [the value of amplitude in the epic] in his infamous last chapter of the *Poetics.*" Tillyard
seems to miss the distinction just made between imaginative and mechanical economy, although, I imagine, no one would want to follow Aristotle's norm today as an exclusive judge of the value of epic.

77. Dryden, *Essays,* II, 158-160. Tillyard modernizes this idea, saying
that the amplitude of the epic, revealing a whole civilization and a world-
view, has a quality which tragedy, since it deals with introversion and at
times with psychologically warped characters, commonly lacks. It is true
that the epic has this broad basis, but critical opinion in the eighteenth
century did not emphasize this fact in any significant way. Tillyard seems
to me to miss the larger meaning in the rich particularity of true tragic
action. In fact Milton is frequently at his best in *Paradise Lost* when he is

Neither the Neoplatonic nor the more empirical noetic of the Enlightenment equipped the critics to see that a genuine tragic view of man is already universal—again the distinction between idealization and ideation. That the symbolic action of a play presents man at his most actual and yet at his most meaningful rarely or never entered the discussion. Two added reasons for their preference may be mentioned. One was the stage deception theory, more prominent in the Italian Renaissance than in eighteenth-century England, though still residual there. The other was the impact of nationalism, whose strong feelings were taken for granted all through Europe at the time. National glory and royal power naturally waxed in epic celebration, much as the actual fate of the king and his national ambitions very realistically affected the fate of the people at large.

SACRED POETRY

Given the strong moral motivation of criticism at large, critical interest in sacred poetry is only natural. Yet the lack of a genuine sense of transcendence and the consequent inability to relate satisfactorily the interests of religion, morality, and poetry disappoint this expectation sharply. Some critics thought sacred poetry presumptuous. The austere mysteries of the Christian revelation are too profound for poets to improve upon. Samuel Johnson's view of this matter is familiar, but its motivation is rather complicated and it will be discussed in the last chapter. This objection usually derived from an inadequate understanding of how imagery works, and from confusion about the meaning and place of wit and judgment in poetry.[78] More fundamentally in many

---

dramatic, though he is masterful, of course, as an epic poet in his sustaining power. Tillyard, *The English Epic*, pp. 8 ff.

78. W. K. Wimsatt and Cleanth Brooks, *Literary Criticism: A Short History* (New York: Knopf, 1957), pp. 221 ff.

cases, critics lacked a clear notion of the probable as a significant response to value rather than as an idealized picture of it, which surely was needed for appreciation of sacred poetry as mimesis.

Addison thought that Milton's poetic treatment of the doctrines of free will, the Incarnation, and the Redemption was "dry . . . to the generality of readers."[79] But he found praise for the style and manner of this treatment, in a fashion typical enough of his rather mechanical approach to poetic excellences. William Temple also disapproved of sacred poetry. The ancients, for example, mixed fables of the gods with their poetry, but this would be degrading to the Christian.[80] Such an approach leaves little place for symbol and myth, separating as it does the mind and the faculty for making images.

But behind these objections lies the fundamentally univocal and monistic Enlightenment noetic, with its characteristically limited sense of the analogy linking God with His creatures. Consequently there was little room for symbol or metaphor, which most readily grasps this analogy in a sacramental way. The Medieval mind had a place for God and religion in its poetry and art because it felt at home with this analogy. The hymns, the cathedrals, and Dante's *Divine Comedy* make this clear. Although poetic theory of the time was more rhetorical and stylistic in interest, the theologians showed a more genuine understanding of religious art than the Neoclassical critics.[81]

John Dennis, on the other hand, offers a contemporary

---

79. Addison and Steele, *Spectator*, IV, 334 (No. 315).
80. Sir William Temple, *Works*, III, 433.
81. See Edgar de Bruyne, *Études d'esthétique médiévale* (Bruges: De Temple, 1946), II, 303–304; *L'Esthétique de moyen âge* (Louvain: L'Institut supérieur de philosophie, 1947), pp. 97–98; C. S. Baldwin, *Medieval Rhetoric and Poetic (to 1400)* (New York: Macmillan, 1928), pp. 239–241, 124.

defense of sacred poetry. He thought of poetry as the rhetoric of the passions, of value in proportion to the nobility of the passions awakened. The nobler "kinds"—epic, tragedy, and the greater lyric—produced enthusiasm; the lesser—comedy, satire, little ode, elegaic, and pastoral—produced the vulgar passions. He pragmatically prefers the lesser because, despite their greater objective didactic potential, the greater are too difficult for the generality of men. But in the case of sacred poetry he changes his norms and sees the greater didactic potential proportioned to its content or subject matter. His argument is syllogistic: those objects of greatest dignity should move the highest passions; religious ideas are of the greatest dignity and most apt to fill the minds of the greatest and wisest of men; therefore . . . "Longinus" is blamed for not seeing religious poetry as the most sublime, and contemporary poetry is inferior precisely because it is not religious. Finally, we should recall his notion of the theological function of the arts: "The great Design of Arts is to restore the Decays that happen'd to human Nature by the Fall, by restoring Order: the design of Logick is to bring back Order, and Rule, and Method to our Conceptions, the want of which causes most of our Ignorance, and all our Errors."[82]

SATIRE

T. S. Eliot characterized Ben Jonson's satiric poetry as "superficial," that is, concerned with the surface of life. Eliot did not argue that satire is artistically or psychologically less complicated, but that, unlike epic and tragedy, satire is not regularly concerned with the deeper metaphysical problems of existence. It focuses attention upon the social context of human life, on "nature" as meaning "that social order

82. Dennis, *Critical Works*, I, 336, 338-342.

which [seems] the best safeguard against individual whim, and to the regulated life of cities."[83] Manners in urban living are the special subject of satire; fate and idealism are left to tragedy and epic poetry. To be sure, the competent satirist can occasionally terrify us with his knowledge of the ultimates, as the endings of *Gulliver's Travels* and *The Dunciad* show. But his normal arena is the surface of life.

Satire flourished as an art at this time in the work of such writers as Addison, Swift, and Pope. The age was receptive to it as a special form of "the proper study of mankind." The compromise of rationalism and skepticism was perhaps most creative in this area. Psychic and moral energy was likely to be more fruitful in dealing judgment upon questions of social behavior than upon metaphysical doubt. The noetic born of the clear and distinct idea could be most useful to the muses in dealing with the closer focus of city life and the abuse of its tidy and well-kept ideal of propriety and correctness in all things. Yet in the hands of a truly gifted artist such as Pope, the satiric pen had tremendous power and vitality, mirrored in the subtlety and variety of his use of the enclosed couplet. Mrs. Baum, in discussing Ben Jonson's notion of satire as distinct from rhetorical suasion, points to a difference one might wish eighteenth-century theorists had seen more clearly, for it surely marks the distinction between the best satire of the time and the critical comment made upon it as a genre. "It is necessary," she says, "to insist that . . . [his] didactic theory is more philosophical than moral, more literary than monitory. As a critic and dramatist Jonson accepts the responsibility of a poet for *perceiving* and *stating values*; he does not restrict the poet to any narrow rôle of writing merely to inculcate a certain idea or body of ideas."[84]

83. *Critical Essays of the Seventeenth Century,* ed. Joel E. Spingarn (Bloomington: Indiana University Press, 1957), I, lxvii.

84. Helena W. Baum, *The Satiric and the Didactic in Ben Jonson's*

Dryden says that urbanity or well-mannered wit is far less important than moral doctrine, which is "the very soul which animates it." Wit is only a tool and a means, for satire is as instructive as moral philosophy. A few pages later he seems to contradict this when discussing the relative merits of Horace and Juvenal as satirists. Horace is a better satirist because his material is more universal and reaches more of an audience by treating folly rather than vice, the latter being less prevalent. Yet he prefers Juvenal for more aesthetic reasons: his intellectual wit and his more masculine thought and verse. Horace's meat is more nourishing but Juvenal's cookery more pleasant; Horace is a "more general philosopher," Juvenal a greater satiric poet. He ends this discussion with an Horatian distinction which we have seen to be rather idle in any truly functional understanding of mimesis. In satire, profit is more honorable but pleasure first in favor. "And who would not choose to be loved better, rather than to be more esteemed?"[85]

Dryden and Addison, among others, however, are Classical in recommending satire above lampoon, because of the advantage of the universally grounded criticism over the petulant complaint. Dryden, though, makes exceptions when one has himself been lampooned, if his subject is a public nuisance![86] Addison is impressed by the didactic value of satire but suggests a broader understanding of it, saying that satire helps to "clear our mind of prejudice and prepossession, and to rectify that narrowness of temper which inclines us to think amiss of those who differ from ourselves." While approving of the didactic value of ancient writings, he says that satire instructs the best (which should make it the highest

Comedy (Chapel Hill: University of North Carolina Press, 1947), p. 22 (italics mine).

85. Dryden, *Essays,* II, 75, 87.

86. *Ibid.,* II, 52-53, 79-80; Addison and Steele, *Spectator,* III, 200-201 (No. 209); V, 184-185 (No. 355).

genre, were he consistent). Yet he is aware of the peculiarly empirical quality of good satire which enters "so directly into the ways of men" and sets "their miscarriages in so strong a light."[87] Goldsmith shares this sense of the empirical quality of satire. It is the sense of the surface Eliot spoke of, the noting of the changes brought about by time in the forms of our follies and vices. We should welcome the up-to-date satirist as a merciful substitute for the legislator! Finally, Fielding, faithful to his interest in "good nature," sees the satirist as a man of good will, a doctor who heals, a friend who will crush the serpent that would kill us. If there is pain in the process, it is better to be laughed at than to die of the pest or malady.[88]

DIDACTIC POETRY

Ideally speaking, there is a place in the mimetic tradition for a genre of didactic poetry. True, such poetry would tend to be abstract or idealistic, and to present materials less creatively transformed. Yet we should recall Mrs. Baum's comment on the talent of the didactic poet "for perceiving and stating values," his responsibility to be "more philosophical than moral, more literary than monitory."[89] In the few statements we have in criticism of such a genre, however, we do not find this distinction. The genre is hardly distinguished from rhetoric. Style is the poetic element, and philosophy or morals the substance. The critics speak even more boldly than Sidney in his *Apologie* of disguising the bitterness of philosophy. That the philosophy itself be part of the poetry seems foreign to their thought.

Lord Kames, for example, distinguishing between a pa-

87. *Ibid.,* III, 196-197 (No. 209).
88. Oliver Goldsmith, *The Works of Oliver Goldsmith,* ed. J. W. M. Gibbs (London, 1885), III, 507-508; Henry Fielding, *The Complete Works of Henry Fielding* (New York: Barnes and Noble, 1967), XV, 259.
89. Baum, *The Satiric and the Didactic,* p. 22.

thetic and a moral composition, the one awakening emotions and sympathy and the other teaching a moral lesson beyond this, prefers the latter. While some of his reasons appear aesthetic, the dominance and importance of moral teaching seem to contradict them.[90] Joseph Warton writes: "To render instruction amiable, to soften the severity of science, and to give virtue and knowledge a captivating and engaging air, is the greatest privilege of the didactic muse."[91] This is not merely high generic praise but an introduction to a more detailed assimilation of the genre with rhetoric as well. Teaching an unlearned audience makes it restive. One must divest the heart of more patent reason and dogmatic stiffness. Warton makes no distinction between the object of imitation and what we would call today the poetic object. The didactic poet should turn rules into images; he should, in the Hobbesian sense, speak of things as already accomplished for persuasive concreteness and use digressions to relieve boredom. This last effect can best be accomplished by a stroke of passion: "Men love to be moved, much better than to be instructed." Although he generally dislikes elaborate style, he urges it upon didactic poetry, especially in the "inactive parts" where style should be as labored as possible.[92] Hugh Blair, usually more perceptive than Warton, speaks of didactic poetry—which he values highly—as no different from rhetoric. Such poetry differs from the philosophical or moral treatise in prose "in form only, not in scope and substance." Form in this context means verse, numbers, and embellishments to engage the fancy and secure in the memory the substance being taught. Poetic form is supposed to amuse and relieve the reader.[93]

90. Henry Home, Lord Kames, *The Elements of Criticism*, 6th ed. (Edinburgh, 1785), II, 374-375.

91. *The Works of Virgil*, ed. Joseph Warton and Christopher Pitt (London, 1763), I, 292.

92. *Ibid.*, I, 292-302.

93. Blair, *Lectures on Rhetoric*, III, 137-141. For several examples of the

CONCLUSION

In any art theory, weakness in the concept of structure indicates essential weakness in conceiving of the art itself. This, in turn, leads to a misunderstanding of the autonomy of the art and of its function. Insight, voice, tone, and all other elements of an art must cohere in a self-sufficient structure, or not be art at all. This is especially true of mimetic art theory, for what is cognitive in mimesis, for all its "representational" character, depends intrinsically upon structure, not only for its particular shape and contour, but for the very substance of its intuition. In mimesis structure is the ultimate guarantee of its autonomy, the action where meaning finds its being in imitation of nature's realism.

This structural autonomy, in turn, governs the audience function of mimesis, pleasurable contemplation. This function must take its cue from structure, not vice versa. Yet most eighteenth-century theory worked in the opposite direction. Such a reverse of process is characteristically rhetorical, for rhetoric is a transitive and not an autonomous art. Since its primary concern is with audience response, its structural considerations follow the lead of the desired reaction. Weinberg points out well that when sixteenth-century Italian critics first blended Platonic, Aristotelian, and Horatian elements into a pragmatic though theoretically unstable account of poetry, this rhetorical orientation toward a predominantly moral end governed their effort. "According to that theory, poetry was by its nature an imitation of reality, made to conform as nearly as possible to that reality in order to produce

---

didactic genre during the eighteenth century in England see Dwight L. Durling, *Georgic Tradition in English Poetry* (Port Washington, N.Y.: Kennikat, 1963), pp. 20 ff. Eighteenth-century treatment of the new genre of the novel was also strongly moralistic, often justifying and condemning works according to their didactic potential. A similar interest was manifested in the fable.

moral effects desirable both for the individual and for the state."[94] This same approach was still very much in evidence at the time of our study. With structure's autonomy thus weakened, the cognitive element was naturally enough thought of as a practical or an ideal source of moral doctrine, a concept, an idea or an abstraction decorated for rhetorical efficacy, not the truly poetic universal. Rationalism and moral idealism dominated structural concerns. Such a climate was not friendly to the legitimate concerns of poetic structure.

Poetry and rhetoric have admitted similarities; all analogies have. But their central dynamisms are different, as are their functions or goals. This comes very clearly to the fore when there is question of the genres and their structures, each of which is supposed to afford its own proper pleasure to the audience. To treat poetry as if it were rhetoric is a disservice to both these arts, and an invitation for one or another formalism to replace the vital form of mimesis. This confusion is most clearly revealed in the treatment of style, the main concern of the next chapter.

One further word about the structure of mimesis. Though structure for Aristotle derived from the poet's artful activity, it was itself the ultimate way in which a play or poem imitated nature, the "action" spoken of above. As a result one can see in the notion of mimetic structure a perennial legacy which transcends its tradition. The need for creative structure generally admitted today does not derive from any merely subjective characteristic of the poet, but is imitative in its deeper roots of the meaningful world he lives in. Eliseo Vivas, who heartily accepts the need of an "objective" world to feed and nourish a poet's mind, seems to miss this demand in Aristotle's notion of mimesis. He rightly rejects the Chicago view that form is taken ready-made from nature and expressed in a different medium, inadequate for ex-

94. Bernard Weinberg, *A History of Literary Criticism in the Italian Renaissance* (Chicago: University of Chicago Press, 1961), II, 801.

plaining what goes on in poetic creation. If this were Aristotle's meaning, I would agree with him. But, it is clear from what we have seen already, it is not. I would suggest that Aristotle's view of how structure imitates nature has much more in common with Vivas' own very fruitful and attractive notion of aesthetics as "creation and discovery," though the latter is understandably much more modern and psychologically nuanced.[95]

95. Eliseo Vivas, *Creation and Discovery: Essays in Criticism and Aesthetics*, 2nd ed. (Chicago: Regnery, 1965), pp. 48, 158–161, 387–388. Also see pp. 135–136, above.

FORM AS PROPRIETY: THE STYLISTIC ELEMENT

Of the three elements isolated in this study, style is the least satisfying to discuss in the context of the *Poetics*. Two fundamental facts must be kept clear from the outset. First, because Aristotle thought of mimesis primarily as drama, dramatic action, not language, was the explicit focus of his concept of poetic structure. The probable, the shaped insight, was embodied in dramatic action. Though language was obviously related to the probable, it was primarily thought of as *a medium for expressing it* rather than as part of the poetic structure itself. Secondly, what was abstract in Aristotle's method of thought tended further to separate the inner poetic movement from its expression. Elements which were thought of as abstractly separable were treated in the concrete as separable and distinct, though somehow as obviously related. Hence the interaction of word and meaning, or better, the status of word as an aspect of meaning in both the genesis of the poem and in the finished poem itself, a status of which theorists today are explicitly aware, was not known. Once the concept of mimesis was applied to other areas of literature, which began even in the *Poetics,* these two facts occasioned serious limits in understanding the place of style and language in poetry. Unfortunate dichotomies, later developed, between "matter" and "form," "form" and "content," as well as the various tendencies to separate language and meaning, all derive, to some extent at least, from thinking of language in poetry as *a medium of expression*. The more subjective emphases of theories of imagination in the nineteenth century and later, culminating in Croce's notion of intuition-expression, were needed to clarify the matter. Yet even today, for all our advances in linguistics and verbal-centered criticism, we are still not out of the dark.

But the concept of style as a medium has a more positive and fruitful aspect. This demands that style have an *adequacy* to the meaning it expresses, both as a sign of meaning's achievement and as a link between speaker and audience. This is what the word *propriety* means in the title of this chapter, a translation of the Greek τὸ πρέπον and the Latin *decorum,* which latter word was often used in this technical meaning in Renaissance and Neoclassical English treatises. There should be a qualitative proportion between what is said and how it is said. It reflects the Classical notions of λόγος and *verbum*, where word and meaning had the one morpheme, used to express the interplay of the linguistic and the rational and reflected also in the Latin pun of *ratio* and *oratio*.[1] Randall, in fact, describes Aristotle's notion of knowledge in terms of language: "Knowledge is a matter of language and saying, of words and sentences, of verbalized distinctions and of precise statements. It is not a mere opening of the eyes, a looking and seeing—though it must start from and be about what we can see. This is why it is so difficult to translate what Aristotle is saying into any other tongue, and also why what his Greek says seems usually so clear." "Man is a 'rational animal'—that is, he is an intelligent living being who uses *logos,* language."[2]

1. Richard McKeon, "Aristotle's Conception of Language and the Arts of Language," in *Critics and Criticism, Ancient and Modern,* ed. R. S. Crane (Chicago: University of Chicago Press, 1952), p. 177.

2. John H. Randall, *Aristotle* (New York: Columbia University Press, 1960), p. 298.

This unity was, to be sure, an ideal, and probably frequently an unconscious presupposition, but unfortunately it was not explicit in Aristotle's discussion of style in poetry. The tradition that followed him, especially during the time of our investigation, tended to separate thought and language overmuch, but this separation had its beginnings in Aristotle alongside his ideal presumption of their unity. This marks an odd ambiguity. In the nineteenth century Cardinal Newman gave splendid expression to the ideal, at least, of the two-fold *logos* in his well-known essay "Literature."

Thought and speech are inseparable from each other. Matter and expression are parts of one: style is a thinking out into language. This is what I have been laying down, and this is literature; not *things,* not the verbal symbols of things; not on the other hand mere *words*; but thoughts expressed in language. Call to mind, Gentlemen, the meaning of the Greek word which expresses this special prerogative of man over the feeble intelligence of the inferior animals. It is called Logos: what does Logos mean? it stands both for *reason* and for *speech,* and it is difficult to say which it means more properly. It means both at once: why? because really they cannot be divided,—because they are in a true sense one. When we can separate light and illumination, life and motion, the convex and the concave of a curve, then it will be possible for thought to tread speech under foot.[3]

Unfortunately this separation not only is possible but has been actual in many a rhetorical and poetic treatise. Later Newman calls language not only thought's "instrument of expression," but "its own double" and the "channel of its speculations and emotions." Style, then, should be considered in a very deep sense *mimetic*; but our problem is more complicated than this might suggest.

3. John Henry Cardinal Newman, *The Idea of a University,* ed. C. F. Harrold (New York: Longmans, Green, 1947), p. 241.

FORM IN STYLE

The two limiting factors in Aristotle's treatment of language in poetry need further comment. It is generally admitted today that the function of language in a drama differs from its function in a lyric. A play can survive translation better than a lyric, even a poetic play. The dominant form in a play is dramatic, in a lyric, verbal. The first part of this statement would be familiar to Aristotle. Susanne Langer, writing from a linguistic and cultural perspective quite different from Aristotle's, echoes him quite closely in saying: "I believe *the drama is not strictly literature at all.* It has a different origin, and uses words only as *utterances.* It is a kindred art, for it produces the same primary illusion as literature, namely the semblance of experienced events, but in a different mode: instead of creating a virtual Past it creates a virtual Present. It is related to literature as sculpture and architecture are related to the graphic arts."[4]

Gerald Else obliquely makes the same point in commenting on Aristotle's disqualifying Empedocles as a poet. "His verdict can be assessed more sympathetically, as a reaction against the verbalism which perennially afflicted Greek literature; and especially it can be welcomed as a necessary and long overdue protest against the other Greek literary vice, didacticism ... It was left for Aristotle to state explicitly what his countrymen were vague about or had forgotten: that philosophy or history versified are not poetry, that literature is essentially *stories.*" And in a note he adds: "the confrontation of Homer and Empedocles [and we recall that Aristotle thought of epic as an analogue of the drama] gives a first rough indication of what [mimesis] includes (*stories* about *men*) and what it does not (exposition, *argument* about elements, principles or things). We may remember that the

4. Susanne Langer, "The Primary Illusions and the Great Orders of Art," in *Hudson Review,* 3 (1950), 233.

first hint to this effect was the apparition of μύθους in the second line of the *Poetics*." This stress is so strong that we find Aristotle weighting plot to the partial neglect of *character* and treating *thought* in a dramatic character as something strictly speaking outside the specifically dramatic structure, to be expressed through the techniques of the rhetoric of speech (1449b). Else says a little earlier in the same passage: "When all is said and done, Aristotle's real conviction about words and word-magic was that they were a necessary evil, 'all imagination and there for the sake of the listener.' "[5] But this last phrase is from the *Rhetoric* (1404a), and was written in the context of his and Plato's desire to keep language as the instrument of reason rather than of mere emotion. Aristotle's notion of poetry as primarily drama was and is often forgotten when extending his comments to other forms of poetry, especially to the lyric. This becomes especially problematic in the matter of style.

But the matter is complicated further by the second of the difficulties mentioned earlier, namely the tendency to treat language and poetic meaning as separable because of what was abstract in Aristotle's methodology, despite the presumption about the two-fold *logos*. Today we tend to think that in lyric poetry and in analogous forms language tends to mold and determine the intuition as well as vice versa. There is a kind of mutual interaction in the creative process as well as in the poem itself. The kind of language a poet speaks, his personal grasp of it, and the pressures of its metrical and hundred other characteristics help characterize his insight. But Aristotle and his tradition, not consciously alert to this, tended to think of the intuition as forming and determining the medium of language. In the second chapter of the *Poetics* (1448a) he makes objects imitated and the mode of imitation the determining factors among differing

5. Gerald F. Else, *Aristotle's Poetics: The Argument* (Cambridge: Harvard University Press, 1957), pp. 52-53.

ways of imitation. These are what we have called the cognitive and structural elements. "Such diversities may be found even in dancing, flute-playing and lyre-playing. So again in language, whether prose or verse unaccompanied by music." Earlier, in the first chapter, we gather the same notion when he denies the name of poet to Empedocles, because all he has in common with Homer is that he writes in meter (1447b). However, when he speaks in the twenty-second chapter of the demands of good poetical language, he seems aware that it adds life to the intuition, though mainly dominated by it; yet his comments on style here are less than satisfying. Poetical language is different from that of prose or rhetoric, one gathers. In poetry:

The perfection of style is to be clear without being mean. The clearest style is that which uses only current or proper words; at the same time it is mean:—witness the poetry of Cleophon and of Sthenelus. That diction, on the other hand, is lofty and raised above the commonplace which employs unusual words. By unusual, I mean strange (or rare) words, metaphorical, lengthened,—anything, in short, that differs from the normal idiom. Yet a style wholly composed of such words is either a riddle or a jargon . . . A certain infusion, therefore, of these elements, is necessary to style; for the strange (or rare) word . . . will raise it above the commonplace and mean, while the use of proper words will make it perspicuous (1458a).

Poetic language seems to have a special character of its own, at least to the extent of being different. Yet it is hard to see that the traits which make it unusual really enter the poetic substance as we think today. Yet, for all its difference, the language of poetry is equated with that of rhetoric in cross references in the *Poetics* and the *Rhetoric*. In the former we read: "Concerning Thought, we may assume what is said in the Rhetoric, to which inquiry the subject more strictly belongs. Under Thought is included every effect which has to be produced by speech" (1456a). He then singles out such elements as proof, refutation, excitation of feelings, and other rhetorical concerns. In the *Rhetoric* (1404b), in turn, he refers back to the passage from the twenty-second chapter of the *Poetics* (quoted above). Else observes revealingly that one reason he declines to treat the chapters on style in the *Poetics* (20-22) is that "they have very little—astonishingly little—connection with any other part of Aristotle's theory of poetry . . . These strictly grammatical definitions and discussions offered a more tempting field for emendation and interpolation than any others in the *Poetics,* because grammar—unlike the theoretical understanding of poetry—did in fact make great strides after Aristotle."[6] Nevertheless one grows impatient with Aristotle's abstractions: "Poetry is treated as such in the *Poetics*; its educational function is taken up in the *Politics*; the statements and arguments of poets and of characters in poetry are analyzed in the *Rhetoric*; the moral situations and moral aphorisms of poets are used in the *Nicomachean Ethics*; and poetry and mythology are quoted as evidence in the *Metaphysics*."[7]

Aristotle's treatment of style, then, is unsatisfying; at best it is ambiguous. Given the limitations of such a treatment, form in style will be thought of as deriving mainly from within the inner movement of the probable, for language will be seen as having propriety to the extent it can express the intuition so structured. Nevertheless, given the principle of the two-fold *logos,* this dependence can be overstated by applying the Aristotelian pattern of matter and form where it will not fit, namely, making language exclusively a passive principle in its union with the determining power of plot or intuition. McKeon seems to do this, much as he and others of the Chicago school tend to apply Aristotle's apparatus for

6. *Ibid.,* p. 567.
7. McKeon, "Aristotle's Conception of Language," p. 214.

analyzing scientific knowledge too readily and univocally to the inner movement of poetry.[8] Although this view of form in style tends to insure for mimesis an organic unity from within and to relate it to form in nature, thus freeing it from the false autonomy of formalism, it does not adequately account for style, nor, indeed, even for Aristotle's inadequate understanding of style. The difference lies in a sense of the potential which language brings to its task in poetry, the shaping, actualizing, and complementary power which it shares in the transactions of the two-fold *logos,* at least somewhat, if inadequately implied and admittedly poorly expressed in the twenty-second chapter of the *Poetics.* Further, what Aristotle considered utterance or diction in drama is left unchanged in its rhetorical conception, once the concept of poetry as drama is broadened to include other, more linguistically demanding kinds. Aristotle at least distinguished the inner movements of poetry and rhetoric, which later treatises, especially those mainly concerned with grammatical and stylistic elements, did not. The Classical and the better part of the Neoclassical traditions had a richer control of their art than their theories of style could account for, or else they would not have achieved as well as they did. Yet Aristotle seemed to show a sense of the vitality inherent in language when he wrote: "It is a great matter to observe propriety in these several modes of expression . . . But the greatest thing by far is to have a command of metaphor. This alone cannot be imparted by another; it is the mark of genius, for to make good metaphors implies an eye for resemblances" (1459a). Since he relates this ability to style or expression, he seems to be at least somewhat aware of the close link of word and image, such a link as we find

8. *Ibid.*, pp. 182–183. Julius Caesar Scaliger, the Renaissance critic, had strong tendencies in the same direction when speaking of style; see W. K. Wimsatt, *The Verbal Icon* (Lexington: University of Kentucky Press, 1954), pp. 282–283.

operative in the "wit tradition" of seventeenth- and eight-eenth-century England. This tradition was quite alive in its poetry, even though theory of the time was not aware as we are today of how metaphor in scientific or expository state-ment differs from metaphor in poetry, or of how the latter depends in great part for its life upon the shaping power of its language.

Finally, because form in style derives largely though am-biguously from form in the inner movement of mimesis, we should stress that it expresses an intuition already trans-formed by the poet's making. Even though the *Poetics* speaks of diction in terms of rhetorical speech, the thoughts and sentiments expressed reveal the motivation of the plot, or, more extensively, the poetic insight. Otherwise we would be back in the Platonic trap of poetry as a copy of the ideal rather than a creative imitation. In practice, as long as good mimetic poetry was produced, this source of vitality was effective. What effect it had as a critical presupposition was revealed in a more or less reasonable treatment of stylistics. But the entire Classical and Neoclassical theoretical traditions offered a weak foundation for both the writing of poetry and its practical criticism. The confusion of poetry with rhetoric, and the treatment of style as a value in itself, a view leading to formalism, make this clear enough.[9]

9. Weinberg notes that Horace's influence in the rhetorical treatment of poetic style during the Italian Renaissance was clearly dominant over any influence of the *Poetics,* inadequate as Aristotle's treatment of language in poetry was. "Rhetorical considerations were strongest, however, in the Renaissance study of poetic language." "As has been abundantly demon-strated throughout the preceding chapters, the Horatian mode was taken as a rhetorical mode." Whatever potentially corrective influence might have been offered by the *Poetics* was never felt on a deeper level. "The *Poetics* tended to subordinate language to all the other poetic considera-tions, whereas for many of these critics it was the most important." Moralistic utility, conceived of rhetorically, is given as part of the motiva-tion behind this stress. This rhetorical dominance was one of the prevailing motives for imposing the *Ars Poetica* on the *Poetics* at the time, and this

STYLE AND FUNCTION

No matter how Aristotle and others explained it, style in mimesis is the local habitation where the audience finds the shaped insight. It is here that the autonomy of art is to find pleasurable contemplation. The Classical sense of ultimate form is there for itself and for its audience without any sense of conflict, for the mutual fulfillment implied in Tate's notion of communion. This demanded singular propriety in style, what Pope was later to call "correctness": polish, refinement, precision, control, succinctness, balance, proportion, clarity. Randall observes of Aristotle's basic attitude toward knowing, not as a problem but as a fact: "we can be said to 'know' a thing only when we can state in precise language what that thing is, and why it is as it is. Knowledge and language are a flowering of the world, an operation of its power to be understood and expressed."[10] Centuries after Aristotle Pope expresses this conviction that intelligible Nature (form) is "At once the *Source,* and *End,* and *Test* of *Art.*" And correctness achieves the ultimate form of the art to insure the pleasurable contemplation. The circuit can now be closed between nature and the audience, and poetic mimesis find its fulfillment. Unfortunately this ideal was rarely held in clear critical focus after Aristotle. Poetry's end was confused all too often with the didactic persuasion proper to rhetoric. And the autonomy both of mimesis and of pleasurable contemplation was lost.

---

union was still strongly felt until the end of the tradition we are studying. Elsewhere Weinberg notes the ineptness of the marriage of these two approaches to poetry at this time: "there was no slightest intimation of the true state of affairs with respect to these two texts: the fact that they address themselves to essentially different problems, that they use widely different methods, and that they produce statements of a completely different nature about poetry . . . Their real opposition was not even suspected." Bernard Weinberg, *A History of Literary Criticism in the Italian Renaissance* (Chicago: University of Chicago Press, 1961), II, 804-805; I, 154-155.

10. Randall, *Aristotle,* p. 7.

POETRY AND RHETORIC

Although Aristotle did not distinguish adequately between the styles of poetry and rhetoric, he clearly differentiated the two arts, their inner movements, and their humane functions. He thought of rhetoric as "the faculty of discovering the possible means of persuasion in reference to any subject whatever" (*Rhetoric*, 1355b). He saw this as something quite different from the power of presenting the poetic probable. The tradition that followed after him as early as the Alexandrian period turned its interests away from the nature of poetry to an emphasis on grammar and style; given the didactic propensities of this tradition, it tended to confuse poetry with rhetoric.

C. S. Baldwin, who has studied this problem in detail from Classical times down through the Renaissance, observes in summary: "Rhetoric meant to the ancient world the art of instructing and moving men in their affairs; poetic the art of sharpening and expanding their vision."[11] (He is thinking of the Classical Greek precritical experience which came to an end about Aristotle's time.) Using "image" and "idea" in a valid, if somewhat more modern, context than the terminology of Aristotle's day would admit, he expands this distinction earlier in his study: "Rhetoric and poetic connoted two fields of composition, two habits of conceiving and ordering, two typical movements. The movement of one the ancients saw as primarily intellectual, a progress from idea to idea determined logically; that of the other as primarily imaginative, a progress from image to image determined emotionally." He adds that, even in seeing a distinction between the two arts, Hugh Blair in his *Lectures* (38) wrongly places it in style alone, and DeQuincey, in the difference between the literature of knowledge and the

11. C. S. Baldwin, *Ancient Rhetoric and Poetic Interpreted from Representative Works* (New York: Macmillan, 1924), p. 134.

literature of power. Balzac saw it more accurately as *"écri-vains des idées—écrivains des images."*[12] Closer to our day, C. S. Lewis, speaking with a clear Classical accent, has much the same to say: "Both these arts, in my opinion, definitely aim at doing something to an audience. And both do it by using language to control what already exists in our minds ... Rhetoric ... wishes to produce in our minds some practical resolve ... and it does this by calling the passions to the aid of reason ... Poetry aims at producing something more like vision than it is like action." In rhetoric, imagination is for the sake of passion, while in poetry passion is for the sake of imagination, the release of vision.[13] We may add that in this tradition poetic style should ideally have an organic quality, wherein the sum of parts is less than the whole, accentuating the autonomy of the poem and its contemplation; whereas rhetorical style, being more discursive and practical in its purpose, is "constructed" with a view to its transitive efficiency.

Distinguishing poetry from rhetoric in this fashion is not splitting hairs. These two kinds of writing reveal two different intentions of the mind at work inside its own deeper unity of insight, the pilot of human life. They form a polarity rather than two separate categories. If this were not so, some compositions would be hard to characterize. There are admittedly many "mixed" writings. What is Newman's sermon "The Second Spring" or his *Apologia Pro Vita Sua*? Yet, as a rule, if the writing is truly unified in structure and purpose, the one movement or the other will tend to dominate and gather in the various parts at work. The human mind is one, and since language forms with it the two-fold *logos,* there is a kind of contemplative insight in all writing that transcends mere report and tends

12. *Ibid.,* pp. 3-4.
13. C. S. Lewis, *A Preface to Paradise Lost* (London: Oxford University Press, 1942), p. 52.

to share more or less fully what Newman in *The Idea of a University* calls "Liberal or Philosophical Knowledge."[14] Nevertheless, the distinction made in this section of our study has as far-reaching import as its neglect has caused widespread confusion in the Classical and Neoclassical traditions.

Furthermore, the word *rhetoric* has had and still has many meanings. To trace its history would be to recount the entire history of letters and of humanism in the West. Apart from the abuse of the word, which usually denotes trickery and insincerity in the use of language, three main uses of the word can be isolated. First, *the oratorical sense*. The art had its historical and etymological origins in oratory: the ῥήτωρ was an orator or speaker in Greek. Today we call the art in this sense the rhetoric of speech, for it deals with the composition of speeches, sermons, and other forms of communication, that have in common the goal of a more or less specific persuasion of a particular audience. Second, *the sense of noncreative prose*. It was natural enough that the art be extended to broader uses as the need presented itself. Prose expositions, history, and other forms of communication with less oratorical and perhaps more general aims of persuasion developed readily under the impact of the art and techniques learned from the orator. This was true in Greece, Rome, and in Renaissance Europe, when prose developed as a broadcast means of instruction and communication. The distinction we draw in this section between poetry and rhetoric includes these first two uses of the word. Third, *the general sense of writing*. In this sense the word is used of all writing that has more than pedestrian character to it, including creative and noncreative prose as well as poetry. It has its basis in antiquity, as we have just seen, where styles were not differentiated too strictly according to the differences of their inner movements.

14. Newman, *The Idea of a University*, pp. 88-109.

In such an inclusive sense as this the Renaissance is frequently said to be a triumph of the rhetorical tradition over the predominantly metaphysical tradition of the Middle Ages. Today this use of the word rhetoric avoids the confusion of the two specific arts of poetry and rhetoric by attending very generically to language, whether creative or not, as the expression of *voice,* varying as author's voice does, which carries his intent and purpose. Thus we read of "the rhetoric of Yeats," "the rhetoric of Eliot," "the rhetoric of Newman," and the like. Brooks' and Warren's *Modern Rhetoric* varies the concept a bit in treating creative and noncreative prose but not poetry. If the purposes behind these various uses are clearly seen, no confusion need arise.

In her formidable study *Elizabethan and Metaphysical Imagery,* Rosemond Tuve looked upon the Renaissance fusion of poetry and rhetoric not as a defect but as a natural result of contemporary psychology and as a value to be approved. Since her analysis reveals a central weakness in poetic theory not only of the Renaissance but of the eighteenth century as well, it is worth some detailed attention at this point. Renaissance art theory, she says, saw the function of poetry as the celebration of essential reality; hence invention (the source of imagery) did not seek out new matter to write about, but tried to stimulate new thought about matter already found in the raw material of experience. From then on it was a question of finding *apt* style, of disposition of the parts of the composition, and the like. "The subject of a poem is an embodied purpose, not a subject matter as such." The didactic element, which follows upon this basic attitude toward the activity of the poet, consists in clarifying, ordering, praising, and adorning the subject, in order to render it a living soul embodied in language. Hence this didactic element is not added gratuitously to the contemplative element but is identified with it.

This analysis presents mimesis in precisely Neoplatonic

and Platonic terms by not distinguishing it from either philosophy or rhetoric. This is mimesis as a copy, not as a structured imitation. While poetry at this time, as well as in its larger tradition, was object-oriented, and although, as Else says, invention sought to uncover the "true relation which already exists somehow in the scheme of things," mimetic poetry did not *report* essential reality but *constructed from its seeds of meaning the probable,* the poet's wrought insight. Further, poetry in which imagination or invention merely clarifies, praises, or adorns an idea or a purpose removes the precisely creative activity from forming the very heart of the poem, from its cognitive and structural center. In such a conception poetry cannot be distinguished essentially from the aims and structure of rhetoric.

Miss Tuve's next step is logical enough: namely, seeing that the function of poetry is "naturally" didactic. She vindicates this claim by applying contemporary psychologies of will and emotion to the experience of reading a poem or seeing a play. "In the total process of perceiving, understanding, and taking an attitude toward reality, the final linkage in the normal chain of intellectual-distinguishing-of-true-from-false-and-moral-choosing-of-good-rather-than-bad was broken only by an 'infected will.'" Though this kind of didacticism is not crass but partakes of the Platonic variety of knowledge-as-virtue, applied here in the milieu of original sin, it is still the function of rhetoric.[15]

She denies that Sidney's view of the pleasure of poetry implies deceit. "When Sidney speaks of poetry as a 'medicine of Cherries' (p. 173), he is not advocating a cheap way of fooling people into virtuous conduct, a kind of propaganda, in which all means will serve, given a good end. He is talking about the fact (or so the Elizabethans saw it) that good-

15. Rosemond Tuve, *Elizabethan and Metaphysical Imagery: Renaissance Poetic and Twentieth-Century Critics* (Chicago: University of Chicago Press, 1947), pp. 388-398, 401.

ness when it is contemplated in its essential nature—the intellect's task—is so lovely that men cannot but reach out after it. So even the hardhearted and blasé, reading a poem, 'steale to see the forme of goodnes, (which seene they cannot but love) ere themselves be aware.' "[16]

Her argument shows more earnestness than coherence. What does Sidney mean in saying that virtue is bitter and unpleasant, if, indeed, it has this irresistible "forme of goodness"? What kind of ontological discontinuity is there in a system where the form is good yet bitter to the taste? This bitterness derives from a Platonic view of the ugliness of matter clouding the image of form in created reality. How, then, can other material images reveal this form? Or, perhaps, he is speaking of the unattractive state of abstract knowledge of what virtue is. In either case, what kind of psychological disharmony makes goodness bitter to experience yet attractive through an image in no way intrinsically related to it? What precisely is meant by adornment, clarity, and praise, by this odd relationship of appearances and reality both inside the poem and out, where appearances both differ from the reality and yet reveal it? Surely Sidney's very words and metaphor can hardly be stripped of implying deceit: "And, *pretending* no more, doth intende the winning of the mind from wickednesse to vertue: even as the childe is often brought to take most *wholsom things by hiding them* in such other *as have a pleasant tast*: which, if one should beginne *to tell them the nature* of *Aloes* or *Rubarb* they shoulde receive, woulde *sooner take their Physicke at their eares* then at their mouth."[17] The italics are mine, except, perhaps ironically, for *Aloes* and *Rubarb*. Time and again in the essay, similar analogies of harmless deceit are used to explain how and why poetry is attractive.

16. *Ibid.,* p. 401.
17. *Elizabethan Critical Essays,* ed. G. Gregory Smith (London: Oxford University Press, 1904), I, 172.

The psychology which Miss Tuve claims as operative here involves too many inconsistencies in the name of the "infected will" to bolster a coherent and satisfying poetic theory. Appearances and reality in it are so constituted as to help through hostility and to reveal through dissimilarity. Neither Sidney's nor Miss Tuve's context means to exploit the sense of paradox at the heart of the conflict between appearances and reality, often only too clear in Renaissance poetry. Rather, neither Platonism nor Neoplatonism can adequately buttress an operative mimetic theory of poetry. Attractive as Sidney's essay is in its intuitive observations and sustained enthusiasm about poetry, it is theoretically inconsistent in its effort to blend Platonism, Aristotelianism, and the notions of Horace, especially in questions of the didactic function of poetry.

The history of the confusion of poetry with rhetoric is a long one. This confusion tended to accompany a decline in a philosophical and metempirical view of nature and of poetry. The vacuum was usually filled by an interest in style and in the didactic efficacy of the art. Atkins points out another reason for this confusion as early as the Alexandrian period: there was virtually no independent audience for poetry, therefore no serious effort at "training rational lovers of literature."[18] It was a derivative rather than creative age, and its educational concerns were largely pragmatic. Later, Cicero and Horace channeled this influence through the Middle Ages and the Renaissance down through the eighteenth century.

Cicero, for example, saw poetry as an instrument for developing the orator's style, for the poet is "closely akin to the

18. J. W. H. Atkins, *Literary Criticism in Antiquity* (London: Methuen, 1952), I, 6-8. See also Baldwin, *Ancient Rhetoric,* pp. 1-5, 224-229; *Renaissance Literary Theory and Practice,* ed. D. L. Clark (New York: Columbia University Press, 1939), pp. 15, 187-189; *Medieval Rhetoric and Poetic (to 1400)* (New York: Macmillan, 1928), pp. 174-176, 179-181. The index of the last volume lists twenty-one entries indicating this confusion of the two arts in medieval texts treated, p. 317.

orator, being somewhat more restricted in rhythm, but freer in his choice of words, and in many kinds of embellishments his rival and almost his equal" (*De Oratore* [1.70]). In this condescending treatment, not only rhetoric but style is the center of attention rather than the inner movement of the art of poetry. M. L. Clarke, in comparing the *De Oratore* with Plato's rhetorical treatise, the *Phaedrus,* points out that Cicero's discussion is only superficially in the intellectual tradition of the Greeks, and lacks the philosophic orientation of Plato. "Immersed as he was in the world of δόξα [political repute] and only fitfully interested in that of ἐπιστήμη [philosophic thought], he could, for all his professed admiration for the founder of the Academy, have little in common with him."[19] Atkins reminds us that "to Cicero and to most of his contemporaries, oratory was queen of the literary 'kinds,' with poetry as her handmaid; and this treatment of poetry from a rhetorical standpoint was to remain a feature of Roman criticism to the end."[20] Competent poet though he was, Horace fostered this same tradition through his *Ars Poetica* during its long ascendancy to the end of the eighteenth century. It is Alexandrian in form and spirit.

This stylistic interest in rhetoric became exaggerated whenever oratory lost its free forum and rhetoric was limited to the schools of declamation. These highly unrealistic schools were interested only in teaching grammar and a formalistic notion of style. They flourished during the "sophistics," periods when oratory had no socially realistic outlet—after Alexander conquered Athens, and during much of the Roman Empire and the dark centuries of the Christian era. If poetic theory had already been absorbed into the rhetorical and stylistic tradition, these several "deaths" of rhetoric removed the understanding of mimesis further still from its

19. M. L. Clarke, *Rhetoric at Rome,* corrected ed. (London: Cohen and West, 1966), p. 3.
20. Atkins, *Literary Criticism in Antiquity,* II, 37.

original philosophic character. And even when rhetoric was reborn, this original character was not revived.[21]

A further constricting circumstance was the early age at which boys learned their poetry and rhetoric, from the Middle Ages well into the eighteenth century and even later. Because literary education was a propaedeutic to philosophy and at times theology, it was imparted in their very early teens. One could hardly expect the manuals which preserved this tradition to be philosophic, given this audience.[22] Even Blair's *Rhetoric,* with its late eighteenth-century new stirrings of thought, shows this same orientation. But this is only a contributing factor to a deep-seated tradition.

The eighteenth century augmented it in its own way. John Brown, for example, though he seems to value pleasure in poetry over instruction, says: "ELOQUENCE then is no other than a Species of Poetry applied to the particular End of Persuasion. For Persuasion can only be effected by rowzing the Passions of the Soul; and these, we have seen, are only to be moved by a Force impressed on the Imagination, assuming the Appearance of Truth; which is the essential Nature of poetical Composition."[23] Although he makes poetry a genus, its function in both species is a rhetorical one. Gildon, mainly a writer of textbooks, says that the poet imitates "only to instruct and delight, to move Mens Inclinations to assume that Goodness to which they are mov'd; which being the noblest Aim to which any Learning was ever directed."[24] We shall see in the sixth chapter that Blair was among those who advocated poetry as a rhetoric of the emotions. He distinguished between the two arts, saying that though they had

21. Baldwin, *Ancient Rhetoric,* pp. 5, 37-39, 62; *Renaissance Literary Theory and Practice,* pp. 41, 44 ff.
22. Walter J. Ong, s.j., *Ramus, Method and Decay of Dialogue* (Cambridge: Harvard University Press, 1958), pp. 136 ff.
23. John Brown, *Essays on the Characteristics of the Earl of Shaftesbury* (London, 1751), p. 21.
24. Charles Gildon, *The Complete Art of Poetry* (London, 1718), I, 26.

a common origin, oratory developed when man became more rational and civic-minded, and so appealed to the mind; but, being more primitive, poetry appealed more to the emotions and imagination. He sees evidences of this in the eloquence of earlier days, which he thought more poetic than oratorical.[25]

Blair also manifests a tendency to treat style as a feature common to poetry and rhetoric, with rhetorical considerations dominating. He devotes the bulk of his *Rhetoric and Belles Lettres* to questions of language, figures, and style; and while he distinguished between the inner movements of the two arts, it is a distinction between two kinds of rhetoric. When he tries to distinguish their stylistic elements from each other, he suggests that the border between them is a twilight land between verse and prose, poetry and eloquence. In speaking more specifically of the differences in cadence and rhythm in the two forms, prose and verse, he says: "It is hardly possible to determine the exact limit where Eloquence [not prose] ends, and Poetry [not verse] begins; nor is there any occasion for being very precise about the boundaries, as long as the nature of each is understood."[26] Surely the nature of each is not very clear to him, when he distinguishes the inner movements with very little difference, makes them both rhetorical, and treats the stylistic problems so univocally. A final passage confirms this impression and reflects the stylistic limits of the tradition from as far back as Aristotle: he distinguishes perspicacity and ornament in style, saying that figurative language is a "deviation from simple form . . . Simple Expression just makes our *idea known* to others; but Figurative Language, *over and above,* bestows a particular *dress* upon that idea; a dress which both makes it to be *remarked,* and *adorns* it."[27]

25. Hugh Blair, *Lectures on Rhetoric and Belles Lettres,* 7th ed. (London, 1798), II, 80-83, 169.
26. *Ibid.,* II, 81.
27. *Ibid.,* I, 316-319 (italics mine).

A third and final example of the confusion of the two arts is from George Campbell's *Philosophy of Rhetoric* (1776). Hamilton's *The Two Harmonies,* to be discussed below, gives ample evidence that the phenomenon was widespread at the time, and so needs no further illustration here. Campbell was a colleague of Blair, Beattie, and Reid in the Scottish psychological school. The twelfth London edition of his work appeared in 1850, and Scott Elledge says it was in popular use in America for over a century. Campbell's opinion combining the two arts is forthrightly put: "Poetry indeed is properly no other than a particular mode or form of certain branches of oratory. But of this more afterwards. Suffice it only to remark at present that the direct end of the former, whether to delight the fancy as in epic, or to move the passions as in tragedy, is avowedly in part the aim, and sometimes the immediate and proposed aim, of the orator. The same medium—language—is made use of; the same general rules of composition in narration, description, argumentation, are observed; and the same tropes and figures, either for beautifying or for invigorating the diction, are employed by both."

Campbell rather vaguely and inadequately distinguishes the "useful" from the "polite, fine, or elegant" arts by their ends, which are either for use or for pleasure (which he calls "mental taste"), and by their means, which are either "mechanical" or "liberal." Yet at times they tend to mix with one another, as is the case with eloquence and architecture, wherein, he says, "utility and beauty have almost equal influence." This eloquence, which, as we have seen, is the genus of poetry, makes use of all the faculties of the mind. It is polite because "with little or no exception . . . it requires the aid of the imagination. Thereby it not only pleases but by pleasing commands attention, rouses the passions, and often at last subdues the most stubborn resolution. It is also a useful art. This is certainly the case if the power of speech be a useful faculty, as it professedly teaches us how to employ that faculty with the greatest probability of success. Further, if the logical art and the ethical be useful, eloquence is useful as it instructs us how these arts must be applied for the conviction and the persuasion of others."

Campbell's categories and distinctions are rather confusing and at best reveal an odd pragmatism that is a blend of the psychologically empirical and the ideal. This same spirit is reflected in an oblique observation he makes about imitation, which interprets it as both photographic and Platonically ideal at once: "where resemblance is the object, as in a picture or a statue, a perfect conformity to its archetype is a thing at least conceivable. In like manner, the utmost pleasure of which the imagination is susceptible by a poetical narrative or exhibition is a thing, in my judgment, not inconceivable."[28]

These passages light up the essentially rhetorical conception of poetry present in the new psychological approach at the time. Its moralistic aims are the overriding concern, and they again link the empirical and the ideal, but now in a subjective framework.

If style in mimesis was this inadequately understood from the beginning, how did the tradition prosper so long among the poets and, within limits, the critics as well? Poetry and criticism are rather ambiguously interrelated. For one thing, poetry is prior to criticism both in time and in the poet's psychology and practice; in fact, some of our best poetry fortunately gainsays its author's theories and practical comment on it. Wordsworth is a fair example of this. Yet Baudelaire once wisely wrote: "Every great poet becomes naturally, inevitably, a critic. I am sorry for poets who are guided by instinct alone; I consider them incomplete." For him, the aim of their critical scrutiny is "to discover the obscure laws by virtue of which they have produced, and to derive . . . a

28. *Eighteenth-Century Critical Essays,* ed. Scott Elledge (Ithaca, N. Y.: Cornell University Press, 1961), II, 935-938, 1181.

set of precepts whose divine aim is infallibility in poetic production."[29] George Watson has seen an analogous motivation in Dryden's launching into descriptive or practical criticism, an activity which "begins introspectively, often as self-justification, with poets discussing their own works, as Dryden in his prefaces defended his plays from his detractors."[30] On the other hand, criticism has been energized, at least in the English and American tradition, by having its best practitioners among the poets, from Sidney and Jonson down to Tate and Eliot. Yet in all this complementary interaction poetry is ultimately prior and the fertile source of life. At the same time, since poetry speaks for an age as well as a poet, it can wither and decay if its age begins to lose its cultural life. Its noetic, then, and its critical comment can indicate symptoms of this decay, as much as they can gracefully illumine poetic achievement and its cultural vitality.

This priority of poetry and its cultural context over criticism is especially intense when there is question of style, because thought and language in poetry must be one, if the poetry is at all alive, no matter how we speak of them critically. Hence, despite its critical limitations, the rhetorical approach to poetry in its stylistic parts was more a catalyst than an active agent in the presence of genuine poetic talent. Chaucer's and Milton's apprenticeships to a rhetorical conception of style are common knowledge, as are the claims of Jonson and Dryden that they wrote their poems first in prose and then in verse, though they are both theoretically and practically inadequate accounts of the matter. A very competent and important study comes to mind in this context, K. G. Hamilton's *The Two Harmonies: Prose and Poetry in*

29. Quoted by Jacques Maritain, *Creative Intuition in Art and Poetry* (New York: Pantheon 1953), p. 65, from Baudelaire's essay "Richard Wagner et Tannhäuser."

30. George Watson, *The Literary Critics* (Baltimore: Penguin Books, 1962), p. 15.

the Seventeenth Century. Among other things, it reveals a stubborn kind of poetic life inhering in the use of language, despite the critical confusion of poetry with rhetoric, and the noetic breakdown which began as early as the Renaissance.

Hamilton studies the slow critical differentiation of poetic style from that of prose from the Renaissance until the latter part of the eighteenth century, against the background, by now well established, of the confusion of poetry with rhetoric in critical theory, didacticism, and the emergence of scientism. The two styles are ultimately distinguished when the claims of scientism—that new knowledge comes rather mechanically from things and words are merely a vehicle of transfer for this new knowledge—replace an accepted premise that all learning comes from words and language. This premise, he claims, united all humanistic endeavors: philosophy, poetry, and rhetoric. According to it knowledge derives from communication and is deeply dependent upon it, and words are the primary means for formulating thought. When an ascendant scientism replaced this attitude, poetry could no longer be explained (nor indeed survive dependent upon such an explanation), for it would then be reduced to the status of being merely a means of retailing knowledge garnered by another activity, namely science. As a result, theories of poetry as emotional self-expression gradually began to form about an incipient awareness of the imagination.[31]

As far as it goes, Hamilton's thesis is, I think, a sound one. It rightly attributes the decay of respect for language to the scientism of the seventeenth and eighteenth centuries and recognizes the need all the humanities have for language that is alive. I wish, however, to make two observations about this thesis that are directly pertinent to our study at this

31. K. G. Hamilton, *The Two Harmonies: Poetry and Prose in the Seventeenth Century* (Oxford: Clarendon, 1963), pp. 196-197.

point. The first deals with the premise that the Renaissance was "a verbally centered world . . . and that words are always the primary means of formulating thought, in all its various forms." This claim is true of the Renaissance in the sense mentioned earlier in this chapter, that it marked the triumph of the rhetorical over the metaphysical tradition of the centuries immediately before it. The vitality of language and its just measure of creative initiative in the poetic process were clearly present wherever good poetry was written; and one thinks especially of poetry of the wit tradition. But it is difficult to find critical awareness of this creative initiative among Renaissance or Neoclassical theorists. We have already seen the inadequacy of Classical theory, as far back as Aristotle, in dealing with the role of language in poetry. Because of the native tendency in such theory to give dominance and priority to the inner movement over style and, indeed, to conceive of the two as separable—a part of the larger tendency toward abstractionism to be discussed in the next chapter—the concept of decorum tends to assign all initiative to the inner movement. Though in the actual practice of the art of poetry language showed a strong staying power, the best that can be said for critical opinion recognizing the importance of language is the claim for ambiguity with which this chapter deals.

This brings me to my second observation. Given this critical assignment of complete initiative to the inner movement, one would expect the vitality of language to be nourished at the deeper roots of form found there, at what in these pages has been treated as the probable. (And no matter what the critical inadequacy in dealing with language, we have seen that a noetic friendly to a metempirical sense of form was needed to keep the probable itself alive.) Though Hamilton quite legitimately disclaims giving a complete account of critical theory of the time, he would have been more helpful had he laid greater stress on the effect of the prevailing noetic not merely upon language but upon the other aspects of poetry which nourish language, the cognitive and structural elements stressed in our two previous chapters. The effects of this noetic on thought and life in general and particularly upon all aspects of poetic theory were very significant. Otherwise why should the centuries-old confusion of poetry with rhetoric not have caused a crisis in poetic theory of mimesis long before such a crisis actually occurred in the eighteenth century? In the Classical and Neoclassical traditions the practice of the art of poetry and the critical ambiguity regarding style were both sustained by a noetic more friendly to the deeper humane claims of mimesis. Once this noetic no longer prevailed and scientism replaced it, poetry had to look elsewhere both for nourishment and for aesthetic justification.[32] We now turn to evidences of an analogous decay, which strongly suggest that formalism, rather than form, had a strong grip on critical notions of style even as early as the Renaissance.

32. A third observation may be made here, one of more oblique interest at this point but of serious concern for our study as a whole. In claiming that Dryden's "poetry is to be understood and appreciated fully only in terms of concepts which, though they recognized the special qualities of poetry, were based ultimately on an acceptance of homogeneity of all discourse as the means by which man, as a rational being, could know and control the universe," and that hence his poetry should be studied "in terms of concepts of the nature and function of poetry that he himself would have understood and accepted," Hamilton becomes involved to some extent in the intentional fallacy and in the kind of historicism we have cited Wellek as opposing (see above, Preface, p. x). If Dryden's poetry "cannot be judged wholly by poetic criteria, because it is never envisaged as having a sufficiently autonomous existence as poetry," it is hard to know how one can even *approach* an absolute judgment about the nature of mimesis and its function, or, indeed, discern what is and what is not precisely poetic about poetry in any tradition. Rosemond Tuve seems to espouse a similar position in the fourteenth chapter of her *Elizabethan and Metaphysical Imagery* in judging Elizabethan poetry by Elizabethan standards of didacticism. Hamilton, *The Two Harmonies*, pp. 200-201; Tuve, pp. 382-410.

STYLE AND FORMALISM

When style in mimesis is not adequately related to its inner movement, its value and function can easily be misunderstood. We have seen one example of this in the confusion of poetry with rhetoric. Another was formalism, where form in style was not thought of as either deriving from the inner movement of the poem or as closely enough related to it, but rather as a kind of form or value in itself. (This error occurred in the rhetoricizing tradition just reviewed, mainly when rhetoric "died" in the schools of declamation and the sophistics, though a hint of it lurked at the time of our study, for example, in the notion that imagery and language were adornments of an idea.) As a consequence of the misunderstanding, techniques and external factors, methods and procedures tended to become stylized and prescriptive for their own sake. The concept of form in the inner movement of mimesis became formalized when form was thought of as superficial both in nature and in the probable. A parallel can be found in those notions of style in which form was seen as a value in itself in the externals of art. Decorum then became an autonomous system of rules, self-regarding and arid. "Poetic diction" in the sense which Wordsworth opposed would be a ready example. Decorum or propriety in the Classical and Neoclassical tradition included, besides grammar and language, all the techniques which rendered the intuition available to the audience. A few instances of formalism in style are listed here as examples of still other ways in which contemporary critics failed to grasp the true meaning of mimesis. Bate has well observed that an approach to decorum ceased to be truly Classical "in either criticism or practice only when the primary law of humanistic decorum, the portrayal of the universal [our concept of form], was breached: when, that is to say, these stylistic intentions were regarded as almost sufficient ends in themselves, or when they were subjected to the authority of a prematurely generalized rationalistic code or to the satisfaction of social demands and fashions which were wholly transitory in character."[33] In such cases the function of poetry for the audience was usually limited to the enjoyment of stylistic tricks, and this at times as a bait to further moral ends.

The first of these tendencies was to be found in the use of the word "imitation" more and more dominantly in the rhetorical sense of copying the manner of writing of a given author. Such imitation has obvious advantages, especially in one's apprenticeship, even if somewhat over-zealously praised by Pope when speaking of Virgil: *"Nature* and *Homer* were, he found, the *same."* But when imitation is an asset, it usually transcends merely stylistic assimilation in the personal control of the maturing apprentice. By the eighteenth century this ideal of rhetorical imitation, an inheritance from the Hellenistic and Roman times, had in many critical texts become a thin and mechanical stylistic practice. McKeon has noted that an inherent limitation of the practice was to lose sight of meaning as the source of attention and pleasure, and to look to style as an extremely refined interest.[34] Draper, who has studied how this practice fared in the eighteenth century, says that it was a contributing factor in the decline of classical values at the time.[35]

Related to the stress on this kind of imitation was the exaggerated respect for "the ancients." Tradition, properly understood, has a very deep value, but only if it has room for development and originality. Those who exclusively favored "the ancients" in their famous controversy with "the mod-

33. W. J. Bate, *From Classic to Romantic* (Cambridge: Harvard University Press, 1949), p. 43.
34. Richard McKeon, "Literary Criticism and the Concept of Imitation in Antiquity," in *Critics and Criticism, Ancient and Modern*, ed. R. S. Crane (Chicago: University of Chicago Press, 1952), p. 174.
35. John W. Draper, "Aristotelian Mimesis in Eighteenth-Century England," in *PMLA*, 36 (1921), 372 ff.

erns" were as formalistic as their opponents were superficial. Dryden's position as Neander in his *Essay on Dramatic Poesy* had a welcome breadth and depth not too common in this discussion.

Though the doctrine of "The Unities" is more directly a matter of structure, it was frequently treated as one of decorum. Had there been question here of a stage convention, the doctrine might have been critically important. Actually precisely the opposite was true, for instead of deepening the aesthetic potential of the drama, the demand for the unities of time and place tended to mechanize it. In this context verisimilitude or truth to life, both good translations of Aristotle's notion of the probable, came more and more to demand that a play show surface and factual likeness to actual life, that it be literally a *facsimile,* an exact copy. Clarence Green in his study of Neoclassical dramatic theory and its origins in the Renaissance says this notion was deemed necessary for what he calls the "stage deception theory" of drama. "Neo-classic theory asserted that the unities of time and place were necessary if the audience was to *believe* that it was actually present at the time and place of representation, and that if this belief were shattered, theatrical illusion vanished."[36] Johnson's devastating rejection of the doctrine makes an important distinction clear: "It is false, that any representation is mistaken for reality; that any dramatick fable in its materiality was ever credible, or, for a single moment, was ever credited . . . Imitations produce pain or pleasure, not because they are mistaken for realities, but because they bring realities to mind."[37] Yet Castelvetro, the

36. Clarence Green, *The Neo-classic Theory of Tragedy in England during the Eighteenth Century* (Cambridge: Harvard University Press, 1934), p. 206.

37. Samuel Johnson, "Preface to Shakespeare," in *Johnson on Shakespeare,* ed. Walter Raleigh (London: Oxford University Press, 1925), pp. 26-28.

most perceptive of the Italian Renaissance critics, gladly accepted Cinthio's demand for a unity of time and added his own for a unity of place, because he thought drama was meant as a delusion, largely as a diversion for the uncultured crowds who were incapable of thinking.[38]

It is interesting to recall here that, of the six "parts" of a tragedy, Aristotle valued as most important Plot (its unity really being the precisely imaginative substance of a play), and the least important Spectacle, or the theatrical. With this physically conceived doctrine of the unities, values were diametrically reversed. It bridled at mistakes of geography or history, while neglecting the roots of drama in the probable; yet we read in the *Poetics*: "not to know that a hind has no horns is a less serious matter than to paint it inartistically" (1460b). This contrast between Aristotle's attitude and that of the Renaissance and some Neoclassical critics on this point of "truth to life" perhaps reveals best Aristotle's dramatic realism. And the empirical ideals of Hollywood in our own day are perhaps its greatest antithesis.

Partly because of English common sense but more so because Shakespeare did not adhere to the unities, English critics did not take to the doctrine overenthusiastically. Green shows that most English critics opposed its unreasonable demands but quotes Gildon, Constable, Henry Boyd, Lord Chesterfield, and Guthrie as favoring it.[39] The French critics, however, largely favored it; and despite English disagreement with it, that it was held at all reveals a critical milieu quite unfavorable to mimesis.

38. H. B. Charlton, *Castelvetro's Theory of Poetry* (Manchester: University of Manchester Press, 1913), pp. 48-49, 60, 66, 73-74, 83-85, 110-111, 173-177. Some critics claim that Aristotle prescribed the unity of time in the fifth chapter of the *Poetics*. Else says that the phrase "a single daylight period" refers to the time it took to produce a play. Whatever Aristotle held, it is clear that it was not what his Renaissance and Neoclassical followers were holding. Else, *Aristotle's Poetics*, pp. 207 ff.

39. Green, *Neo-classic Theory*, pp. 206, 194-196.

The "Rules mentality" should also be mentioned in the context of formalism. Though here again the French critics offended more than the English—Bossu, Dacier, Rapin, and Voltaire may be mentioned in passing—England was not without critics who fostered the cult. The more reasonable and profitable attitude implied in Pope's notion of the rules as *"Nature Methodiz'd"* and freedom to *"snatch* a *Grace* beyond the Reach of Art"* was not shared by all. Johnson, Beattie, and Welsted agreed that certain general rules should be kept, while particular rules varied with the exigencies of circumstances. Yet we read in John Dennis: "They are eternal and irrevocable, and never to be dispens'd with but by Nature that made them, and the only Rule for that Dispensation is this, that a less Law may be violated to avoid the infringing of a greater." And again: "this is undeniable, that there are proper Means for the attaining of every End, and those proper Means in Poetry we call Rules." Others were to speak of means and ends, usually with less rigidity than Dennis, although we read in Gilson: "For where there is a *Right* and a *Wrong,* there must be some Art or Rules to avoid the one and arrive at the other."[40] Here again, where a strong position was held it tended to be rigid and mechanical and to reveal the formalism we are discussing.

Finally, a word about "wit." At its healthiest, wit was to the Renaissance and Neoclassical tradition what image and symbol have been to the Romantic poets and those who succeeded them. It was the imaginative center of an intellectual poetry. The trope of the rhetorical tradition was its forebear, and in order to keep healthy, wit had to tie word and idea, creativity and judgment, closely together. It is well known that the critical history of the word resembles a maze. Here it will be pertinent simply to note that the changing meaning of the word is an index of the growth of the scientistic

40. *Ibid.,* pp. 73-74.

noetic, and when wit finally disappears as a value in the critical tradition, it has lost its life at the hands of the formalism and decay of a decaying tradition. The Romantics, Hazlitt for example, will treat it as mere cleverness, preferring a more humane *humor* to it.

Wimsatt, who has chased the elusive rabbit, wit, through the maze, offers a helpful suggestion for following its course under the impact of the new scientism and schematism.[41] "Bacon had described the two powers—that of perceiving resemblances and that of perceiving differences—in the Latin of his *Novum Organum* (I, 55) without recourse to either of the terms 'wit' or 'judgment.' And it may be well if we try to think of those powers, or the concepts of them, taken neutrally, as relatively stable concepts behind a considerable activity of the term 'wit,' an effort as it were on the part of that agile term to keep up with the center of value which not only in philosophy but in poetry was shifting from the pole of imagination or seeing resemblances to that of judgment or seeing differences. 'Imagination' and 'fancy' had to stay more or less on one side of the polarity, and so did 'judgment.' But 'wit,' because of its near synonymity with 'poetry,' had to move as the implicit concept of good poetry moved." He then surveys comments on wit from Jonson, through Hobbes, Dryden, Locke, Addison, and Pope. The last named tried to offer a balance between the meaning of wit and judgment, to restore the word "wit" after its impoverization by the rationalist philosophers. It was also under the attack of moralistic Puritans who identified the poet as a wit with a bawdy rake. Johnson found fault with Pope's separation of word and idea in his well known couplet:

41. W. K. Wimsatt and Cleanth Brooks, *Literary Criticism: A Short History* (New York: Knopf, 1957), p. 229. The entire chapter "Rhetoric and Neo-classic Wit" deals with the problem at length.

> *True Wit* is *Nature* to Advantage drest,
> What oft' was *Thought,* but ne'er so well Exprest.

Bate agrees with Johnson in this, though Hooker, Audra, and Williams have defended Pope.[42] At least he offers another view in the same *Essay on Criticism* in this couplet:

> For *Wit* and *Judgment* often are at strife,
> Tho' meant each other's Aid, like *Man* and *Wife.*

At any rate, Pope himself saw the handwriting on the wall at the end of the *Dunciad,* which Wimsatt quotes as symbolic of the end of the wit tradition:

The concluding crescendo of the poem is an extraordinary re-capitulation in negative of the rhetorico-metaphysical tradition.

> *Wit* shoots in vain its momentary fires,
> *Art* after *Art* goes out, and all is Night.
> *Physic* of *Metaphysic* begs defence
> And *Metaphysic* calls for aid on *Sense!*

The last lines reach out for the utmost metaphysical and theological implications of the "word," not only the human but the divine creative act, the "logos." Not only grammarian, rhetorician, and poet, but Academician, Church Father, neo-Platonist, scholastic theologian, and aesthetician of "light," have contributed to the edifice of humanistic intelligence which appears in the darkly brilliant subverted image of this denouement.

---

42. W. J. Bate, *The Achievement of Samuel Johnson* (New York: Oxford University Press, 1955), pp. 214-215; E. N. Hooker, "Pope on Wit: the *Essay on Criticism,*" in Richard F. Jones, et al., *The Seventeenth Century* (Stanford: Stanford University Press, 1951), pp. 225-246; Alexander Pope, *Pastoral Poetry and An Essay on Criticism,* ed. E. Audra and Aubrey Williams (London and New Haven: Methuen and Yale University Press, 1961), pp. 209 ff., especially 218-223.

Lo! thy dread Empire, CHAOS! is restor'd;
Light dies before thy uncreating word.[43]

CONCLUSION

The rhythm of this chapter began with the concept of stylistic propriety involving the imperfectly understood ideal of the two-fold *logos*. It developed through considering the rather ambiguous staying power of language, verified better in the practice of poets than in critical formulations, and the long-lived confusion of poetics with rhetorical criticism. It ended with our seeing how this tradition, more and more under the influence of a scientistic and moralistic noetic, turned further away from the native demands of mimesis toward a formalism of one sort or another. Where a poetic tradition is truly alive, the importance of the creative word is at least implicitly divined. The poet "has a way with words," we say; he is a shaper of words. This has been rather simply put: "A poem is a word for things."[44] Though the Classical tradition had at its best an implicit and healthy sense of this, its tendency toward abstractionism caused a built-in weakness even in the best of its critical accounts of style. The imperfect help which the rhetorical tradition offered was even at its best inadequate. Under the impact of an intensified moralism from the Renaissance through the eighteenth century, it could bolster less and less a dying poetic. And an interesting paradox ensued: the more exclusive and detailed the attention given to style, the less its place in poetry was understood. Form had become formalism.

Further, in any kind of poetry, including mimesis, words have a paramount importance for the audience. The iconic quality of a fully achieved verbal structure is the most con-

43. Wimsatt and Brooks, *Literary Criticism*, p. 247.
44. Hugh McCarron, s.j., *Realization* (New York: Sheed and Ward, 1937), p. 129.

vincing evidence of its potential for contemplation, and the pleasure it rightly affords the ultimate fruition of the two-fold *logos* in the audience. But the didactic concerns of the tradition we have been studying turned the function of words into likely vehicles of instruction, forgetting the legitimate autonomy of language. In the next chapter we shall study two limitations of mimesis, the one from within its own make-up, the danger of abstractionism, the other from without, the narrow moral climate into which it was received in the eighteenth century. This will prepare us for an accurate reading of the Horatian formula in Chapter 6, itself by this time something of an uncreating word.

5

LIMITS TO FORM

Until now we have been concerned with the positive contribution of form in constituting mimesis and then relating
it to its audience. But form in mimesis has built-in limits,
and throughout its tradition it also met limits from its cultural milieu. Both these sets of restrictions should be discussed in order to understand the explicit eighteenth-century
statements about the humane function of literature, the subject matter of the chapter that follows this one.

By its nature the methodology of any system of thought
limits the reality it deals with. Judgment specifies, defines,
clarifies; appreciative synthesis unifies and tries to vitalize
what it perceives; but some part of the richness to be com-
prehended always eludes the system, even when the knowing process is thought of as a part of the reality known.
(Nonsystematic thought has analogous difficulties of at least
equal dimensions.) To say all this is merely to recognize the
limits of the human mind. The philosophies of Plato and
Aristotle through their various descendants can safely be
said to have dominated the period of our study; hence a brief
view of the limits of these systems reflected in our subject
matter will be helpful.

Among the many polarities of the human mind, now
taken as commonplaces, these two systems tend to illustrate
opposing tendencies in the polarity of the empirical and the
ideal, both, however, still within the tradition of objective
philosophies. Both sought in form the roots of reality and

of its intelligibility. For Plato, since form transcended experience, the transcendent thrust of the mind characterized his method and patterns of thought; for Aristotle, with his focus on the emerging real of experience, the empirical thrust of the mind was dominant. Because of these orientations Plato's method tended to be more generic, Aristotle's more categorical. Plato's thrust toward the ideal tended to be vague about the shadowy areas of experience, in the interest of the more inclusive unity exercised by the master forms which they obscurely reflected. Aristotle's search for the forms in experience tended naturally to specify and characterize them according to their genus and species. Plato tended to overlook differences among things and processes in the interest of a higher unity. Aristotle was interested in differences among things and processes, for the form of the mind was actualized by the form of the objects it knew; hence "aspect," or what is technically called "formal object," was very characteristic of his method. Further, for Plato the ascetical quest of the soul for the ultimate forms threw a unifying aura on all human activity and tended to erase the differences among means for the sake of the end. Aristotle's more scientific approach was more interested in cataloging reality as he experienced it. Platonism, the least methodical of methods, at best made for a valuable higher synthesis of knowledge, at worst for vagueness and confusion of opposites. Aristotelianism, the most methodical of methods, at best made for clarity and a realism of sorts, at worst for formalism. These distinctions apply significantly to the way each tended to look at how poetry and morals relate to each other, which will be discussed a little later in the chapter.

Both Plato and Aristotle, being Greeks, were objective philosophers whose systems were mimetic of "the given," the universal in nature. Together they form another polarity with the more subjective philosophers and their various systems which have influenced literary theory, beginning with the Associationists and extending to Kant and the post-Kantian philosophers of imagination. As we have already seen, the mimetic theory of poetry is best understood against the background of the older, Greek philosophies. Yet there are limits to this theory of poetry, precisely because of its more or less exclusive reliance upon the objective and universal characteristics of these philosophies. A third polarity should be kept in mind, that which exists between the essentialist and the existentialist thrust in our processes of knowing and perceiving. Without being overly categorical, we may truly say that both the Greek philosophies which influenced much eighteenth-century thinking about poetry and morals were mainly essentialist.

The limits to be traced in the succeeding pages should be understood against the background of these three polarities. Those that derive from the concept of mimesis itself are Aristotelian in origin. Although Platonic elements entered the discussion of the cognitive and structural elements of imitation, it was usually through a misunderstanding of the theory, and these limits have been pointed out already. The limits of a more external sort, deriving from the milieu and lying behind much of the moralism, are in origin either Platonic or Aristotelian, in the sense that the logic of scientism and rationalism derive from Aristotle as a kind of great-grandfather, though, it must be admitted, out of the more spurious Ramist and Cartesian matrices.

THE CRITICAL LIMITS OF FORM

Both the strength and weakness of the Classical approach to art lie in its respect for the universal. Form in the real world of experience is meaningful in itself before it is universal, before one notes its reference to other similar forms or its significance for many minds. The same is true of mimesis. An insight is significant to many because it is already meaningful. We have seen that the vitality of mimesis depends upon its objective orientation toward human values, and there is no doubt that here is the prime factor in the greatness of Western realism in art as well as in philosophy. Interest in the universal saved mimesis from the extravagance and whim of individualism. *But universality is secondary to the significance of form itself.* Vitality is usually preserved where this priority is remembered. The word "universal" is an epistemological strategy required by the limits of our minds, to which "the given" quality of things is prior, at least for the mimetic philosopher and critic. When this is forgotten, we usually find the conceptual limitations of the universal becoming more prominent, and method replaces substance. Nevertheless, respect for the universal understood as significant in itself lies behind Classical art and theory at their best. This is the source of humanism. What is human recurs generation after generation, and the continued induction it affords constitutes a community of cultural experiences and values. We are reminded of Doctor Johnson's satisfaction with that which has pleased many and pleased long. It is a guarantee against the clandestine, the esoteric, and the private. Humanism has always sought both an intellectual self-confidence and an intellectual humility which can only come from a sense of a shared humanity. Here is the main contribution of the universal to form in the cognitive element in mimesis.

Yet the universal has its limits. Things do not exist in an abstract manner, bereft of individual differences, adrift in time and space. Fear of whim and the private vision can tend to cloud the importance of the singular elements in experience. While it is true that the poetic universal was one of probability rather than of fact, subsisting in a creative structure and hence free from an overeasy abstractionism, still it lacked, critically speaking at least, the variety and richness of a more personally conceived insight. The recurrence of stock types in plots and characters shows this in many an eighteenth-century play. Even Ben Johnson did not always succeed in keeping his types from becoming abstractions. Critics like Dennis, Collier, and Rymer, and at times even Dryden and Addison, stress the universal in such a way as to turn the probable of the *Poetics* into the Neoplatonic ideal.

Besides this, both the early and late mimetic tradition possessed a rather inadequate sense of the place of history in human experience. Since the nineteenth century we have become much more aware of man's evolutionary nature. Rightly understood, historicism has enriched the humanist tradition. Related to this is the part played by geography, climate, national, personal, and social factors in constituting man's form or nature. Finally, Associationism and other subjective sources of knowledge, once they were freed of their early mechanical conceptions, have enriched the potential of both philosopher and poet alike for speaking of the human situation.

Form in the structural element gave creative substance to the poet's insight, the term of his making. In so doing, it caught by analogy what was meaningfully concrete and dramatic in actual life. The genres served as special modes of realizing this fundamental goal and were thought of as tidily revealing the aesthetic intention of the poet and achieving in each case a peculiar and proper pleasure in the audience. Conceived of by analogy with biological species, the genres offered handy categories for understanding peculiar and specific qualities of given poems and made comparative criticism possible. The concept of genres, however, could and did turn into a system of mechanical a-prioris, with almost metaphysical demands for an artificial conformity. Wimsatt finds something of this defect in the modern instance of the Chicago Critics' calling poems "things."[1] The Neoclassical

1. W. K. Wimsatt, *The Verbal Icon* (Lexington: University of Kentucky Press, 1954), p. 50.

storms about the mixing of the genres also manifest the limit of such criticism. English common sense and an appreciation of Shakespeare's genius, however, kept this tendency to a minimum.

We have already discussed the built-in limitations to form in style in the previous chapter. Formalism, rhetorical stresses, "the Rules," and the phenomenon of "poetic diction" at the end of the eighteenth century all indicate the need for a more subjective link between language and the inner movement of a poem in the mimetic concept. Though the Romantic reactions to many traditional stylistic premises admittedly attacked caricatures rather than established practices, their reaction pointed out well the need of a fresh approach to the problem of language in poetry.

In discussing admitted limits of a system, one readily crosses over to defects and positive abuses. The limits just reviewed indicate a constant temptation to abstractionism in a mimetic culture fundamentally rational in its approach. This defect has been well described by Alfred North Whitehead as the Fallacy of Misplaced Concreteness, discussed in the context of the eighteenth-century noetic of *Les Philosophes*. It should be kept in mind as a radical cause of formalism in the tradition we are studying, and a fundamental reason for its eventual decay.

POETIC FUNCTION AND THE MORAL CLIMATE

The problem of how poetry affects its audience is a complicated one. By now it has many sophisticated developments in critical writing. But today, as in the eighteenth century, the problem must be discussed against the background of the moral climate both of the critics involved and of their time. The importance of the noetic in forming the critic's view of the making of literature has a parallel importance in determining how he thinks of the effect it has on its audience.

Today we are much more theoretically explicit in relating ethics and poetics when discussing this problem than eighteenth-century critics were. Yet the basic demand of relating the two sets of values is implicit in any treatment of the problem. This is particularly true in the case of mimesis, which should be conceived of as both autonomous and as a source of wisdom. This autonomy is contemplative, and both Plato and Aristotle thought of ethics as beginning with understanding. Finally, mimesis is metempirical at its roots; hence any defense of its autonomy and any relation of it to the ethical sphere seem to demand at least an implicit ontology and psychology that can offer a ground common to both poetics and ethics. These, we shall see, were not readily available in the eighteenth-century moral climate.

A further point should be remembered here. Mimesis was developed in the Greek climate, and its theoretical elaboration reflects Aristotle's larger philosophic premises. In eighteenth-century England its climate was quite different. By then it had passed from a Greek (and Roman), through a deeply religious Christian, milieu to one that was gradually being secularized while still nominally and pragmatically Christian. Plato and Aristotle thought of ethics as beginning with a knowledge of the Good. For Plato the good life consisted in a fuller and fuller contemplative possession of the absolute form of the Good. All other aspects of ethical effort subserved this contemplative goal. Aristotle thought of ethical perfection more in terms of action. Believing in the reality of the forms in the world of experience, he thought that the good life consisted in the cumulative happiness derived from actions dictated by one's human nature in its quest for fulfillment.[2] Early in its history, Christianity adopted elements

2. Two points should be noted here. (a) In the Platonic, Aristotelian, and various Christian systems of ethics, both mind and will, contemplation and action, are involved. The differences, apart from premises and values, are in emphasis, though they are strongly characteristic and marked.

of both these ethical systems to help explain its own moral goals, but these were completely transformed in accord with a totally other sense of destiny and purpose of the New Creature, as St. Paul calls the Christian, not merely a human person, but a creature and indeed a child of the Living God.

Randall reminds us that "for Aristotle the fullest and most intense activity of man's characteristic function, the completest fulfillment of man's distinctive 'nature,' is the operation of *nous,* of reason, in knowing . . . The fullest development of human nature, of human *nous,* leads men beyond human nature itself to the 'life of the gods,' to participation in what is 'deathless and eternal'—to the supreme, continuous, and never-ending blessedness of sheer *nousing,* sheer knowing," in John H. Randall, *Aristotle* (New York: Columbia University Press, 1960), pp. 270-271. But for Aristotle day-to-day ethical living issued in voluntary action, in analogy with his empirical notion of the forms. So did Christian moral action, given its supernatural transformation being discussed at this point of our study and its motivation in faith and reason.

The divine destiny of which Randall speaks should not be confused with the Christian notion of personal, divine adoption, issuing in the Beatific Vision of God. The first is thought of as natural to man, an exigency of his human constitution, the second as gratuitous, supernatural, and knowable only through Revelation. In the Christian scheme of things too, both on earth and in heaven, love had a more transcendent place in the last analysis. This is clear in the systems of Augustine and Bonaventure. But even in the more characteristically Aristotelian system of Aquinas, the term of the Christian life in the Beatific Vision was an affective state: the soul and whole person *loved* God *by knowing* Him.

(b) Later manipulation of the Platonic concern, when there was question of poetry, frequently lacked the contemplative orientation of Plato, it must be said in fairness to him. Those who opposed poetry as "lies" were usually quite voluntaristic. Those who favored it as a rhetoric of morals were either pragmatic in their thought, and hence not worried by intellectual inconsistencies, or at best failed to consider the psychological and doctrinal differences between Christian and natural ethics. The *psychology* behind Platonic ethics (its dominant contemplative orientation) was not the same as that of the Christian milieu (one more voluntary, though surely not voluntaristic, in orientation); yet compensation for the differences was not made when a didactic or rhetorical view of poetry was urged for moral purposes. This was compounded when the *doctrinal* differences between Christianity and Greek philosophy were ignored, differences which are involved in these pages in the distinction between the concerns of salvation and the concerns of culture. In such a milieu even the rather pragmatic Horatian formula becomes immensely more pragmatic.

No matter what intimations of immortality have been found in Greek and Roman beliefs, the Christian sense of the meaning of time and of eternity essentially transformed the moral climate into which such a tradition as mimesis was received.

THE CHRISTIAN MORAL CLIMATE

It would be idle to try to define the Christian moral climate in a few pages. The varying forms of Christianity, the various emphases in doctrine, and the many cultural contexts in which it has been operative make the task impossible. I shall merely point to certain radical shifts in attitudes that originally formed the basic pattern of Christian moral values and to some changes that had become influential by the eighteenth century.

The most fundamental change to be noted from pre-Christian times is the conviction that God plays an intimate role in the life of man. His revelation, which was begun with the Hebrews, culminated with the Incarnation of the Second Person of the Divine Trinity as Christ; with the doctrines of God's personal providence, of sin as a personal offense against God, of man's redemption by Christ from personal and original sin, of a deep corporate union of all in His Church, reflecting the analogy of the human body in a mystical though very real sense, as the achievement of this redemption, of grace, its life-line with God, the mysterious means of the Trinity dwelling with man, and of the final affective vision of the Trinity as the goal of human life and its fulfillment. Though these doctrines evolved to greater explicitness under the pressure of historical factors and through theological development, they formed the prephilosophic and precritical noetic of both philosopher and peasant from the earliest Christian times and thus rendered the Christian moral climate radically different. It may be characterized as divinely human.

The New Creature must now find his happiness and fulfillment in following a divine wisdom and keeping to the
promptings of a divine will. His ethical climate was "otherworldly," but in a manner more personal, realistic, and imperative than Plato had conceived of, wonderful though that
was. Though eye had not seen, nor ear heard, nor mind
conceived of it, the "heaven haven of the reward" was as
actual and convincing as its loss in hell was terrifying. What
had been error to the Greek was now sin to the Christian;
what had been moderation and self-control was now a deepened share in the divine life. The divine dimension of this
climate naturally expanded the meaning of human action
and responsibility, and among the theologians of the Middle
Ages this new ethical relationship helped develop a Christian
sense of analogy between man and God. Ideally speaking at
least, in this scheme of thought there was no conflict but
rather identity between sin as a human failure and as a divine
offense, between vice as a human surrender and as a cause
of eternal punishment, between virtue as human perfection
and as cause of reward in heaven, between the love of God
and one's self-fulfillment, between a desire for personal
happiness and the triumphant glory of God. This basic conviction, implicit though it often was in the Medieval scheme
of things, was forgotten in great part in the eighteenth century—another measure of its univocal thinking—and this
caused a significant change in ethical considerations.

Through this analogy the earlier Christian "otherworldly"
orientation also had a strong human dimension. Chaucer,
Dante, and Aquinas, to mention only a few, understood the
far-reaching implications of the Incarnation for a life here and
now on earth. The instinctive rejection over the centuries by
the Christian conscience of the Manichean, Albigensian, and
Jansenistic doctrines bears witness to this balance, which is
often forgotten when the Christian moral climate is discussed. Despite the very many limits of theory in practice,

this human dimension should be remembered when one discusses the relationship of the Christian belief to the development of human culture.

The opposition between a more optimistic and a more dour Christian view of ethics and culture that has see-sawed through the centuries must be understood in the context of the limiting factor of the doctrine of original sin. Man's divine and supernatural destiny finds a roadblock in this fact. The Pauline description of the human predicament has a psychological validity that is timeless, and of which both Plato and Aristotle were sufficiently aware: "I do not do the good that I wish, but the evil that I do not wish, that I do" (*Romans*, VII, 19). The doctrine, which has had various shades of interpretation throughout the Christian centuries, basically spoke of man's relapse from God and hence from his intended integrity described above. This left him prone to further, personal sin, and despite Christ's redemption, in a state of combat and conflict with himself and his environment.

Man's supernatural destiny, then, and the mitigating factor of original sin determine the basic difference between the Christian moral climate and that of pre-Christian times. Within this climate two fundamental attitudes toward art and culture developed, which have persisted with varying intensity and stress until today. The one, more conscious of man's native weakness and of the intensified moral seriousness of his life, longed for a resolution of tensions in eternity, while looking at life on earth largely as a trial and hazard to be endured. This predominantly otherworldly view is often called eschatological. The other, while aware of the inroads of original sin and of man's eternal transcendent destiny, appreciated with more relish the earth as "charged with the grandeur of God," a place of pilgrimage rather than a mere vale of tears. Its optimism derived from a more thorough sense of the pattern of redemption through the Incarnate

God, a sense of its powers of renewal, a sacramental view of the universe and an awareness of the need for a humane and social culture for a full Christian life on earth. This view is called incarnational and is favorable to culture and the arts.[3]

Many studies have been made of these polarities in the history of Christianity. At different times one has received greater stress than the other; and all the implications of how Christianity relates to culture and the arts are as far from full theoretical clarity as they are from practical realization. This is not the place to discuss this special and complicated problem. It is enough to outline the two main tendencies of the debate and to mention what is not always taken as true, that there has always been in Christianity a tradition that is friendly to the arts. As recently as 1956 David Daiches took the opposite for granted: "If one takes the Christian position on Original Sin, one cannot of course take the view that what is *humanum* is good—the Latin proverb *humanum est errare,* 'to err is human,' would be the appropriate one there rather than the famous declaration *'homo sum, et nihil humani a me alienum puto.'*" Although he was speaking of a context that was rather puritan in character, his generalization was historically and critically unsound.[4] The Middle Ages, the last period, perhaps, when culture and the Christian religion were quite closely integrated, give ample proof that the incarnational attitude was working at a very deep level in Dante, Aquinas, and Chaucer, in the drama, the hymns, and the drinking songs of the day. It was a time far from exclusively eschatological.

Yet the Church, which admittedly had a predominating influence upon the culture of the time, both then and always has had goals deemed larger and further-reaching than those

3. A later study of the problem is B. Besret, *Incarnation ou eschatologie* (Paris: Cerf, 1964).

4. David Daiches, *Critical Approaches to Literature* (Englewood Cliffs: Prentice Hall, 1956), p. 55.

of any school or culture. In the Middle Ages, though culture was important, its role was other and much less important than salvation and sanctification. Cultural theory was far from being the recognized area of academic concern it is in modern times. Further, practically speaking, it could be misleading for us to try to piece together such a theory in order to understand how Medieval thinkers would relate art and morality. Apart from the thoroughgoing transcendence of the concerns of salvation and sanctification over those of culture, there is an added semantic difficulty: the meanings Medieval thinkers gave words and concepts dealing with the arts differ greatly from those we are accustomed to. They thought of poetry as a part of grammar and rhetoric, interesting mainly for stylistic reasons and for the limited didactic value it might have for the young schoolboys (in their very early teens) to whom it was taught and for whom the Horatian formula was considered apt. It was deemed inferior to philosophy and theology and a propaedeutic to them. Yet the theological works of Augustine, Aquinas, Bonaventure, and Hugh of St. Victor, among others, show constant and ample respect for culture; and they are now being culled for valuable oblique awareness of the nature of symbol, the relationship of the crafts and prudence, and a rather hard-headed sense of the autonomy of these crafts as activities. Aquinas, for example, saw the perfection of the crafts in the dance or game (*ludus*), because it served no proximate finality beyond itself, having completed its reason for being in its performance.[5]

Again, aesthetics, as we know it, is a mid-eighteenth-century German invention, yet Aquinas and other Medieval theologians had much to say about beauty. Joyce, for example, thought his own aesthetics deeply Thomistic. Actually he and others have misunderstood Aquinas by reading

5. Edgar de Bruyne, *Études d'esthétique médiévale* (Bruges: De Temple, 1946), III, 295–296.

him in too modern a context. When Aquinas spoke of beauty, he was thinking of ontology rather than aesthetics. Moreover, for him *ars* meant something more like *craft*, an activity that produced either a practical or a fine art, as we would think of them today. Yet anything like Aristotle's notion of the probable was far from operative in his notions of poetry. Nevertheless, William Noon, whose admirable study *Joyce and Aquinas* handles this complicated problem of Thomistic "aesthetics" with great clarity, wisely recalls Thomas Gilby's remark about Aquinas' appreciation of the autonomy of the crafts, that it was the artists at the University of Paris, not the students of divinity, medicine, or law, who mourned most for him when he died.[6]

These ambiguities in Aquinas the Aristotelian put in sharper focus the complexities of the larger Medieval milieu into which the Classical tradition was received and in whose moral climate the function of art was discussed. From our point of view no adequate solution was achieved. Yet the noetic supporting Christian culture and various Christian approaches to the problem of morality was more favorable to the legitimate claims of both than that which prevailed in the eighteenth century. The Medieval noetic was clearly metempirical, with its emphasis on the transcendence of faith and salvation, its effort among the Schoolmen to find a synthesis of faith and reason, its respect for reason's own transcendence and for much of the humane Classical tradition to which it was heir, and, finally, its respect for analogy as a pervasive habit of mind. In such a climate salvation and culture were not likely to be confused, for the stakes were too high. What use was made of the please-and-teach formula must be understood against this background. In such a situation men would not be likely to look to poetry and

6. *Ibid.*, II, 302 ff.; III, 219–226, 340–344; William T. Noon, s.j., *Joyce and Aquinas* (New Haven: Yale University Press, 1957), pp. 18 ff.; Walter J. Ong, s.j., "Wit and Mystery: a Revaluation," in *Speculum*, 22 (1947), 324.

the arts for their ultimate ethical motivation, simply because their faith and the social unity it afforded them offered a much surer and a more convincing guide. With the later break-up of Christendom, this assurance and conviction were impaired by the splintering of doctrinal opinion and ecclesiastical allegiance. The moral imperatives of the Christian tradition remained strong, but the noetic framework that had supported it was gradually shaken. Poetry and the arts might well be expected, then, to attract men more strongly as sources of wisdom to live by, especially because the renewed emphasis on Classical studies and the new native exuberance of the Renaissance coincided with this dissolution, particularly in England.

If the discussion of the past few pages has seemed a curious way of backing into a discussion of the moral climate of the eighteenth century into which theories of the function of poetry were received, I think it nonetheless pertinent and necessary. The new dimension which Christianity brought to ethical living was first absorbed into the Medieval cultural milieu and was concretely shaped by and helped shape this milieu. By the time of the Enlightenment, though the Christian ethical imperative was still widespread and strong, its noetic backgrounds had changed radically and were no longer adequate to it. Reason and faith had largely been estranged through overconfidence in reason on the part of the rationalists (not without their own brand of skepticism), a lack of confidence in reason on the part of the Puritan tradition, and later a strong reaction to rationalism among the various sects and schools of emotionalism. Rationalism, as we have already seen, dispensed more and more with the humane context of mystery—especially the Christian sense of mystery. In Pieper's terms, it was an age of *ratio* without an adequate sense of *intellectus*. In the moral sphere this eventually led to voluntarism. For example, despite their various forms of empirical rationalism, Locke, Newton, Hartley, and Priestley were known to be moral and pious Christians.

Voluntarism, then—often the ethical ally of fideism—best describes the moral climate of the time, a climate in which ethical action and attitudes derive from an imperative not adequately motivated by knowledge—this inadequacy deriving either paradoxically from an oversimple understanding of human, and especially Christian, moral activity, or from its dim shadow, skepticism. While the Cambridge Platonists strove mightily against this tendency, their effects were limited and long delayed. This voluntarism greatly supported the tendency to interpret the function of mimesis in a moralistic fashion. We should remember that Classical poetics was conceived in a milieu where ultimates were in great part political—with varying degrees of emphasis and difference, of course, in Plato, Aristotle, and Horace. The Christian ultimate, even in its most incarnational form, is never this. As a result, when these Classical structures for evaluating literature were used in the Enlightenment context, in which the Christian moral imperative was still strong but without a sufficient intellectual backing, the perennial conflict between the claims of art and the claims of morality were intensified because they were caught in the tension and confusion of the claims of salvation and of culture. Added to this, there had been no sufficiently theoretical facing of this problem, even in the comparatively more metaphysically minded Middle Ages. So we see that the fundamental forces muddying the waters of this problem were neither Puritanism nor the doctrine of original sin—though they were, of course, contributory—but rather the inability of rationalism to deal with the Christian imperative, and later in the century, the inadequacy of the emotionalist reactions to this rationalism. This conflict may have been muted in the case of some critics, especially where good sense and poetic insight were somewhat stronger. But it surely was pervasive of the times. I have no doubt that it was important, to some extent, in spite of his deep intelligence and common sense, in Johnson's bouts with melancholy and the strong moralistic judgments he occasionally made about morality in literature.[7]

EIGHTEENTH-CENTURY MORAL CLIMATE

It has been helpful to ascertain the Christian moral climate as it affected our problem by seeing its formation in the Middle Ages, not because it was perfected there, nor because it has not in some significant ways been deepened since then. The Protestant sense of interiority, for example, has added a valuable dimension. Rather it has been helpful because in the Middle Ages a synthesis of faith and reason was attempted and in good part achieved, a synthesis which was needful in order to deal with the tension of the concerns of salvation and culture. Alfred North Whitehead has drawn an interesting contrast between the noetics of the Middle Ages and the Enlightenment which suggests that my strategy has been a wise one:

In so far as the intellectual climates of different epochs can be contrasted, the eighteenth century in Europe was the complete antithesis to the Middle Ages. The contrast is symbolised by the difference between the cathedral of Chartres and the Parisian salons, where D'Alembert conversed with Voltaire. The Middle Ages were haunted with the desire to rationalise the infinite: the men of the eighteenth century rationalised the social life of modern communities, and based their sociological theories on an appeal to the facts of nature. The earlier period was the age of faith, based upon reason. In the later period, they let sleeping dogs lie: it was the age of reason based upon faith. To illustrate

7. The problem of Johnson's occasional lapses into moralism is treated below, pp. 290–293.

my meaning:—St. Anselm would have been distressed if he had failed to find a convincing argument for the existence of God, and on this argument he based his edifice of faith, whereas Hume based his *Dissertation on the Natural History of Religion* upon his faith in the order of nature. In comparing these epochs it is well to remember that reason can err, and that faith may be misplaced.[8]

While one might wish to distinguish and, perhaps, cavil at some of the details of this antithesis, its central thrust is very perceptive. For our purposes it helps point to the basic rationalistic quality which paradoxically occasioned the various forms of voluntarism in the eighteenth-century moral climate. It was a situation which should not be oversimplified. But three elements which were mixed in various ways should be stressed as operative in this voluntarism: empirical rationalism, the Christian ethical imperative not sufficiently aware of its complexities, and the various forms of emotive reaction to rationalism, whether in a religious or a nonreligious context. This is not to suggest a tidy or pat picture, but these elements were surely at work. Hence three phases or kinds of voluntarism will be suggested to describe the moral climate of this century against which the critical judgments of the function of literature should be viewed. These are rationalistic voluntarism, Christian voluntarism, and voluntarism and the emotions.

(a) *Rationalistic Voluntarism.* The intellectual climate of empirical rationalism outlined in Chapter 2 is the familiar basis of this kind of voluntarism, in which the humane context and values are inadequately accounted for by the new scientific and mathematical methodologies. The surface elements of life and experience become more important than the deeper roots of human value and desire; human nature,

8. Alfred North Whitehead, *Science and the Modern World* (New York: Macmillan, 1948), p. 83.

finality, and mystery are relatively neglected. As was true in the case of most concepts of mimesis, the rewards of deeper intuitive and metaphysical insights into the moral nature of man are neglected in favor of a more empirical and mathematical simplicity. Appetite and desire are moral, for example, merely because they are facts, not because they reveal a drive toward human value and finality. Hobbes writes: "Whatsoever is the object of any man's appetite or desire, that it is which he for his part calleth *good*: and the object of his hate and aversion, *evil*; and of his contempt, *vile* and *inconsiderable*. For these words of good, evil and contemptible, are ever used in relation to the person that useth them: there being nothing simply and absolutely so; nor any common rule of good and evil, to be taken from the nature of the objects themselves." When this nominalism is applied to the question of justice, there is nothing objectively just, so constituted in the nature of things, but only such justice as comes from positive, arbitrary law, the will of the community. "Force and fraud [are] the two cardinal virtues" in the social war.[9]

John Locke followed Hobbes in his denial of innate principles of human action and his stress of association as the key to human value. For all his show of rationalism, he denied the mind's ability to reach beyond the empirical. God's existence was established by experiencing one's own existence and an empirical causality—we remember that he denied metaphysical causality. He rejected an intellectual approach to religion: "The Writers and Wranglers in Religion fill it with niceties, and dress it up with notions; which they make necessary and fundamental parts of it; As if there were no way into the Church, but through the Academy or Lyceum. The bulk of Mankind have not leisure for Learning and Logick, and superfine distinctions of the Schools." This

9. *The Classical Moralists*, ed. Benjamin Rand (Boston: Houghton Mifflin, [1909]), pp. 215, 221.

simplistic rejection of theology through caricature neglects the cognitive though mysterious nature of the Revelation, the social nature of the Church, and uses pragmatic difficulties as a pretext for simplifying what had for centuries been found to be nourishing precisely because it was mysterious. His rejection of poetry as a waste of time reflects the same intellectual impatience.[10] When his empirical methodology turns to ethics, we read this determination of moral good and evil: "*Moral Good and Evil.*—Good and evil, as hath been shown . . . are nothing but pleasure or pain, or that which occasions or procures pleasure or pain to us. Moral good and evil, then, is only the conformity or disagreement of our voluntary actions to some law, whereby good and evil is drawn on us from the will and power of the law-maker; which good and evil, pleasure and pain, attending our observance or breach of the law, by the decree of the law-maker, is what we call 'reward' and 'punishment.' "[11]

Though Locke postulates a divine law as the norm of sin and duty, and of rewards and punishments, he undercuts its availability to the mind through his empiricist principles, saying that this law can only be known through the experience it offers of pleasure and pain. Having destroyed the intellectual bases of ethics, he then demands a man of strong moral concern: "Hence I think I may conclude, that *morality* is *the proper science and business of mankind in general.*"[12] Throughout *Human Understanding,* Locke shows himself constantly intent upon Christian morals, though he had removed their foundation stone by stone.

David Hume carried on the same tradition. "It must be

10. *Religious Thought in the Eighteenth Century*, ed. John M. Creed and John S. Boys Smith (Cambridge: Cambridge University Press, 1934), pp. 6–8, quoted from *Human Understanding*, IV, x.

11. *The Classical Moralists*, ed. Rand, pp. 306–307.

12. Kenneth McLean, *John Locke and English Literature of the Eighteenth Century* (New Haven: Yale University Press, 1936), p. 164.

allowed that every quality of the mind, which is *useful,* or *agreeable* to the *person himself* or to *others,* communicates a pleasure to the spectator, engages his esteem, and is admitted under the honorable denomination of virtue or merit."[13] David Hartley, heir to Locke's Associationism, solves the question of morality with his empirical key: "And thus we may perceive, that all pleasures and pains of sensation, imagination, ambition, self-interest, sympathy, and theopathy, as far as they are consistent with one another, with the frame of our natures, and with the course of the world, beget in us a moral sense, and lead us to the love and approbation of virtue, and to the fear, hatred, and abhorrence of vice. This moral sense therefore carries its own authority with it, inasmuch as it is the sum total of all the rest, and the ultimate result from them; and employs the force and authority of the whole nature of man against any particular part of it, that rebels against the determinations and commands of the conscience or moral judgment."[14] This pan-sensationism, though veering toward a sense of intuition, does not transcend Associationism. Experience, rather than any intelligible notion of it, is the norm of judgment of right and wrong, a far cry from the universal idea of the Western tradition.

It is clear that such a moral climate was ultimately hostile to the Western humane tradition, Classical and Christian, incapable, short of the violence characteristic of voluntarism, of yoking moral action to the metempirical values needed for its proper motivation. Yet, as we have seen, traditional moral values were still claimed as imperatives of human conduct. On the Continent, Enlightenment morality followed the logic of its empiricism and rationalism, culminating in the French Revolution (though one must not forget French fideism). But England, always more deeply concerned with a more traditional moral code, preferred a voluntarism,

13. *The Classical Moralists,* ed. Rand, p. 442.
14. *Ibid.,* p. 425.

largely of a Christian variety. Among the critics we have been studying, Dryden, Pope, Dennis, and Addison, to mention but a few, have been found to share the confusion caused by this rationalistic voluntarism. Bredvold's detailed study of Dryden's fideism, Lovejoy's comments on Pope's cosmic toryism, and Fairchild's treatment of Addison's and Dennis' confused voluntarist opinions come to mind in this context.[15]

(b) *Christian Voluntarism.* The Christian moral climate was analogous to the rationalist climate just reviewed. In fact, it was deeply influenced by it, though it also contained constraining factors of its own. We have seen ample evidences of the transforming influences of this rationalism upon contemporary thinking about God and religion. Both what Michael Macklem calls a "Physics of Theology" and the deism of such men as John Toland and Charles Blount, a deism which attacked the transcendent principles behind a reasonable faith, were in a more optimistic vein, whereas fideism and other forms of skepticism were more pessimistic. All tended to undermine the intelligible bases of the Christian moral climate. Macklem's *The Anatomy of the World* is an interesting and detailed study, using Donne and Pope as termini, of how in the course of a century the theological understanding of moral and physical evil shifted radically

15. Louis I. Bredvold, *The Intellectual Milieu of John Dryden* (Ann Arbor: University of Michigan Press, 1934), pp. 73 ff.; Arthur O. Lovejoy, *The Great Chain of Being* (Cambridge: Harvard University Press, 1936), pp. 192 ff.; Hoxie N. Fairchild, *Religious Trends in English Poetry* (New York: Columbia University Press, 1939), I, 71, 179-180. Bredvold in a later study, *The Brave New World of the Enlightenment* (Ann Arbor: University of Michigan Press, 1961), shows how several splintered views of nature and of morals followed upon the abandonment of the traditional notions of nature and of nature's law. Of special interest to us here is his stress on the materialistic basis of ethical doctrine in the empirical tradition, on how moral human nature was considered merely an extension of physical nature, and on how problems of morals were treated as if they were problems in mathematics or mechanics. See pp. 28 ff. and 45.

from the context of the Christian doctrine of original sin to the cosmological context of "whatever is, is right"—and wrong. Summing up the significant turnover in theological opinion on how moral law was conceived, and especially on how it was related to physical and moral agents, he says: "For Donne this relationship is productive of disorder in both man and the world; for Pope it is productive of order. The difference is not simply that between affirmative and negative answers to the question of the existence of evil. It is rather that between a conception of evil as sin or the consequence of sin and a conception of evil as a condition of existence."[16] This is a clear example of the univocal leveling of heaven and earth spoken of above in Chapter 2. Perhaps there is no more revealing rejection of the essential human awareness of mystery in the Christian context than the denial or exaggeration, at any time in history, of the doctrine of original sin and its effects. For a sense both of the complexity of the mystery of evil at this level and of an integration of what it means with other Christian values is most necessary, if one is to perceive how Christianity is densely human and truly realistic. A lack of this awareness is analogous to the lack in philosophy and aesthetics of a sense of mystery and myth, paradox and ambiguity. In its brilliant tradition of tragedy the Greek mind shows its own dark awareness of the mystery Christians call original sin, and most eloquently dramatizes how profoundly its spirit differs from that of the Enlightenment.

Horton Davies offers other evidence of how rationalism produced, in part at least, this Christian moral climate in his study of liturgy and worship of the time. To begin with, he calls the section of his study covering the period 1690–1740 "The Dominance of Rationalistic Moralism." He has

16. Michael Macklem, *The Anatomy of the World* (Minneapolis: University of Minnesota Press, 1958), p. 4.

done this, he says, "since the characteristic marks of the theology of the period are the reduction of the supernatural to the natural, the mysterious to the rational, and the depreciation of faith in favour of the good works of charity." His study is valuable for us because it goes beyond the history of ideas into something of their practical impact upon the devotional life of the Church. He thinks the stress is important because a study of the liturgy "is a profound clue to the interpretation of religious life at any period," and quotes with agreement Canon Roger Lloyd: "The true history of the Church is therefore the history of its worship." Davies then goes into detail: from the stripping of the Church of England of its sense of the numinous, through a rationalistic sense of Deity, a tendency to downgrade interest in the Trinity, neglect of certain forms of worship, the Sacraments, and the Pulpit, to a softening of original sin, the atonement, and a sense of sacrifice. In summary, his judgment of the impact of the Enlightenment on the life of the Church is this: "Such an age will relegate to the background whatever is paradoxical and remote from the ordinary ways of thinking. In religion this will mean a reduction of revelation to the limits of the rational and a distaste for such a speculative doctrine as the Holy Trinity, and such a mystical doctrine as salvation through the atoning sacrifice of Christ. Morality, as related to religion, will come into prominence because the intuitions of the conscience are comparatively clear, and the general distinction between good and evil widely accepted."[17] This last claim highlights the inadequacy of the clear and distinct idea to deal with the mystery of iniquity.

We draw the same impression of the numinous being replaced by a deceptive clarity in a study of contemporary religious literature by A. R. Humphreys, who is, perhaps, a

17. Horton Davies, *Worship and Theology in England from Watts and Wesley to Maurice: 1690-1850* (Princeton: Princeton University Press, 1961), pp. 3, 6-7, 52, and pp. 52-93, chs. iii-iv *passim*.

little less severe than Davies in his final judgment of the situation. While he finds in Thomson's *Seasons* both awe and exaltation, "the awe is simply awe that the Almighty has designed the universe to give man unmitigated satisfaction, and the exaltation inspires only a glowing rhetoric." Speaking of Law's *Serious Call* and Butler's *Analogy,* he remarks: "Even these, standing out as they do against an apparently widespread unbelief, seem to witness rather to the strength of the tide against which they strain than to any general faith."[18]

From what we have seen, it is clear that one cannot separate the influence of this rationalism from the indigenous factors of contemporary Christianity. But a few of these factors should be stressed. If a sense of original sin and of the misery of its evil effects should not be forgotten, there is also danger in overemphasizing them. The Protestant dogmas on fallen man still had much of the severity of Lutheran and Calvinist doctrines of an earlier era, of the darkness of mind and the weakness of will, of the emphasis on a fiducial faith rather than on confidence in good works, in the face of a God who was conceived of largely in terms of Will. Puritan doctrine especially would illustrate this tradition, even though the word can admittedly have many meanings and the Puritans had gained a fairly substantial economic and this-worldly status in English life. Nevertheless, Lawrence Sasek, an *amicus curiae* for contemporary Puritan literary taste

18. A. R. Humphreys, "Literature and Religion in Eighteenth-Century England," in *Journal of Ecclesiastical History,* 3 (1952), 159-190, especially 159 and 188-189. Hiram Haydn in his *The Counter-Renaissance* (New York: Scribners, 1950), especially chs. i and iii, discusses the retarding influence of Puritan doctrines on the Humanist aims of the Renaissance, as does C. S. Lewis in his *English Literature in the Sixteenth Century Excluding Drama* (Oxford: Clarendon, 1954), pp. 157 ff. An older book, J. W. Krutch, *Comedy and Conscience after the Restoration* (New York: Columbia University Press, 1924), is also pertinent reading on the moral climate of the time.

which has perhaps been caricatured in the past, finds this taste highly moralistic. Attitudes toward the theater are predominantly hostile, and even where some literature is approved of for "recreation," didactic and moralistic motives predominate. It is all in the tradition of Gosson and thinly veiled philistinism.[19] Again, Creed and Boys Smith point out that after the seventeenth century the tradition of metaphysical theology was largely neglected, and an analogous theology of Reformation dogmas, which might have expanded some of the more positive elements of the tradition, was not developed.[20]

The Cambridge Platonists can stand as transitional to the third group which formed the moral climate of the century. Such men as Cudworth and More seriously tried to establish a Christian moral climate that would have some metaphysical validity to transcend the merely empirical world. They espoused, besides the Platonic tradition, the Stoic and Medieval Scholastic traditions of natural law, relating law to God's will and thus to religion. Although this type of thought naturally abetted a more metempirical moral climate, its influence was not too far-reaching; and Bredvold points out its tendency toward contemporary sentimentality, for example, in espousing the concept of the "noble savage," which in principle it should disavow. At any rate, while this kind of Platonism tried to foster a metempirical moral climate, the general structure of Platonic thought, as we have seen, was basically not favorable to the demands of mimesis.[21]

19. Lawrence A. Sasek, *The Literary Temper of the English Puritans* (Baton Rouge: Louisiana State University Press, 1961), chs. vi and vii *passim*.

20. *Religious Thought in the Eighteenth Century,* ed. Creed and Boys Smith, p. xxii.

21. Eugene M. Austin, *The Ethics of the Cambridge Platonists* (Philadelphia: University of Pennsylvania Press, 1935), pp. 20 ff. and 43 ff. Bredvold, *The Brave New World of the Enlightenment,* pp. 60 ff.

(c) *Voluntarism and the Emotions.* Eighteenth-century interest in the emotions grew in marked intensity as the century drew to a close. This can be explained in good part as a reaction to the two kinds of voluntarism just discussed. Those favoring this reaction tended to agree in finding man's moral perfection in good feeling. This common denominator of belief in man's good instincts as the basis of a good moral life derived in great measure from Shaftesbury, Hutcheson, and the Latitudinarian religious leaders: Isaac Barrow, Robert Smith, John Tillotson, Richard Cumberland, and Samuel Parker.[22]

Shaftesbury had reacted strongly against Hobbes' materialism and his ethical doctrine of self-interest, as well as against Puritan Christianity. Because his thought is deceptively Platonic, it has little of the Greek vigor of mind and sense of objective transcendence. He chose to look at man as essentially benevolent and susceptible to the charms of beauty, goodness, and truth. He considered virtue its own reward, rejecting the doctrine of divine rewards and punishments as a motive for moral action. He compared the beauty of moral action to the beauty of form in the world of experience: "The shapes, motions, colours and proportions of these latter being presented to our eye, there necessarily results a beauty or deformity, according to the different measure, arrangement and disposition of their several parts. So in behaviour and actions, when presented to our understanding, there must be found, of necessity, an apparent difference, according to the regularity or irregularity of the subjects."[23] "Thank heaven I can do good and find heaven in it. I know nothing else that is heavenly. And if this disposition fits me not for

22. R. S. Crane, "Genealogy of the Man of Feeling," in *ELH*, I (1934), 205-230.

23. Anthony, Earl of Shaftesbury, *Characteristics of Men, Manners, Opinions, Times, etc.*, ed. John M. Robertson (London: Richards, 1900), I, 251.

heaven, I desire never to be fitted for it, nor come into the place. I ask no reward from heaven for that which is reward itself."[24] Such simplistic thinking, univocal in a manner diametrically opposite to that of materialism, does not face the mystery of evil, its complexity and paradoxes; and such distortion of the place of rewards and punishments in the larger frame of Christian values reveals the shallowness of his thought. What of virtue that is unpleasant and vice that is attractive? Again an interesting bit of univocal thinking, as unreal as its opposite, poetic justice.

Robert Marsh has tried to tone down the excesses of Shaftesbury's moral theorizing. It is fair enough to say that Shaftesbury's various "senses" are closer to being predispositions rather than faculties or perfections of the soul, and to stress the notion of the inward colloquy of the soul with itself as a way of making his moral optimism less than naive. But his writings are still predominantly misty when speaking of moral goodness in the man of feeling, and one wonders how sharply he faced the critical barrier Newman was to speak of: "those giants, the passion and the pride of man." Bredvold rightly stresses the influence of Shaftesbury's more sentimental and naive view on the thought and literature of the century following his death. One has but to think of the only really substantial blemish in Fielding's *Tom Jones,* his reliance on this sentimental philosophy to bring Tom to his happy ending, which would have been an even greater structural weakness, were it not artfully undercut by Fielding's brilliant sense of comedy.[25] Shaftesbury's influence was in-

24. Shaftesbury, *The Life, Unpublished Letters, and Philosophic Regimen of Anthony, Earl of Shaftesbury,* ed. Benjamin Rand (London and New York: Swan Sonnenschein and Macmillan, 1900), p. 347.

25. Robert Marsh, "Shaftesbury's Theory of Poetry: The Importance of the 'Inward Colloquy,'" in *ELH,* 28 (1961), 54-67; John Henry Cardinal Newman, *The Idea of a University,* ed. C. F. Harrold (New York: Longmans, Green, 1947), p. 107; Bredvold, *The Brave New World of the Enlightenment,* p. 70.

tensified by the work of Hutcheson, who systematized his ideas. And as a result the Scottish school of taste, in turn, came under his sway.[26]

Hutcheson defines the moral sense in this way: "We mean by it only a determination of our minds to receive amiable or disagreeable ideas [in the context *mind* and *ideas* do not denote the intellectual penetration of what is real, but merely the psychological experience] of actions when they occur to our observation, antecedent to any opinions of advantage or loss to redound to ourselves from them; even as we are pleased with a regular form, or an harmonious composition, without having any knowledge of mathematics, or seeing any advantage in that form, or composition, different from the immediate pleasure."[27]

Moral sense, then, for both Shaftesbury and Hutcheson, looked characteristically to instinctive approbation or disapprobation as the main criterion of good and evil, separating moral science in good part from understanding and setting it ahead of religious doctrine in importance. The imperative of feeling, even given the "Inward Colloquy," seems a weak arbiter of moral value, a fairly ineffectual slayer of the dragon of evil. Yet in one way or the other it influenced Fielding, Smollett, Cowper, Akenside, Shenstone, Goldsmith, and the sentimental dramatists, together with the entire Scottish school of critics. Also under this influence, poetry was conceived of as a rhetorical means of wakening emotions for moral ends.[28]

The concept of the moral man of good feeling was also

26. W. J. Bate, *From Classic to Romantic* (Cambridge: Harvard University Press, 1946), p. 51; Crane, "Genealogy of the Man of Feeling," p. 230.

27. *The Classical Moralists,* ed. Rand, pp. 399-400.

28. William E. Alderman, "Shaftesbury and the Doctrine of Moral Sense in the Eighteenth Century," in *PMLA,* 46 (1931), 1087-1094, especially 1088-1089.

formed by Latitudinarian preaching, which was very popular as an answer to the Puritan call for the man of righteousness. Universal benevolence, the Latitudinarians said, was an expression of Christian charity and a general sign of virtue. It derived from feeling, not from Stoical reason; and it brought with it feelings of self-approval. The good man could thus find "moral weeping" a "self-approving joy." Two brief passages describe this benevolence. The first is from Samuel Parker: "As for the generality of Men their hearts are so tender and their natural affections so humane, that they cannot but pity and commiserate the afflicted with a kind of fatal and mechanical Sympathy; their groans force tears and sighs from the unafflicted, and 'tis a pain to them not to be able to relieve their miseries." In the second passage Sir William Dawes assigns the origin of these feelings to nature: "Nature has implanted in us a most tender and compassionate Sense and Fellow-feeling of one anothers miseries, a most ready and prevailing propension and inclination to assist and relieve them; insomuch that pity and kindness towards our Brethren have a long time, passed under the name of Humanity, as properties essential to and not without Violence to be separated from humane Nature."[29]

CONCLUSION

My intent, in great part, in this study is to show how the eighteenth-century noetic shaped contemporary opinion about the value of poetry to man. If critical theory fell into formalism, and then by reaction into an emotionalism of sorts, the same noetic supplied a parallel in the moral climate in which the function of poetry was judged. Rhetoric and didacticism found congenial lairs. If a transcendence of

29. Quoted in Crane, "Genealogy of the Man of Feeling," pp. 205-206 and 224-225.

some sort was needed to relate mimesis to its subject matter and to judge its nature aright, it was just as important for understanding its function. This was especially true given the Christian cultural context in which it was to function. If salvation and culture were to find genuine accord rather than mutual confusion or substitution, some sense of the metempirical, from which to judge the claims of both, was necessary. But none was forthcoming. We find a strange set of univocal judgments about the many different aspects of morality, all of which purport to be Christian, but which are actually parallels of the cosmological noetic described in the second chapter. Christian morality is human and divine in its demands. It requires that the goodness or evil of moral actions be judged by their intrinsic value, by their augmentation or hindrance of the pilgrim's quest for a real goal; that rewards and punishments be seen as salutary comment on this value and on the difficulty of the effort, as well as on the dignity of man as a Child of God; that this interest in no way deny the intrinsic beauty of virtue and the ugliness of vice. It insists that pleasure and pain are not ready signals of the value of a human act, the best of which may well at times be irksome and unattractive, and that the will of God is identical with man's fulfillment. The needed perilous balance, demanding a sense of analogy, was eminently lacking. When the Horatian formula is judged against this background, we can see in this climate an added impetus to the long tradition it had already fostered by turning Aristotle's concept of pleasurable contemplation into a rhetorical aim of pleasing in order to teach what was otherwise hard to make attractive. The fate of this formula is the subject of the next chapter. Meanwhile we may close these remarks with a wise statement of Étienne Gilson, calling for some semblance of the metempirical, if the complexities of human life are to be reconciled with intelligence: "Skepticism is a philosophical disease which either moralism or pseudo-mysticism can ease, but for which there is no other cure than to come back to the science of being as being, metaphysics."[30]

30. Étienne Gilson, *Being and Some Philosophers* (Toronto: Pontifical Institute of Mediaeval Studies, 1949), pp. 1-2.

6

FORM AND THE FORMULA

Up to this point our study has presented and has tried to evaluate the indirect and oblique evidence of eighteenth-century critical opinion of the function of literature. It is by far the most important evidence, because it reveals the actual contours of this critical thought. The direct evidence was usually expressed in the Horatian please-and-teach formula, popular ever since the Middle Ages and enjoying canonical status in any codification of Renaissance and Neoclassical tenets. To refer to it alone would be to catalogue a commonplace of this critical tradition. Hence it was important for us to get behind the façade of the formula. Now we may select a few of its important treatments and the direct evidence they reveal of the moralistic tendencies of contemporary critical opinion. Our findings rather closely parallel those of former chapters, with the bulk of opinion favoring either a Cartesian formalism or a Platonic or Neoplatonic moralism, or both. In general the use of the formula has a decidedly rhetorical emphasis and intent.

PLEASURE AS A BAIT

The formula, of course, was Horatian. If one were to relate Aristotle's notion of poetry's function to this formula—which we have seen would entail some warping of it—one would have to see the pleasure as an outgrowth and natural overflow of insight, the two organically one. This was rarely the case among the eighteenth-century critics. Pleasure was largely a bait or an instrument, and only rarely spoken of as organically one with insight. Pleasure as a bait or instrument is clearly a rhetorical conception. Further, Aristotle would prefer to say that the audience saw, or came to know, rather than that it was taught. Sidney, whose *Apologie* was the best all-around Renaissance critical statement, early took this position that pleasure was a bait, and many subsequently followed his lead. After his memorable applause for the poet, who comes "with a tale which holdeth children from play, and old men from the chimney corner," he likens poetry to a pleasant deception, disguising the bitter taste of *"Aloes* or *Rubarb,"* that is, moral doctrine. Though this essay does include a fair account of Aristotelian mimesis as "figuring forth," in the next sentence it asserts the purpose of poetry as Aristotelian: "with this end, to teach and delight."[1] Elsewhere in the essay Sidney frequently voices a strong Renaissance Neoplatonic moral bias when speaking of both the nature and the function of poetry.

John Dennis often shows himself to be a rationalist critic. In the following passages he makes a rationalistic appeal to reject reason as a source of pleasure in poetry and to substitute passion for it. For him poetry is a rhetoric of the emotions in the service of virtue. His syllogism runs as follows: "By Happiness, then, I could never understand any thing else but pleasure." It is false to attribute happiness to reason, for reason shows us only our weakness. Passion, "which Reason pretends to combat," alone can please us. "For when any Man is pleas'd, he may find by Reflection, that at the same time he is mov'd." In actual life the passions are not under the control of reason, but in the drama they

---

1. *Elizabethan Critical Essays,* ed. G. Gregory Smith (London: Oxford University Press, 1904), I, 172, 158. This passage has been discussed at greater length earlier; see pp. 196–199.

are; and that is why they can move properly, and hence properly instruct. This is the place of the purgation in drama. "Poetry then is an Art, by which a Poet excites Passion (and for that very Cause entertains Sense) in order to satisfy and improve, to delight and reform the Mind, and so to make Mankind happier and better: from which it appears that Poetry has two Ends, a subordinate, and a final one; the subordinate one is Pleasure, and the final one is Instruction."[2]

Dennis' analysis hardly fits the demands of mimesis, and at the same time it offers a confused psychology of the emotions for a poetic of the new directions. For Aristotle pleasure was in the mind, a guarantee of the rightness of its automatically satisfying function. For Dennis it is in the senses and the passions, both presumed to be in conflict and compromise with each other and with the mind. Further, the experience of emotion, pleasure, and suasive moving to virtue seem confused. At this point he elaborates on the importance of moral instruction and on the means to this end, namely, impassioned rhetoric. Religious poetry is important in this context, and even moral philosophy should attempt to instruct through passion, else it would not persuade. But poetry is more powerful to this end. Because philosophy only moves gently, the reformer should use poetry, or the strong emotions "will fly to their old objects; whereas Poetry, at the same time that it instructs us powerfully, must reform us easily; because it makes the very Violence of the Passions contribute to our Reformation."[3] One is reminded that only the violent bear Heaven away!

Addison can be expected to urge the moral values of literature. He too subscribes to the Horatian formula, but he has a more perceptive sense than Dennis of the aesthetic

2. John Dennis, *The Critical Works of John Dennis,* ed. E. N. Hooker (Baltimore: Johns Hopkins Press, 1939-1943), I, 148-151.
3. *Ibid.,* I, 336-338.

values involved in poetry. Like Johnson he respected the common-sense taste of the general audience and preferred its approval to the carping approval of the esoteric critic, "as though the first precept in poetry were not to please."[4] Yet he primly rejects the antics of an acrobat because they cause admiration for the distortion of nature and for buffoonery. Human nature's dignity should be studied for the audience's benefit.[5] Both here and in his strict rebuke of those who represent vice he seems to miss the precise nature of mimesis and the contemplative quality involved in the enjoyment of poetry. Pleasure is rather a means to virtuous knowledge, and so a species of rhetoric. His zeal in rebuking "evil writers" even goes so far as to approve of the sentiment, while rejecting the doctrine, of a Roman Catholic divine who taught that an evil author who repents of his sin must abide in Purgatory as long as the evil effects of his writings endure![6]

Gildon, the compiler and writer of textbooks, looks for both profit and pleasure in poetry, explicitly using the Horatian formula, but he relates the two elements in a clearly pragmatic way. Poetry teaches by pleasing. "Whatever instruction we receive from poetry must be deliver'd with pleasure, which if wanting, we never can arrive at the profitable; and this is the reason why *Horace* will not admit of mediocrity in poetry, because an indifferent poet can never give us that delight which is absolutely necessary to make his instructions of any force, since the very instructions themselves are the effect of the pleasure we receive from the performance." He adds, however, that, even if poetry gives only

4. Joseph Addison and Richard Steele, *The Spectator,* ed. George A. Aitken (London, 1898), VIII, 160 (No. 592).

5. Joseph Addison and Richard Steele, *The Tatler,* ed. George A. Aitken (London, 1898-1899), II, 388 ff. (No. 108).

6. Addison and Steele, *Spectator,* II, 407-411 (No. 166).

pleasure *per impossibile,* it should not be scorned, life being as difficult as it is![7]

Thomas Rymer sees the need for state censorship to safeguard the didactic function of the drama. There should be a committee of lay bishops who, just as clerical bishops oversee orthodoxy in the pulpit, would ensure "that no doctrine be there broached, but what tends to the Edification, as well as to the Delight of the Spectator."[8]

John Hughes, a minor critic, turns the didactic interest of contemporary criticism to his analysis of allegory, which he sees as a "Fable or Story, in which, under imaginary Persons or Things, is shadow'd some real Action or Instructive Moral." He agrees with Plutarch's argument for fiction: truth is austere and rigid. This is the honey-on-the-cup approach already found in Sidney. The author of an allegory "covertly instructs Mankind in the most important Incidents and Concerns of their lives."[9]

Steele was more explicitly moralistic than Addison, possibly because he was more sentimental. He considered all audiences to be composed of those who seek gross pleasures of the flesh and those who overcome this desire "by addition of fine sentiments of the mind."[10] In *Tatler* 98 we read: "I have always been of the opinion that virtue sinks deepest into the heart of man when it comes recommended by the powerful charms of poetry." Imagination and passions yield to the pleasure of poetry and "our reason surrenders itself with pleasure in the end. Thus the whole soul is insensibly betrayed into morality, by bribing the fancy with beautiful and agreeable images of those very things that in the books of

7. Charles Gildon, *The Laws of Poetry* (London, 1721), pp. 17, 125.
8. T[homas] R[ymer], *A Short View of Tragedy* (London, 1693), p. 48.
9. John Hughes, "An Essay on Allegorical Poetry," in *Critical Essays of the Eighteenth Century 1700-1728,* ed. Willard H. Durham (New Haven: Yale University Press, 1915), pp. 88-91.
10. Addison and Steele, *Spectator,* VII, 137 (No. 502).

the philosophers appear austere, and have at the best but a kind of forbidden aspect."[11] "Bold metaphors and sounding numbers" can "rouse up all our sleeping faculties, and alarm the whole powers of the soul." Here style is the instrument of rhetoric. Raphael's paintings, among others, are more swift and direct in performing a similar function than philosophy and moral science. "What strong images of virtue and humanity might we not expect would be instilled into the mind from the labours of the pencil?"[12] Finally, in a gesture of liberality, he (unlike Addison) would allow such indifferent presentations as horseplay, ghosts, and the other "well-drawn rusticities" found in the *Country Wake*, provided these do not offend good manners and are of indifferent nature.[13]

It is a commonplace of Fielding criticism today to accept as serious his claims to being a writer with a moral purpose. Yet we know his *Tom Jones,* among other things a moral book, shocked some of his contemporaries, including so sensitive a humanist as Johnson. One presumes that Fielding's own reactions were more liberal. Yet one is surprised to read his critical comments on the purpose of literature. He echoes Rymer's metaphor: as the ministry is to the state, the bishop to the church, the general to the army, such "is a great and good writer over the morals of his countrymen." He bases his claims on the close analogy between taste and morals in an age. "True taste is indeed no other than the knowledge of what is right and fit in every thing."[14] Here we see a belief in the identity or near-identity of moral and aesthetic sense (a point that will arise again later). Fielding was a Shaftesburian, believing in the morals of good feeling.

11. Addison and Steele, *Tatler,* II, 331 (No. 98).
12. Addison and Steele, *Spectator*, III, 275-276 (No. 226).
13. *Ibid.,* VII, 137-138 (No. 502).
14. Henry Fielding, *The Complete Works of Henry Fielding* (New York: Barnes and Noble, 1967), XVI, 28-29.

Yet in his *Covent Garden Journal* we read rather severe strictures on what he considers writing for mere amusement. *"Pleasantry . . . should be made only the Vehicle of Instruction."* "But when no Moral, no Lesson, no Instruction is conveyed to the Reader, where the whole Design of Composition is no more than to make us laugh, the Writer comes very near to the Character of a Buffoon." Though Fielding is writing against those who claim the "utmost Scope and End of Reading is Amusement" (presumably an irresponsible group), it is difficult to reconcile these remarks with his own novels, and his own best humorous writing in them with his rejection of Aristophanes and Rabelais. These men, he says, aim to "ridicule all Sobriety, Modesty, Decency, Virtue, and Religion, out of the world."[15] Surely it would be unpleasant to think of Fielding as he did of Thwackum and Square!

Though Dryden wrote at an earlier period, he may be mentioned here in conclusion as one of the more reasonable critics holding to a view of pleasure as a rhetorical instrument. As usual, he has little to offer in the line of theory, and even in that little he is inconsistent; but his practical judgments show his characteristic common sense and shrewdness. Aden's dictionary of his critical opinions lists several columns of entries on the purpose of poetry and literature. A few of them speak of pleasure as its sole purpose, but the vast majority derive from the Horatian formula, pleasure usually being some kind of medium of instruction.

For instance, in his "Defense of an Essay of Dramatic Poesy" we read: "for delight is the chief, if not the only, end of poesy: instruction can be admitted but in the second place, for poesy instructs as it delights." Then in "Heads of an

15. Henry Fielding, *The Covent Garden Journal,* ed. G. E. Jensen (New Haven: Yale University Press, 1915), I, 193-194.

Answer to Rymer," with the Horatian formula in mind he says: "And these two ends may be thus distinguished. The chief end of the poet is to please; for his immediate reputation depends on it. The great end of the poem is to instruct, which is performed by making pleasure the vehicle of that instruction; for poesy is an art, and all arts are made to profit." In "A Parallel of Poetry and Painting" he makes the same distinction, and adds: "the means of this pleasure is by deceit; one imposes on the sight [painting], and the other on the understanding." And in his "Discourse on Satire" he voices the familiar idea of pleasure as a bait: "without the means of pleasure, the instruction is but a bare and dry philosophy: a crude preparation of morals, which we may have from Aristotle and Epictetus, with more profit than from any poet."[16]

Yet we find a more broadly conceived view of how the two ends in the formula should relate in "A Parallel of Poetry and Painting": "As truth is the end of all our speculations, so the discovery of it is the pleasure of them; and since a true knowledge of Nature gives us pleasure, a lively imitation of it . . . must of necessity produce a much greater: for both these arts . . . are not only true imitations of Nature, but of the best Nature, of that which is wrought up to a nobler pitch." This sense of verisimilitude as the basis of satisfaction in art is truly Classical in spirit, reminiscent of what we readily associate with Johnson. For Dryden it should also be the basis of moral interest. "Moral [here, human] truth is the mistress of the poet as much as of the philosopher"; and hence poetry "must *be* ethical." The epic shows "nature beautified, as in a picture of a fair woman." This beautifica-

16. John Dryden, *Essays of John Dryden,* ed. W. P. Ker (Oxford: Clarendon, 1926), I, 113; II, 112, 128; *The Critical Opinions of John Dryden,* ed. John M. Aden (Nashville: Vanderbilt University Press, 1963), pp. 80-82, 250.

tion is the basis of true admiration, whereas burlesque "shows her deformed . . . at which we cannot forbear to laugh, because it is a deviation from Nature."[17]

He even rejects poetry that is too didactic, and therefore, to this extent, not poetry. He says of Lucretius: "there is no doubt to be made, but that he could have been everywhere as poetical, as he is in his descriptions, and in the moral part of his philosophy, if he had not aimed more to instruct, in his System of Nature, than to delight. But he was bent upon making Memmius a materialist, and teaching him to defy an invisible power: in short he was so much an atheist, that he forgot sometimes to be a poet." Yet one wonders whether doctrinal error rather than a lack of verisimilitude was his real motive for this judgment. For a few pages later, presumably asserting that the purpose of poetry is to express morally ideal truth when he says that "barefacèd bawdry is the poorest pretense to wit imaginable," he still has no trouble defending his own translation of objectionable materials from Lucretius on the grounds that he is only the translator of what is already set together in this fashion, and secondly, that the absence of gross words and filthy metaphors tends to palliate the meaning. "He has carried the poetical part no further, than the philosophical exacted."[18] This separation of poetry and idea does not seem strange to him, nor does his inconsistency in calling any unbecoming part unpoetical, after claiming that Lucretius' errors have stripped it of its poetical quality. But the see-saw tips the other way when we read of the nobler pleasure of comedy: "the business of the poet is to make you laugh: when he writes humour, he makes folly ridiculous; when wit, he moves you, if not always to laughter, yet to a pleasure that is more

17. Dryden, *Essays*, II, 137–138; I, 121, 18.
18. *Ibid.*, I, 260, 263.

noble." Then back again, for comedy's laughter "teaches us to amend what is ridiculous in our manners."[19]

Yet one learns to appreciate Dryden's common sense and to understand him with a certain ambiguity. In his "Prologue to *The Assignation*" he wryly laments that, whereas it pertains to the office of a priest to correct his audience and the audience usually accepts the rebuke, the poet, a priest in his own way, is only vilified for doing the same. He also shows no illusion about the efficacy of poetry or the drama to reform morals:

> For, when a Fop's presented on the Stage,
> Straight all the Coxcombs in the Town ingage:
> For his deliverance, and revenge they joyn:
> And grunt, like Hogs, about their Captive Swine.

And in the "Prologue to Love Triumphant":

> The Fable has a Moral too, if sought:
> But let that go; for upon second Thought,
> He fears but few come hither to be Taught.[20]

RHETORIC OF THE EMOTIONS

Henry Home, Lord Kames, is transitional between the critics just reviewed, who favored a rationalistically conceived rhetorical function of poetry, and those to follow, who tended to think of this function largely in terms of the emotions. Although Dennis and Fielding show tendencies in this latter

19. Quoted from Dryden's "Preface to *An Evening's Love*," in Frank H. Moore, *The Nobler Pleasure: Dryden's Comedy in Theory and Practice* (Chapel Hill: University of North Carolina Press, 1963), pp. 94-97.

20. John Dryden, *The Prologues and Epilogues of John Dryden*, ed. William B. Gardner (New York: Columbia University Press, 1951), pp. 50, 175.

direction, their methodology tends to be more rationalistic in character. Kames shares both methodologies and is also somewhat unusual in his interest in Associationism, which serves as a link between the two approaches.

In his effort to evolve a psychology of criticism that would blend the best elements of both approaches, Kames comes up with an oversimple and facile picture of the world and of man's place in it. He postulates a new "sense" at almost every turn, thus giving man an enviably ready control of his affairs. The clarity of sight and hearing recommends these senses as especially important for the arts; the others are not of consequence to them. "Ideas in a train," his phrase for the association of ideas, put these sense data to use.[21] Then Kames postulates as self-evident in our experience several inner "senses." The divine sense or "sense of deity" gives universal and certain assent to God's existence without need of reasoning. Good morals are braced by this sense, but they derive more directly from another special sense, the "moral sense," which distinguishes good from bad. Finally there is "a sense of taste" with which to recognize the ugly and the beautiful, and hence of importance in dealing with the arts. The "moral sense" is not to be confused with the "sense of taste," though they work in close cooperation. All these senses are clear to our consciousness and in their operations, but they need development in each individual.[22]

Kames approaches the function of literature from this psychological system. "No occupation attaches a man more to his duty, than that of cultivating a taste in the fine arts: a just relish of what is beautiful, proper, elegant, and ornamental, in writing or painting, in architecture or gardening, is a fine preparation for the same just relish of these qualities

21. Henry Home, Lord Kames, *The Elements of Criticism,* 6th ed. (Edinburgh, 1785), I, 6, 17.

22. Lord Kames, *Sketches of the History of Man,* 2nd ed. (Edinburgh, 1778), IV, 199-201; I, 196; IV, 9 ff.

in character and behaviour. To the man who has acquired a taste so acute and accomplished, every action wrong or improper must be highly disgustful." If passion should overcome him, he is more easily won back. Kames reasserts this confidence in the power of literature to help educate the young and to foster morals in his *Loose Hints upon Education* and in his somewhat naive enthusiasm for the power of the *Songs of Ossian* to purify manners, refine love, and inspire armies to valor! "Tho' that poem is of great antiquity it is replete with good lessons and judicious reflections."[23]

Hugh Blair also stresses the power of poetry's emotional appeal in the service of virtue, but more moderately. "I will not go so far as to say that the improvement of taste and of virtue is the same; or that they may always be expected to co-exist in an equal degree. More powerful correctives than taste can apply, are necessary for reforming the corrupt propensities which too frequently prevail among mankind." His reasoning is interesting in one given to stressing the emotional values of poetry. "Eloquent speculations are sometimes found to float on the surface of the mind, while bad passions possess the interior regions of the heart. At the same time this cannot but be admitted, that the exercise of taste is, in its native tendency, moral and purifying. From reading the most admired productions of genius, whether in poetry or prose, almost everyone rises with some good impressions left on his mind: and though these may not always be durable, they are at least to be ranked among the means of disposing the heart to virtue." These remarks close with the claim that eminence in the "sublime" parts of eloquence cannot be attained "without virtuous affections in a strong degree."[24] To relish this sublimity in the reading of poetry

23. Kames, *Elements of Criticism*, I, 11; *Sketches*, I, 470.
24. Hugh Blair, *Lectures on Rhetoric and Belles Lettres*, 7th ed. (London, 1798), I, 15-16.

makes the same demands of an audience. This old rhetorical association of virtue and appreciation reminiscent of the notion of *bonus vir poeta* (*et orator*) indicates Blair's ultimate context and reflects the popularity of "Longinus" in the contemporary shift from the premise of form to the premise of feeling.

In his treatise "Concerning Moral Good and Evil" Francis Hutcheson argues in a similar manner. Though he is a bit more detailed and analytic, he is less perceptive. "We shall find this [moral] *Sense* to be the Foundation also of the chief Pleasures of POETRY. We hinted, in the former Treatise, at the Foundation of Delight in the *Numbers, Measures, Metaphors, Similitudes.* But as the Contemplation of *moral Objects,* either of *Vice* or *Virtue,* affects us more strongly, and moves our Passions in a quite different and a more powerful manner, than *natural Beauty,* or (what we commonly call) *Deformity,* so the most moving Beautys bear a Relation to our *Moral Sense,* and affect us more vehemently, than the Representations of *natural Objects* in the liveliest descriptions."[25] Reflecting the new interest in psychology and the greater dignity of its material for poetic discourse, this passage associates morals and aesthetics through poetry's rhetorical appeal to human emotions.

Young's *Conjectures* shares this same conception. Literature "opens a back-door out of the bustle of this busy, and idle world, into the delicious garden of moral and intellectual fruits and flowers; the key of which is denied to the rest of mankind." Literature makes us self-reliant in our pleasures, especially "if the country is our choice, or fate, there it rescues us from *sloth* and *sensuality.*"[26]

Finally, two variations on the theme show some common

25. Francis Hutcheson, *An Inquiry into the Original of our Ideas of Beauty and Virtue: in Two Treatises,* 4th ed. (London, 1738), pp. 262-265.
26. Edward Young, *Conjectures on Original Composition,* ed. Edith J. Morley (Manchester: Manchester University Press, 1918), pp. 4-5.

sense in dealing with the matter. William Temple, who lived considerably earlier than most of this group, sees the power of emotion to convince one to live a moral life, but he is not too enthusiastic about the human potential for success. "When all is said, human life is, at the greatest and the best, but like a froward child, that must be played with and humoured a little to keep it quiet till it fall asleep, and then the care is over." Goldsmith, while opposing rationalism and espousing an emotional appeal to moral living, has enough humor to see that much of the claim of emotive didacticism may well be cant. Unlike the vice-purveying French writings, English "publications, in general, aim either at mending the heart, or improving the commonweal. The dullest writer talks of virtue, and liberty, and benevolence, with esteem; tells his true story, filled with good and wholesome advice; warns against slavery, bribery, or the bite of a mad dog; and dresses up his little useful magazine of knowledge and entertainment at least with a good intention."[27]

PLEASURE AS A VALUE

Toward the end of the century we find a growing if frequently inadequate appreciation both of the value of pleasure as an autonomous end of poetry and occasionally even of the Aristotelian understanding of mimesis, though more often it is linked with growing stress on taste and the emotional value of poetry. Richard Hurd, for example, complained that "the unnatural separation of the DULCE ET UTILE hath done almost as much hurt in *Letters* as that of the HONESTUM ET UTILE, which Tully somewhere complains of, hath done in *morals*." In his essay "On the Idea of Universal Poetry" he says that pleasure of the mind is the purpose of

27. Sir William Temple, *The Works of Sir William Temple, Bart.* (London, 1814), III, 443; Oliver Goldsmith, *The Works of Oliver Goldsmith,* ed. J. W. M. Gibbs (Covent Garden, 1884-1886), III, 285.

poetry. Quoting Francis Bacon, he agrees that while reason buckles the mind to the nature of things, poetry "SUBMITS THE SHEWS OF THINGS TO THE DESIRES OF THE MIND." But in saying this he misses with Bacon the organic nature of mimesis. The remainder of his essay tends to reinforce this impression by showing that the pleasure of poetry resides in rhythm, metaphor, and other superficial elements, superficial at least as far as the substance of poetry is concerned. History may please, he says; but if it does, this is pure gain. But if poetry please not, all is lost; for this is its very nature. Finally, instruction and precept, though not required, may be included. This seems like the familiar patchwork of unorganically related ends.[28]

Here and elsewhere Hurd shows more good will than theoretical understanding. The following passage, for example, is puzzling. "Though the poets . . . frequently *instruct us* by a true and faithful representation of things; yet even this instructive air is only assumed for the sake of *pleasing,* which, as the human mind is constituted, they could not so well do, if they did not instruct at all, that is, if *truth* were wholly neglected by them."[29] This is a curious statement. Though his thought seems to lead to the opposite conclusion from that of the didactic critics, the patchwork of ends unorganically conceived within the Horatian tradition is evident.

Beattie is more satisfying when he comes to deal with the purpose of poetry in his *Essays: On Poetry and Music.* He claims unequivocally that poetry in every period of its progress was primarily meant for pleasure. But when he explains his meaning his focus seems to slip toward the pragmatic and rhetorical interpretation. He says, for example, that when a poet chooses materials that would be useful "in giving them

28. Richard Hurd, *The Works of Richard Hurd, D. D., Lord Bishop of Worcester* (London, 1811), I, 267; II, 2-3, 15-16.
29. *Ibid.,* II, 16.

form (and it is the *form* chiefly that distinguishes poetry from other writings) [he] has always made the entertainment of mankind its principal concern." "Form" here has largely stylistic reference. Beattie adds that nothing but this form can account for men's serious application to the difficult arts of painting, poetry, and music.

Yet he returns to a more organic concept of the place of pleasure in reading poetry when he says that instruction can better be obtained elsewhere. Philosophers and historians please, the better to instruct; but poets instruct, the better to please—a claim rare in that time. The real pleasure of poetry is such that it holds the interest of intelligent and rational creatures. Poetry that appeals to the light and giddy, or to the profligate, corrupts the heart; but poetry that appeals to *"general taste"* cannot be immoral or insignificant. "The necessity of this arises from a circumstance in human nature ... namely that the human mind, unless when debased by passion and prejudice, never fails to take the side of truth and virtue." "To favour virtue, and speak truth, and take pleasure in those who do so, is natural to man; to act otherwise, requires an effort, does violence to nature, and always implies some evil purpose in the agent." Though perhaps somewhat optimistic, this line of thought tries to relate poetry to its true roots in intellectual human nature.[30]

In *Dissertations Moral and Critical* he returns to the problem, but in a context more directly ethical than aesthetic. "Every composition ought to have a moral tendency, or at least be innocent. That mind is perverted, which can either produce an immoral book, or be pleased with one." This is a commonplace of eighteenth-century critical judgment, which today can be more readily understood in terms of how the truth of literature differs from the truth of science and philosophy. Beattie seems to be aware of the inadequacies

30. James Beattie, *Essays: On Poetry and Music*, 3rd cor. ed. (London, 1779), pp. 8-9.

of this judgment when he observes that it is unfortunate when the hero of a novel or play is captivating in his vice. He admits the aesthetic appeal involved, yet he cautions that a good artist should keep his presentation under control "without any perversion of our faculties, or any confusion of right or wrong, [so as] to make the same person the object of very different emotions of pity and hatred, of admiration and horror." This view goes well beyond the typical plea for poetic justice. He sums up his position thus: "Let this, therefore, be established as a truth of criticism, that the end of poetry is TO PLEASE. Verses, if pleasing, may be poetical, though they convey little or no instruction; but verses whose sole merit is, that they convey instruction, are not poetical. Instruction, however, especially in poems of length, is necessary to their *perfection,* because they would not be perfectly agreeable without it."[31]

In no critic of the time apart from Johnson is the vitality of the Classical tradition so articulate as in Sir Joshua Reynolds. His *Discourses* on art delivered to the Royal Academy reveal his large concept of imitation and its human finality. He had the advantage of not having to deal with the minutiae of literary style and with rhetoric, and hence he was free to stress the philosophic premises at the heart of mimesis. What attention he gave to artistic techniques was quite adequate and pointed. Yet these techniques were specifically artistic and could hardly lead him into moralistic or rhetorical considerations. At a time when scientism and mechanical views of nature filtered into the writers of manuals of poetry and rhetoric, the *Discourses* come back again and again to consider the object-orientation of Classical mimesis and the need of great art in this tradition to feed upon the real.

The lectures regularly express a balanced view of the function of art, and a few sentences will suffice to indicate his

31. Beattie, *Dissertations Moral and Critical* (London, 1783), pp. 184-185.

mind in the matter: "The value and rank of every art is in proportion to the mental labour employed in it, or the mental pleasure produced by it." "The great end of the Art [painting] is to strike the imagination . . . the spectator is only to feel the result in his bosom."[32] In the ninth Discourse he treats the familiar problem of the relationship of art and virtue, basing his view that each helps the other upon the broad premise of general nature as the proper food of the mind. The pleasures of the mind broaden the human personality. In this respect he reminds us of Johnson. But he shows, nevertheless, something of the limits of the Classical psychology he inherited: "Whatever abstracts the thoughts from sensual gratifications, whatever teaches us to look for happiness within ourselves, must advance in some measure the dignity of our nature." "Our art, like all arts which address the imagination, is applied to somewhat a lower faculty of the mind, which approaches nearer to sensuality; but through sense and fancy it must make its way to reason; for such is the progress of thought, that we perceive by sense, we combine by fancy, and distinguish by reason." Yet in all this the artist is helpful to society in various ways, especially in raising the standards of taste.[33] Reynolds' meaning is usually much broader than that of his contemporaries, who may share his words but not his accent; he speaks from the deep and stable premises of the Classical tradition.

Again there is Twining, that careful student of the *Poetics*. When discussing the function of poetry, he leaves no doubt of his position or of its identity with that of Aristotle. "For that this [pleasure], in Aristotle's view, was the great end of the art, and of all its branches, appears, if I mistake not, evidently, from many other passages of this treatise, as well as from that now before us. Nor does he any where, appear to

32. Sir Joshua Reynolds, *The Discourses of Sir Joshua Reynolds*, ed. John Burnet (London, 1842), pp. 52-56 (Discourse IV).
33. *Ibid.*, pp. 165-166 (Discourse IX).

me to give any countenance to an idea, which rational criticism has, now, pretty well exploded—that *utility* and *instruction* are the end of Poetry. That it may indeed be rendered, in some degree, useful and improving, few will deny; none, that it *ought* to be made so, if it can. But that the *chief end* and *purpose* of Poetry is to *instruct*—that Homer wrote his *Iliad* on purpose to teach mankind the mischiefs of discord among chiefs, and his *Odyssey,* to prove to them the advantages of staying at home and taking care of their families—this is so manifestly absurd, that one is really astonished to see so many writers, one after the other, discoursing gravely in defence of it."[34] His use of Homer highlights well the difference between instruction and contemplation as the poem's goal.

CONCLUSION

This survey of the career of the Horatian formula in the eighteenth century confirms the findings of the earlier chapters of our study. This formula spoke of a clearly rhetorical view of poetry and conceived of the purposes of poetry in a pragmatic and nonorganic fashion, revealing a moralistic rather than a contemplative understanding of the mimetic tradition. It is understandable that the critical tradition that consolidated this view had lost its vitality. It was gradually being replaced by a critical approach that was quite differently oriented. Although the subjectivity noted toward the end of this chapter was a boon and entirely to be expected, it suffered in being estranged from the deeper and still viable premises of the mimetic tradition. The last voice of this tradition was sane, firm, and, as we have since been able to judge, transcendent. It was the voice of Samuel Johnson.

34. Thomas Twining, *Aristotle's "Treatise on Poetry"* (London, 1789), p. 561.

7

FORM AS PROCESS:
SAMUEL JOHNSON

In such a study as this it may seem strange at first sight
to have mentioned the opinions of Dr. Johnson only in
passing. Surely he was the greatest of the eighteenth-century
critics; in fact, no other was in a class with him. This is the
obvious reason for discussing him apart from the rest, and
for separating his copious texts from the more general context
of even the best of the other critics. The methods and per-
ceptions of his great and restless mind differ too radically
from the rest; his premises are always larger, his grasp more
alive and incisive.

For one thing, he is generally opposed to merely theoretical
inquiries, yet every serious problem he addresses awakens
penetrating judgments of broader inference than the particular situation would normally warrant. Again, though he
does not confuse literature with other human endeavors, it
is always a part of the larger human scheme of things. He
is unique in his sense of the dynamic importance of experience, yet he is rational to the core. Conversely, though
planted firmly in the rational Classical tradition, he is always
prepared to shift his premises of judgment, not from weari-
ness or the need to compromise, but the better to encompass
the ever-widening vistas of truth which new and varied experience opens to his eager mind. Though never static, he is
not addicted to change for its own sake. For him originality
is not at odds with tradition but its natural outgrowth.

While other critics shared these qualities singly with him,

none had them all together and in dynamic fusion. He was unique in his constant awareness of literature and life not merely as fact but as process. Modern philosophers of existence have made this word commonplace among us, but the phenomenon was unique in the days of Cartesian static clarity. As Bate has well observed, "The force of Johnson's example is not that he abstractly describes the obvious process of experience as it applies to art, but that he is unable to forget it in his actual practice."[1] Fact, history, and induction from rich experience are the sources of his deeper judgments about general nature. He could appreciate the harvest of the new empirical method without losing the older sense of the universal and of the human values involved at all levels of experience. His critical performance, like Coleridge's a half a century later, proved that the Classical and the Modern sensibilities and discoveries in art and theory were not inimical but mutually enriching. "Process," perhaps, best suggests the multiple and dynamic approach he assumed toward literature and its criticism, which let form in all three phases spoken of in this study shine forth as a basis for a reasonable understanding of mimesis and its function of pleasurable contemplation.

LITERATURE AND GENERAL NATURE

Johnson's use of the phrase "general nature" has long been familiar. It and the methodology through which it is derived are the best key to his noetic, the broad basis of his critical judgments. W. R. Keast deals well with the paradox involved in his critical performance. Though he wished to discredit the unwarrantably "scientific" method of earlier prescriptive critics, Johnson himself was intent upon reducing to "science" those areas of literature which were considered the do-

1. W. J. Bate, *The Achievement of Samuel Johnson* (New York: Oxford University Press, 1955), p. 182.

main of caprice and the irrational. This, of course, was not inconsistent, when one recalls his unwillingness to depend upon simply achieved a-priori generalizations about the infinitely complex realm of the poet's mind and the human concerns he commented upon; yet it was his firm conviction that human life, for all its mystery and unpredictability, was at root reasonable and had an available universal meaning. Keast's treatment of his methodology is helpful in understanding this consistency. For Johnson, he says, quoting from the "Preface to Shakespeare," " 'Demonstration,' the work of the scientist . . . 'immediately displays its power, and has nothing to hope or fear from the flux of years.' Science, he tells us elsewhere, pursues truth simply; and since scientific statements bear a fixed and necessary relation to nature, their force is immediately evident to the rational mind. But 'works tentative and experimental,' he continues, 'must be estimated by their proportion to the general and collective ability of man, as it is discovered in a long succession of endeavours.' " One can readily see the perfection of the Pythagorean scale of numbers, but the richness of Homer's poems begins to dawn upon us only when we see so much of subsequent literature as variations of his achievement in transposing his incidents, new naming of his characters, and paraphrasing of his sentiments.[2]

Here we find Johnson clearly aware of the difference between necessity in material things and the probability that marks the human and the human involvement with things. Though both are ultimately reasonable, this analogy must be reached with clear respect for the differences. The univocal quality of so much thinking of his time is shown to be inadequate for dealing with human concerns. As we shall presently see, his empirical sense was even sharper than Aris-

2. W. R. Keast, "The Theoretical Foundations of Johnson's Criticism," in *Critics and Criticism, Ancient and Modern,* ed. R. S. Crane (Chicago: University of Chicago Press, 1952), pp. 396-398.

totle's, and hence his universal, which he called "general nature," was conceived of with greater complexity. From the new empiricism he absorbed a greater sense of the variety of human experience and he had as a result a greater sense of its unpredictability. But his firm Classical sense of the transcendence of the true universal removed him from the company of Locke and the later empiricists. The higher and lower reason, which Pieper speaks of as a Classical and Medieval heritage, was his own, but with an even more enriched sense of the complication, mystery, and ambiguity of human affairs. The mind must be supple enough to cope with "the real state of sublunary nature, which partakes of good and evil, joy and sorrow, mingled with endless variety of proportion and innumerable modes of combination; and expressing the course of the world, in which the loss of one is the gain of another; in which, at the same time, the reveller is hasting to his wine, and the mourner burying his friend; in which the malignity of one is sometimes defeated by the frolick of another; and many mischiefs and many benefits are done and hindered without design."[3] He says this apropos of Shakespeare's mingling of tragedy and comedy, in the face of which the concept of genre must yield to the richer concept of the life it imitates. Hagstrum sums up Johnson's sense of life and of art as processes: "The poet ranges, observes, wanders, converses, learns, estimates, traces. The verbs all come from the tenth chapter of *Rasselas,* the portrait of the ideal poet. The process is an empirical one: as the poet perseveres, he enters into nature. He ultimately will 'rise to general and transcendental truths, which will always be the same . . .' But he must rise to them; they will not descend to him. It is in this way—and in this way alone—that art can

3. Samuel Johnson, "Preface to Shakespeare," in *Johnson on Shakespeare,* ed. Walter Raleigh (London: Oxford University Press, 1925), pp. 15-16.

attain moral validity."[4] Thus Johnson, treading a perilous balance between a Lockean and a Neoplatonic approach to nature, achieves a noetic most hospitable to Aristotle's concept of imitation.

How rich his view of form in human nature was, both in the three phases of imitation and in the mind of its audience, can be seen from a variety of comments on poetry and other forms of literature. Often an oblique observation is more revealing than his normally masterful, direct treatment; but

---

4. Jean H. Hagstrum, *Samuel Johnson's Literary Criticism* (Minneapolis: University of Minnesota Press, 1952), p. 75. On pp. 15 ff. and earlier in "The Nature of Dr. Johnson's Rationalism," in *ELH*, 17 (1950), 191-205, Hagstrum, and more recently Robert Voitle in his *Samuel Johnson the Moralist* (Cambridge: Harvard University Press, 1961), both rightly stress the influence of Locke on Johnson's notions of reason and of the mind. We should be careful, however, in making Johnson simply an empiricist. We should distinguish, I think, between Johnson's empiricism, a strong homing instinct for the concrete, and Locke's empiricism, which viewed the universal idea as a composite sensation and mistrusted metaphysical causality. Although both these kinds of empiricism affect epistemology, Johnson's does so mainly in a psychological manner, while Locke's denies the ontological validity of any knowledge that would transcend the data of experience. Both Voitle and Hagstrum are mainly interested in the psychology of Johnson's thought when speaking of his empiricism. Yet Voitle goes beyond Hagstrum, and rightly, I think, in making Johnson much more an old-fashioned man of reason when there is question of his moral values and judgments. The distinction I have offered is an important one both for epistemology in general and for the claims made in this study: that mimesis demands a mind in poet and audience that is open to the metempirical, which hence rejects empiricism in the Lockean sense. Randall, it will be recalled, denies that Aristotle is an empiricist in this Lockean sense—in *Aristotle* (New York: Columbia University Press, 1960), pp. 95-97, 299. In fact, any description of Johnson's notion of the human mind has to imply a strong influence of the Aristotelian notion of *nous*. In a sense similar to Johnson Aquinas and all the Scholastic realists were empiricists—*nihil est in intellectu quod non prius fuerit in sensu*. Hagstrum, however, seems to underestimate Coleridge's empirical thrust in this same non-Lockean sense. Coleridge's "On Poesy or Art" reveals an important corrective, in its discussion of imitation, to the German idealism often taken too exclusively as the source of his theory of imagination.

behind most statements looms the rich point of return, a purposeful and very complicated sense of human life, which is always the ultimate court of appeal when the normal conceptions of art need revision.

Speaking with deep approval of Dryden's mind, he wrote: "There is scarcely any science or faculty that does not supply him with occasional images and lucky similitudes; every page discovers a mind very widely acquainted with both art and nature, and in full possession of great stores of intellectual wealth." This, he says, Dryden obtained "from accidental intelligence and various conversation; by a quick apprehension, a judicious selection and a happy memory, a keen appetite of knowledge and a powerful digestion; by vigilance that permitted nothing to pass without notice, and a habit of reflection that suffered nothing useful to be lost."[5] He is equally enthusiastic about Aristotle's inductive method, to understand the experience of politics before theorizing. "The same method must be pursued by him who hopes to become eminent in any other part of knowledge. The first task is to search books, the next to contemplate nature. He must first possess himself of the intellectual treasures which the diligence of former ages has accumulated, and then endeavour to increase them by his own collections."[6] But historical empiricism has its own limits, and direct experience offers a needed supplement. " 'Books,' says Bacon, 'can never teach the use of books.' The student must learn by commerce with mankind to reduce his speculations to practice, and accommodate his knowledge to the purposes of life."[7]

His famous discussion of Metaphysical poetry reveals his view of how the mind works. While he found such poetry

5. Samuel Johnson, "Dryden," in *Lives of the English Poets,* ed. George B. Hill (Oxford: Clarendon, 1905), I, 417.

6. Samuel Johnson, *Rambler* No. 154, in *The Works of Samuel Johnson* (Oxford, 1825), III, 230.

7. *Rambler* No. 137, in *Works,* III, 150.

a challenge to the reader's intellectual ingenuity, it did not trace "intellectual pleasure to its natural sources in the mind of man." These poets wrote as beholders rather than partakers of human nature, lacking feeling and a sense of the sublime, "for they never attempted that comprehension and expanse of thought which at once fills the whole mind, and of which the first effect is sudden astonishment, and the second rational admiration. Sublimity is produced by aggregation, and littleness by dispersion. Great thoughts are always general, and consist in positions not limited by exceptions, and in descriptions not descending to minuteness."[8] And in *Rasselas* Imlac advises: "The business of a poet is to examine, not the individual, but the species; to remark general properties and large appearances: he does not number the streaks of the tulip, or describe the different shades in the verdure of the forest." He must "divest himself of the prejudices of his age and country . . . he must disregard present laws and opinions, and rise to general and transcendental truths, which will always be the same."[9]

Johnson's empiricism and rational generality are not in conflict, but rather reveal the need of an active mind not so much for synthesizing as for perceiving unity. There is no question here of Lockean composite sensation or association of ideas. "Johnson's position, in short, avoids the usual monotonous quarrel over the issue of generality versus particularity in art. It avoids this debate by subsuming it within a larger framework. What is wanted is detail—the familiar, the concrete, the vivid, and sensory—for the sake of the form; and what is desired in the form is the ability to apply not only to the particular details that serve as the immediate vestibule or conductor to it, in a work of art, but also to others that are cousin to them."[10]

8. Johnson, "Cowley," in *Lives*, I, 20-21.
9. Johnson, *Rasselas* (ch. x), in *Works*, I, 222.
10. Bate, *Achievement of Samuel Johnson*, p. 199.

The ultimately humanistic orientation of all thought for Johnson, whether inside art or not, indicates the truly metempirical range and quality of his concept of general nature. In no other fashion can man's mind be "filled." "Nothing can please many, and please long, but the just representations of general nature," he wrote in the "Preface to Shakespeare." External nature is only a human context. "A blade of grass is always a blade of grass, whether in one country or another . . . Men and women are my subjects of enquiry; let us see how these differ from those we have left behind."[11] "He who thinks reasonably must think morally." "The truth is that the knowledge of external nature, and the sciences which that knowledge requires or includes, are not the great or frequent business of the human mind." Moral and religious knowledge (and in the context, "moral" is always "humanly important") have a universal and transcendent value, for "we are perpetually moralists, but we are geometricians only by chance. Our intercourse with intellectual nature is necessary; our speculations upon matter are voluntary and at leisure."[12]

These passages help form for us a notion of Johnson's noetic, whether he is thinking of poetry or of some other form of intellectual endeavor. The familiar passage from the "Preface to Shakespeare," that begins "Nothing can please many, and please long, but the just representations of general nature," shows effectively and at some length this noetic working directly in forming his view of poetry as mimesis.[13]

11. Hester L. Piozzi, *Anecdotes of the Late Samuel Johnson, LL.D.*, ed. S. C. Roberts (Cambridge: Cambridge University Press, 1925), p. 66.

12. Johnson, "Milton," in *Lives*, I, 99–100. Voitle's stress on Johnson's strong appeal to a more traditional "reason" where morality was at stake should be recalled here. See above, p. 273 and Voitle, *Samuel Johnson the Moralist*, ch. ii.

13. Johnson, "Preface to Shakespeare," in Raleigh, *Johnson on Shakespeare*, pp. 11–12.

This passage reveals Johnson's central position as a critic, and must always be the point of return in understanding his judgments, especially when they seem to lapse—and at times do—from a sane humanism to a more didactic view of literature. Practical concerns, related to certain psychological fears, at times seem to overcome his basic and broader convictions. But the limits which these occasioned, to be treated later in this chapter, should not be allowed to dwarf the essential Johnson.

Further, general nature in poetry verifies in a very vital way the Aristotelian probable outlined earlier in this study. The universality which Johnson demands in and through the concreteness of character and plot makes this clear. The unique whim or idiosyncrasy pleases neither many nor long. Nor does the static impress of the *type*. Rather, as in Shakespeare, the continued and creative flow of character and action is what achieves poetry and its universal meaning. Even in Shakespeare's poorer plays this life is to be found. "The meek sorrows and virtuous distress of *Catherine* have furnished some scenes which may be justly numbered among the greatest efforts of tragedy. But the genius of *Shakespeare* comes in and goes out with *Catherine*."[14] This last sentence is eloquent. But normally he looks for this life not in separate parts, for the parts live in the whole—surely an Aristotelian view. The value in contemplating the probable thus elaborated, the "practical axioms and domestick wisdom," the "system of civil and oeconomical prudence," is not that derived from pedestrian didacticism. Rather it is the vision of the whole, such as one finds in Shakespeare's plays, where "persons act and speak by the influence of those general passions and principles by which all minds are agitated, and the whole system of life is continued in motion." Characters and their actions thus constitute a "species" rather than an

14. *Ibid.,* p. 152.

"individual," and are clearly neither type nor abstractly philosophic class, no more than they are the whisp of a whim, but are clearly the Aristotelian probable and permanent humanity, worthy of satisfying contemplation. They lift aesthetic considerations far above any particular moral lesson. What moral learning there is must be distilled from the wine of creation, from which alone "a hermit may estimate the transactions of the world, and a confessor predict the progress of the passions."[15] "In this," says Hagstrum, "Johnson's central conception of the way in which art instructs, morality is neither a kind of didactic appendage, artificially attached to the work, nor any kind of direct homiletic appeal. Art is moral because it is the mirror of life, which in its variety and reality is always instructive; and because it is a representation of general nature, which is itself morally constituted into 'standing relations and general passions.' "[16] For "he who thinks reasonably must think morally." Bate's comprehensive treatment of Johnson's dynamic critical sense reveals this basic conviction of his mind at every turn, but especially when he turns to the problems of originality amid tradition, of convention, and of vitality, and to the explicit sense of human purpose as a norm of evaluating literature.[17]

FUNCTION

With general nature thus understood, we may turn to a more detailed view of Johnson's conception of the function of poetry. For all his rich stress on the cognitive value of literature, some have been surprised by his equally strong stress on pleasure as the unique factor for the audience which

15. *Ibid.*, pp. 12-14.
16. Hagstrum, *Johnson's Criticism*, p. 72.
17. Bate, *Achievement of Samuel Johnson*, ch. v *passim*.

differentiates poetic contemplation from other kinds. Here again he is deeply Aristotelian. The organic unity of the two remove him far from contemporary interpretations of the Horatian formula, as many of the passages still to be cited will show.

Another related problem suggests itself here. Some have noted that Johnson's norm for judging poetry was its success in affording pleasure to its audience. In the article already cited, Keast rightly points to this as a significant ingredient in Johnson's treatment of literature and life as processes rather than as statically defined entities. To the extent that Johnson's stress aims to defeat the attempts of lesser critics to set up false concepts of genres and their specific pleasures, it is reasonable enough. But Keast seems extreme in suggesting that literature had no specific character for Johnson and hence was considered as a relatively undefined part of the vital process. In one sense Wimsatt is justified in calling this kind of criticism affective to a fault. Nevertheless, from the passages dealt with in this chapter, it seems clear that Johnson was quite aware of how literary knowledge is uniquely determined by its structure, and hence aware, too, of the structural autonomy which, I have earlier claimed, saves criticism from being called affective. Stress on variety of the possibilities available in poetry does not deny the actuality of poetry's uniqueness.[18]

Broadly speaking, Johnson's appeal to the audience's response was due partly to impatience with overeasy prescriptive critics, partly to a keen sense of the dynamic human process involved in the experiencing of the arts, and hence of its variety, given the variety of human kind, and partly due, by way of compensation for this last reason, to his belief that men were fundamentally the same in their reac-

18. Keast, "Theoretical Foundations," pp. 395-397.

tions: their variety enriched rather than confounded his concept of human experience. Keast points to the psychological orientation of Johnson's notion of general nature:

> For Johnson, nature is not an ontological, but a psychological, concept: it is defined, that is, not in terms of properties independent of the mind but in terms of its capacity to produce certain responses in men. General nature is thus what all men everywhere recognize as like themselves, and particular nature is what men in general recognize as present only at certain times, under certain conditions, or among certain men. Both truth and variety [Johnson's ingredients for pleasurable contemplation of poetry] arise from the constant linkage between human passions and their effects: the regularity with which the same passions produce effects of the same kind permits recognition and hence truth; the infinite accidental modifications in the actual manner in which the passions do their uniform work afford novelty and variety.[19]

The statement would be more accurate had he said that the ontology of nature was psychologically conceived, because this psychology is anything but whimsical in its process and its properties are indeed quite independent of the mind. They are the given roots of the mind's activity and the source of the sameness involved in the truth and, paradoxically, in its variety as well. But Keast's point is well made, and suggests that Johnson was existentialist without ceasing to be essentialist in the habits of his mind, and personalist without losing his larger social perspective.

In looking to the audience, then, for a judgment of the value of literature, Johnson rested on quite substantial though dynamically mobile critical fundations. While he did not set up mob reaction as an automatic critical norm—"The greatest part of human kind have no other reason for their opinions than that they are in fashion"—universal appeal

19. *Ibid.*, pp. 399-400.

still carried with it strong recommendation: "the common voice of the multitude unrestricted by precept, and unprejudiced by authority . . . in questions that relate to the heart of man, is, in my opinion, more decisive than the learning of Lipsius."[20] This comment, of course, if taken outside the context that has been developed so far in this chapter, could suggest a naive and foolish anti-intellectualism. But the context insures his deeper concerns. Again, Akenside's *Odes* are too tedious to be read, Blackmore's *New Version of the Psalms* puts him in the large number of those who "have obtained only the praise of meaning well," and in general, "That book is good in vain which the reader throws away."[21] This universality of appeal becomes more genuine when it can be tested by time. "Boileau justly remarks, that the books which have stood the test of time . . . have a better claim to our regard than any modern can boast, because the long continuance of their reputation proves that they are adequate to our faculties, and agreeable to nature."[22] Finally, a similar view in the "Preface to Shakespeare" is familiar to all: "What mankind have long possessed they have often examined and compared; and if they persist to value the possession, it is because frequent comparisons have confirmed opinion in its favour."[23]

Like any substantial Classicist, Johnson saw a serious purpose in poetry and literature. Yet in holding such an opinion he has often unfairly been called moralistic. A few interesting observations of Johnson, usually overlooked by his more facile critics, should help us appreciate the deep balance of his central position in the matter. Although Blackmore's

20. Johnson, *Works*, V, 58; *Rambler* No. 52, II, 250; see also "Gray," in *Lives*, III, 441; "Addison," II, 136.
21. Johnson, "Blackmore," in *Lives*, II, 249; "Akenside," III, 420; "Dryden," I, 454.
22. Johnson, *Rambler* No. 92, in *Works*, II, 431-432.
23. *Ibid.*, V, 104.

essays serve humanity well, they are not to be confused with literature. They "can be commended only as they are written for the highest and noblest purpose, the promotion of religion."[24] This more urgent statement is very revealing: "The only end of writing is to enable the readers better to enjoy life, or better to endure it."[25] He considers artful trifles as poetry, though they are surely of no ethical moment: "Genius now and then produces a lucky trifle. We still read the *Dove* of Anacreon and *Sparrow* of Catullus, and a writer naturally pleases himself with a performance which owes nothing to the subject."[26] He once remarked to Garrick that Congreve's description of the temple in *The Mourning Bride* was the finest poetical passage he had ever read and that he recollected nothing in Shakespeare equal to it. "What I mean is, that you can show me no passage where there is simply a description of material objects, without any admixture of moral notions, which produces such an effect."[27] A variation of this reason will be used later when he rejects merely descriptive poetry as being very important. If Johnson's view of literature were moralistic, he would hardly have written that *Paradise Lost* "is one of the books which the reader admires and lays down, and forgets to take up again. No one ever wished it longer than it is. Its perusal is a duty rather than a pleasure. We read Milton for instruction, retire harassed and over-burdened, and look elsewhere for recreation; we desert our master, and seek for companions."[28] Though Johnson's melancholy is partially at work here, the statement is not that of a moralist. Finally, an interesting *obiter dictum* in Boswell confirms this tendency of his mind: "As there is

24. Johnson, "Blackmore," in *Lives*, II, 246.
25. Johnson, *Works*, VI, 66.
26. Johnson, "Waller," in *Lives*, I, 284.
27. James Boswell, *Boswell's Life of Johnson*, ed. George B. Hill and L. F. Powell (Oxford: Clarendon, 1934-1950), II, 86.
28. Johnson, "Milton," in *Lives*, I, 183-184.

no necessity for our having poetry at all, it being merely a luxury, an instrument of pleasure, it can have no value unless when exquisite in its kind."[29]

The finer Classical minds, it is interesting to note, valued specifically didactic poetry least of the genres, partly because of its rhetorical tendencies but especially because of its "particularity of moral" as opposed to the breadth of vision supplied in great poetry (again the autonomy implied in the concept of the probable). We find echoes of these claims everywhere in Johnson but particularly in the "Preface to Shakespeare": "The noblest beauties of art are those of which the effect is coextended with rational nature, or at least with the whole circle of polished life; what is less than this can be only pretty, the plaything of fashion, and the amusement of a day." "From poetry the reader justly expects, and from good poetry always obtains, the enlargement of his comprehension and elevation of his fancy."[30]

Didactic poetry resembles rhetoric more closely than any other kind of poetry, its main function being to teach and its secondary function to please. This tendency so to split the functions of the didactic emphasizes Johnson's identification of them in the case of poetry in general, for he sees the very nature of didactic poetry, with its stress on a pragmatic goal, as minimally poetic at best. Of Pope's *Essay on Man* he says: "The subject is perhaps not very proper for poetry."[31] His reason is made explicit in another context: "To reason in verse is allowed to be difficult; but Blackmore not only reasons in verse, but very often reasons poetically."[32] Because a didactic poem stresses philosophic or doctrinal content so heavily, it usually achieves its didactic goal at the expense of

29. Boswell, *Life of Johnson,* II, 351-352; but see Hagstrum, *Johnson's Criticism,* pp. 77, 189, n. 3.
30. Johnson, "Waller," in *Lives,* I, 292; "West," III, 333.
31. "Pope," *ibid.,* III, 242.
32. "Blackmore," *ibid.,* II, 254.

passion. Again, blank verse, generally disapproved of, for being diffusive, is especially inept in a didactic poem: "A poem frigidly didactick without rhyme is so near to prose that the reader only scorns it for pretending to be verse."[33] Finally Johnson distinguishes between the use of imagery in epic and in didactic poetry, with pejorative reference to the latter: "In didactick poetry, of which the great purpose is instruction, a simile may be praised which illustrates, though it does not ennoble; in heroicks that may be admitted which ennobles, though it does not illustrate."[34] The distinction between "illustrate" and "ennoble" is a technical one touching on the use of imagery in a rhetorical and in a poetic fashion.

Two refreshing and hearteningly human comments should be recalled here. "The world is full of fraud and corruption, rapine or malignity; interest is the ruling motive of mankind . . . in this state of things a book of morality is published, in which charity and benevolence are strongly enforced; and it is proved beyond opposition, that men are happy in proportion as they are virtuous, and rich as they are liberal. The book is applauded . . . Let us look again upon mankind: interest is still the ruling motive, and the world is yet full of fraud and corruption, malevolence and rapine."[35] Johnson then counsels patience and confidence in the slow but sure effectiveness of books. Again, of Gay's *Beggar's Opera*: "I do not believe that any man was made a rogue by being present at its representation . . . [And yet] there is in it such a *labefaction* of all principles, as may be injurious to morality." "The play, like many of others, was plainly written only to divert without any moral purpose,

33. "Roscommon," *ibid.*, I, 237.
34. "Pope," *ibid.*, III, 229.
35. Samuel Johnson, *The Idler and the Adventurer*, ed. W. J. Bate, John M. Bullitt and L. F. Powell (New Haven: Yale University Press, 1963), pp. 488-489 (*Adventurer* No. 137).

and is therefore not likely to do good; nor can it be conceived, without more speculation than life requires or admits, to be productive of much evil. Highwaymen and housebreakers seldom frequent the playhouse."[36]

In the familiar *Rambler* 4, Johnson writes at some length on the novel, the form then being developed by Richardson, Fielding, and Smollett. He is guided throughout by an unusual mixture of a sense of literary verisimilitude and what at first sight might seem an overly strong moral interest. His problem is not unlike the one faced by Plato: how protect an audience from literature which may endanger its moral life in its use? There is the same prudential concern for the audience, which in this case is largely composed of "the young, the ignorant, and the idle." But his sense of the value of literature and its verisimilitude makes his observations more complex and perceptive.

The novel form is valuable, unlike the ancient romance, because it depends on "that experience which can never be attained by solitary diligence, but must arise from the general converse and accurate observation of the living world." This is the "formal realism" which Ian Watt finds characteristic of the novel form then emerging. Johnson sees them, as many at this time did, as conduct books; hence their detailed imitation of life is valuable. When the adventurer of a novel "is levelled with the rest of the world, and acts in such scenes of the universal drama, as may be the lot of any other man; young spectators fix their eyes on him with closer attention, and hope, by observing his behaviour and success, to regulate their own practices, when they shall be engaged in the like part." With this fairly didactic emphasis he turns to a very perceptive psychological observation about the attractiveness of evil inside or outside literature. "There have been men, indeed, splendidly wicked, whose endowments

36. Boswell, *Life of Johnson*, II, 367; Johnson, "Gay," in *Lives*, II, 278.

threw a brightness on their crimes, and whom scarce any villany made perfectly detestable, because they never could be wholly divested of their excellencies; but such have been in all ages the great corrupters of the world, and their resemblance ought no more to be preserved, than the art of murdering without pain." The passage is worth study for its mixture of admiration and disgust with great evil, and it is reflected in the mixed motivation, moral and literary, of his final judgment. It reveals the moralist victorious over the man of literary interest because the human stakes are high. Yet a little later in the same essay, the complexity of the problem is revealed along with broader critical premises than might appear on the surface, and to which we have otherwise grown used. The mind is not to be made the pragmatic slave of puritan virtue in this conflict of art and morality. "It is therefore steadily to be inculcated, that virtue is the highest proof of understanding, and the only solid basis of greatness; and that vice is the natural consequence of narrow thoughts; that it begins in mistake, and ends in ignominy."[37]

When speaking of satire, Johnson again points to truth and probability as sources of human benefit from it. "All truth is valuable, and satirical criticism may be considered as useful when it rectifies error and improves judgment: he that refines the publick taste is a publick benefactor."[38] Yet he saw dangers in its use. "He did not however encourage general satire, and for the most part professed himself to feel directly contrary to Dr. Swift; 'who (says he) hates the world, though he loves John and Robert, and certain individuals.' "[39] He had the Classical dislike of the lampoon because it frequently exhausted its virulence upon imaginary

37. Johnson, *Rambler* No. 4, in *Works*, II, 16-20.
38. Johnson, "Pope," in *Lives*, III, 242.
39. Samuel Johnson, *Johnsonian Miscellanies*, ed. G. B. Hill (Oxford, 1897), I, 327.

crimes and was too singular in the object of its critic
thus tended to lack literary import.[40] He also disli
depressing effects which satire often produced. F
suggests a further reason for this dislike. "Possess
humble spirit, he knew only too well his own failing
felt that he himself was a fellow-sinner and fellow-su
and his heart conceived too strong a sympathy for oth
permit him to be long indignant at their follies or their v
ness. This sense of sharing in human struggle, which c
such scanty rewards of happiness, pervades the moral re
tions of the *Rambler* and the *Idler,* and lacks the animc
and the bitterness of the truest satire. Johnson's humai
preserved him from the vehement indignation of Juvenal.

The Classical tradition rated satire relatively low on t
scale of the genres, just above the didactic poem. Its limitt
subject matter, its pragmatic turn, its closeness to factu.
report, and hence its limited potential for poetic transform;
tion, all restricted its poetic value, and placed it close t
rhetoric. Its characteristically sharp tone tended also tc
estrange it from the more humane spirit behind the rest of
mimesis. These points should be related to Johnson's own
humaneness and his preoccupation with the concrete process
of life and its earnestness when we appraise his view of
satire's function. His moral concern is strong, but his critical
context is too complex to be didactic.

Johnson greatly approved of biography. Its realistic source
in actual life appealed to his appetite for the empirical. "The
minute details of daily life, where exterior appendages are
cast aside, and men excell each other only by prudence and
virtue," made this kind of writing "enchain the heart by
irresistible interest." Yet a valid universality lay hidden in

40. Johnson, *Rambler* No. 22, in *Works,* II, 109-113.
41. P. H. Houston, *Doctor Johnson: A Study in Eighteenth-Century Humanism* (Cambridge: Harvard University Press, 1923), p. 26.

this minute detail. "There is such an uniformity in the state of man, considered apart from adventitious and separable decorations and disguises, that there is scarce any possibility of good or ill, but is common to human kind."[42] Here again imaginative interest and practical moral concern blend to form his judgment of literature. If it is not quite as detached as one might wish, it is clearly more faithful to the autonomy of mimesis than most critical judgments of the time.

Johnson shared Aristotle's preference for tragedy over the epic, despite overwhelming contemporaneous opinion to the contrary.[43] He recognized the essentially dramatic nature of poetry and hence the primacy of drama in vital mimetic theory. Structural considerations dictated this preference, whereas those who preferred the epic were attracted by its ability to present an ideal hero for moral motivation. Johnson's intuitive appreciation of Shakespeare's greatness was largely responsible for his judgment. As we have already seen, his "Preface to Shakespeare" is a monumental statement of what is involved in mimesis, with drama as its metonym: a mirror held up to evolving life. His memorable destruction of the "unities," his defense of tragi-comedy, his rejection of the "stage deception theory," his demand for wholeness and structure in a play, and his ridicule of the "petty cavils of petty minds" derive from this massive view of mimesis and its function, and of drama as its most genuine achievement.

Even when practical moral concerns tend to tip the scales of Johnson's judgment in their favor, one is regularly aware of the solid critical base beneath. While perhaps impatient with the bawdiness of the Restoration stage, he also objected to what he considered the "unreality" of characters, plot, and language in the heroic plays.[44] Again, the "domestic drama"

42. Johnson, *Rambler* No. 60, in *Works*, II, 285-289.
43. *Ibid.*, I, 170; *Rambler* No. 156, III, 242; Johnson, "Milton," in *Lives*, I, 189.
44. *Ibid.*, I, 23-24; *Rambler* No. 125, III, 97-98.

of such as Rowe, though far from Shakespearean in depth, had real value. *Jane Shore,* "consisting chiefly of domestic scenes and private distress, lays hold upon the heart. The wife is forgiven because she repents, and the husband is honoured because he forgives. This therefore is one of those pieces which we still welcome on the stage."[45]

Finally, a word about Johnson's use of the Horation formula. Bate has treated the problem thoroughly and with point. In deriving the real sense of Johnson's altered version of the traditional phrase, he argues from the thoroughgoing context of the "Preface to Shakespeare" and avoids abstract quibbling. This, indeed, was Johnson's own method when he casually shifted the older wording of the formula to "instruct by pleasing." We should stress the context of the "Preface," and even the more extensive contexts just reviewed; for, unlike many of his contemporaries, Johnson neither hid behind the formula nor played with it like an isolated element of criticism or a catch-all for didactic theory. "We are dealing," says Bate, "with a conception of form that is altogether functional, and in a massive and reassuring sense of the word. In fact, it evolves from Johnson's conception of the function of literature itself, and is completely dependent on it. And the principle function of literature, as Johnson said, is to *'instruct by pleasing.'* The growth in awareness, the process of enlightenment, is not apart from the process of 'pleasing,' but rather by reason of it. So the generality that we want in literature—any meaning, order or point—is not apart from the details that appeal to both 'familiarity' and 'novelty,' but rather a deepening and clarification that proceeds by means of them."[46] Here the probable is operative; there is no question of rhetoric.

45. Johnson, "Rowe," in *Lives,* II, 69-70.

46. Bate, *Achievement of Samuel Johnson,* pp. 206-207. While I thoroughly agree with the explanation offered here, I do not believe the phrase "instruct by pleasing" is a very happy one. Of itself it may have an unsatisfactory rhetorical meaning.

LIMITS

Earlier in this Chapter we have seen Johnson veering now and then in the direction of a narrow moralism, despite his fundamental conviction, of which there can be no serious doubt, about the humane autonomy of poetry and the arts. Broadly speaking, this tendency issues from the excess of a good thing, from his conception of life and art as dynamic processes, and from a germane concern for the moral soundness of an audience involved in these processes. In the long run, though somewhat ambiguous, this tendency should be considered a critical defect; it does not, however, justify the popular image, even in some circles today, of Johnson as a narrow moralist. Yet for the sake of a full picture of his approach to the function of literature, we should look at his limits as well as at his pervasive vitality. These critical limits have two more specific sources, pale analogues of the dominant limits traced in Chapter 5. The one is his Classical bias for the universal, even though for him it was richly fed by the empirical. It accounts for his impatience with myth and with certain "unrealistic" elements usually associated with romance and wonder, and for his inability to cope with such conventions as pastoral and bawdy wit, which he thought of as limiting the imaginative potential for the audience of general nature. The second source was his personal psychological and religious bent, which tended to limit the scope of legitimate art. His anxieties robbed him at times of critical distance.[47] These two elements in varying mixture account for what moralism we find in him.

47. One need not adopt Miss Balderston's rather grim view of Johnson's emotional troubles to see this influence. His letters, book of prayers and devotions, and Rasselas all bear witness to his melancholy. See Katherine C. Balderston, "Johnson's Vile Melancholy," in The Age of Johnson (New Haven: Yale University Press, 1949), pp. 3-14. See also Jean H. Hagstrum, "On Dr. Johnson's Fear of Death," in ELH, 14 (1947), 308-319; and

Johnson frequently censured an author for representing immorality in a way that might seem to abet it. Dryden, Pope, Swift, Fielding, and even Shakespeare were all rebuked. "The greatest difficulty that occurs, in analysing his character," he writes of Swift, "is to discover by what depravity of intellect he took delight in revolving ideas from which almost every other mind shrinks with disgust. The ideas of pleasure, even when criminal, may solicit the imagination; but what has disease, deformity, and filth upon which the thoughts can be allured to dwell?"[48] Of the *Dunciad* he wrote: "The beauties of this poem are well known; its fault is the grossness of its images. Pope and Swift had an unnatural delight in ideas physically impure, such as every other tongue utters with unwillingness, and of which every ear shrinks from the mention."[49] Of Dryden: "His works afford too many examples of dissolute licentiousness and abject adulation . . . Such degradation of the dignity of genius, such abuse of superlative abilities, cannot be contemplated but with grief and indignation. What consolation can be had Dryden has afforded by living to repent, and to testify his repentance."[50] And, finally, Shakespeare: "His first defect is that to which may be imputed most of the evil in book or in men. He sacrifices virtue to convenience, and is so much more careful to please than to instruct, that he seems to write without any moral purpose." He continues with the well-known aphorism that he who thinks reasonably must think morally, rising to: "he makes no just distribution of good or evil, nor is always careful to show in the virtuous a disapprobation of the wicked; he carries his persons indifferently through right and wrong, and at the close dismisses

Maurice Quinlan, *Samuel Johnson: A Layman's Religion* (Madison: University of Wisconsin Press, 1964), pp. 126-140.

48. Johnson, "Swift," in *Lives*, III, 62.
49. "Pope," *ibid.*, III, 242.
50. "Dryden," *ibid.*, I, 398-399.

them without further care, and leaves their examples to operate by chance. This fault the barbarity of his age cannot extenuate; for it is always a writer's duty to make the world better, and justice is a virtue independent on time or place."[51] Of Falstaff he writes: "The moral to be drawn from this representation is, that no man is more dangerous than he that, with a will to corrupt, hath the power to please; and that neither wit nor honesty ought to think themselves safe with such a companion, when they see *Henry* seduced by *Falstaff*."[52] Finally, he delivers this broadside against immoral writers in *Rambler* 77: "What punishment can be adequate to the crime of him who retires to solitudes for the refinement of debauchery; who tortures his fancy, and ransacks his memory, only that he may leave the world less virtuous than he found it; that he may intercept the hopes of the rising generation? and spread snares for the soul with more dexterity?"[53] These passages and others like them make interesting reading. They show mature concern with the psychology of author and reader alike and ask shrewd questions that still trouble the minds of parents and educators. But they fail to cope subtly with the relationship of art and morality. Our literature must always be witness to a fallen race without being any the less successful because of its subject matter. Wit and verbal play, irony, humor, and fancy offer, on the contrary, a built-in redemptive answer of imaginative insight, one that is neither an escape nor an indulgence.

A word about poetic justice. We have just seen Johnson chide Shakespeare for lacking it, and in other passages we find similar impatience. But it is important to see that, though attracted to it as a pragmatic convention, he never

51. Johnson, "Preface to Shakespeare," in *Johnson on Shakespeare*, pp. 20-21.

52. *Ibid.*, p. 125.

53. Johnson, *Rambler* No. 77, in *Works*, II, 365.

lets it become a critical principle. On several occasions he actually opposes it as principle. "Dryden," says Bate, quoting
Johnson, " 'petulantly' denies that Milton's Adam can be a
hero 'because he was overcome; but there is no reason why
the hero should not be unfortunate *except established practice,* since success and virtue do not necessarily go together.' "
He further suggests that though Johnson's strong empathy at
times drew him to favor poetic justice, several plays observing
it left him cold. He sums the problem up in this way: "His
undeniable attraction to it is always being cited; and it does
show a rather pathetic tug toward wish-fulfillment. But it is
never permitted to serve as a primary critical principle by
which to accept or reject."[54]

Johnson also tended to be impatient with literary modes,
conventions, and techniques which at first sight seem "unreal." It is an excess of a good thing, of his intellectual realism
and sense of the probable growing out of experience. It readily joined hands with his fear of fancy and morbid imagination and his serious moral interest. In some cases his religious
sense of awe was also involved. Gray's *Bard,* for example,
forsakes the probable and so achieves less moral usefulness.[55]
He also thought that romances, which were factually improbable and hence read with wonder, were useless, because
in them virtue "is unattainable, is recommended in vain;
that good may be endeavoured, it must be shown to be
possible."[56] (An improbable impossibility!) Granted the
absurdity of many situations in the romances, something
deeper underlies the better of them which feeds our sense of
wonder and mystery. Johnson's rational turn of mind, his
cultural climate, and his unusual fear of life's uncertainties
all worked against his developing an appetite for the
mysterious.

54. Bate, *Achievement of Samuel Johnson,* pp. 201-202.
55. Johnson, "Gray," in *Lives,* III, 438.
56. "Waller," *ibid.,* I, 295.

His dislike of mythology is well known. Waller "borrows too many of his sentiments and illustrations from the old mythology, for which it is vain to plead the example of ancient poets: the deities which they introduced so frequently were considered as realities, so far as to be received by the imagination, whatever sober reason might even then determine. But of these images time has tarnished the splendor. A fiction, not only detected but despised, can never afford a solid basis to any position, though sometimes it may furnish a transient allusion, or slight illustration. No modern monarch can be much exalted by hearing that, as Hercules had had his *club,* he has his *navy."* His rejection of pagan mythology, and especially of its mixture with Christian imagery in *Lycidas,* will be recalled. What is not factually real cannot be material for imagery, and since imagery for him tended to be somewhat decorative, it was unfitting to mix the elements of true and false religion in the same poem. Myth and symbol enjoy a greater reputation today because their subjective function is more clearly understood both in life and in art.[57]

Mention of *Lycidas* reminds us of Johnson's dislike of pastoral: "easy, vulgar, and therefore disgusting." Lyttelton's *Progress of Love* is no better: "it is sufficient blame to say that it is pastoral."[58] The genre was patently unreal: it glorified country life (Johnson was for London); learned shepherds were out of date, and, when airing political and theological opinions, out of character; the language tended to be staid, the psychology escapist, and the imitation slavish. Such a genre had no moral value for it could not move the human passions nor touch the human heart. "A Pastoral of an hundred lines may be endured; but who will hear of sheep and goats, and myrtle bowers and purling rivulets,

---

57. "Waller," *ibid.,* I, 295; "Milton," I, 163-164.
58. "Lyttelton," *ibid.,* III, 456.

through five acts? Such scenes please barbarians in the dawn of literature, and children in the dawn of life; but will be for the most part thrown away as men grow wise, and nations grow learned."[59] While much of this merits a hearty "Amen!," the critical limit involved is clear.

The last limit to be mentioned involves Johnson's attitude toward religious poetry. Johnson was a deeply religious man, who looked to his faith for moral guidance. His sense of awe of the "Supreme Being" filled all corners of his consciousness. Further, it fed his temperamental anxieties, which were in turn both source and further issue of his turbulent imagination. Much as his moral earnestness was an effective climate for several critical judgments already seen, this rather overpowering religious attitude joined with certain contemporary critical limitations in his rejection of religious poetry. Poetry and imagery in particular are meant to adorn and enhance their subject matter. God and divine things greatly transcend our ability to perfect with praise. Besides, religion is an act to be performed with simplicity.[60] Had Johnson enjoyed a cultural and religious climate more open to the sacramental view of the universe, as did Dante, Donne, Hopkins, and Eliot; had his personal religious attitude held more familiarity and less anxiety; and had he thought of religious poetry—as he surely proportionately did of other kinds—as revealing human experience of the divine rather than idealizing it: his judgment would surely have been other than it was.

CONCLUSION

No matter what the limits of Johnson's criticism, one must always return to its massive achievements. These reveal a pervasive sense of life in being so sound and right about

59. "Gay," *ibid.*, II, 284-285.
60. "Waller," *ibid.*, I, 291-292.

literature. For him, the process of art in the last analysis always looked to the complicated process of life for its source as well as its purpose. If the final arbiter of a play or a poem was to be a living audience, this audience had to be spread out in time and place like the entire gamut of human life. Of necessity, then, his criticism will always have about it an untidy and yet very suggestive quality. In trying to measure its richness, one is tempted to tax it as Fergusson taxed *Hamlet* for being too alive in its imitation of life. For this reason this chapter has treated mimesis as form in process, in, for, and about life—perhaps the best account that can be given of it and its function—reflected in a critical methodology that is itself dynamic.

Johnson was most unusual in manifesting this thorough sense of life in mimesis. Almost alone among critics he saw that it had to thrive on life, while so many others let it die or left it for dead. Their schematic methodology or a vague methodology of feeling contrasted sharply with his vital sense of process. Had there been more like Johnson, the changeover in critical theory and practice at the end of the eighteenth century might have been more substantial. As the last great voice of Classicism, Johnson called very substantially to Coleridge, the only great new critical figure in England. We see today that they were often saying the same thing from different sides of a wall. Their views, surely, were richly continuous rather than inimical. Had Johnson's contemporaries been more alive, the wall need not have existed.

But beyond being a great transitional critic, Johnson also transcends history. He does this most vividly by asserting the perennially mimetic quality in all great art. Though Coleridge had the advantage of the new awareness of imagination and of the subjective element in art, he knew well, along with Johnson, that all art achieves its meaning, and hence its human appeal, by being open to human life in its source and purposes. More recent critical theory has rightly stressed the personal aspects of creativity, but never fruitfully when it wanted them to be private. It has seen more subtly and even more profoundly into the ways of art and its concerns, but it has never surpassed in quality Johnson's conviction that all art, and poetry in particular, is human to the core. Here is the appreciation of mimesis at its critical best.

How art and life are related was considered a relatively simple critical problem in Johnson's day. In our own it has branched in a score of directions. Psychology, sociology, propaganda, ethics, and theology have all become much more sophisticated, and critics have discovered ties between them and the arts, ties hardly dreamed of in Johnson's day. But the saner among them reflect his legacy. In this he and they have a poet's instinct for the humane center of the arts. Yeats, surely worlds and centuries apart from Johnson, once wrote that "man cannot know truth," because human life is too complicated. Yet he also said that, as artist, "man can embody truth." Nevertheless, the lords and ladies of Byzantium could never be satisfied in their heavenly city of art unless it fed upon mortal human life and sang "Of what is past, or passing, or to come." The language is the same, though the accent may differ, as that of the last restless voice of Classicism: "the pleasures of sudden wonder are soon exhausted, and the mind can only repose on the stability of truth."

EPILOGUE

This study has peered into one small corner of the large critical problem of how poetry relates to life. This, in turn, is but a small corner of the limitless problem which the Greeks first set themselves in taking on the task of understanding the universe. Of course, one no longer seriously tries to take on the universe in quite the confident way of Plato and Aristotle. But from Aristotle, at least, we have inherited a method that is encouraging for any intellectual task, in large or in small. This is the method of metonymous realism, a method that looks for the whole through a patient, teleological exploration of the parts experienced.

This is not the truism it may at first appear to be. When fruitful, this kind of realism is aware of a pervasive analogy at work in any situation in which limit implies inference: analogy between part and whole, subject and object, mutable and permanent. Most of all, it warns against the perennial temptation of the mind to level, to substitute one thing for another. Eliot once wisely said: "nothing in this world or the next is a substitute for anything else." His context was a discussion of the same problem as this study's, the function of poetry, specifically Arnold's prophecy that poetry would replace religion and philosophy.[1] We have encountered this pattern of substitution frequently in the critical opinions we have reviewed, deriving from either idealistic or rationalistic

1. T. S. Eliot, *The Use of Poetry and the Use of Criticism* (Cambridge: Harvard University Press, 1933), p. 113.

premises, and in both cases resulting in an univocal leveling. Poetry and its function will never yield to this treatment. If analogy has always been the way of the poet's mind, critics who wish to explain what the poets are about must always be patient friends of the ways of analogy.

Against this background we may sum up what we have found. Aristotle saw that the Greek poet was characteristically an imitator precisely in being a maker of plots. In his firm, if tantalizingly sketchy concept of the dramatic probable, he divined what was at the heart of mimesis and, by intense metonymy, at the heart of what was best in Greek culture. The native activity of the mind was to look and to see, and in seeing to be fulfilled. This autonomy was fundamental to all further meaningful activity of the person. In the case of poetry this goal of contemplation was most simply yet transcendently affirmed, for through τέχνη the mind put its seal upon things. The Classical heritage, which had its origin in this milieu, was able to vivify, to some degree at least, more than two thousand years of Western Culture. But by the eighteenth century this tradition was greatly attenuated. Its cultural climate could adequately support these ideals no longer, especially in the area of literary theory. Though the skeletal framework of its discussions was still that of the *Poetics*, its substance had largely been lost, and so one or another rhetorical form of moralism had thoroughly replaced pleasurable contemplation as the central function of poetry. To this extent at least—though other areas of human endeavor at the time reveal the same phenomenon—knowledge was no longer valued primarily for the vision of the truth it afforded, but more for the power it gave, important to man though this power was in ethics or morals. By an odd irony, neither the quest for the "really real" nor the belief that "whatever is, is right" proved to be realistic enough; and moral power issued, for the most part, in one or another form of voluntarism. And so at this point the fate of the function of mimesis emerges as a small but stubborn metonym of the state of Western cultural history.

It may be argued that this conclusion and the perspective in which it was drawn tend to exaggerate, and hence to falsify. If the cultural climate were as bleak as has been claimed, how are we to account for the admittedly distinguished literature of the time? As a part of the discursive effort of an age, critical theory will always more directly and openly reveal its philosophic premises than will literature and the arts. To a substantial extent the gifted imagination will usually transcend the discursive limitations of a given mind or of his age. Otherwise we would have little of Wordsworth's great poetry. Pope's *Essay on Man* is considerably more successful than the philosophy which he espouses in it, though the limits of his philosophy tend to limit the poetry in an oblique fashion. While in one sense Dryden's fideism and skepticism were fruitful sources of his poetry, in another they served to limit its potential. To say this one need not be involved in the Platonic fallacy of judging a poem by the philosophic truth of its statement. If mimesis truly feeds upon the richness of form in nature, this richness will be limited in a poem nourished in a less bountiful milieu. Distinguished as is the poetry of Dryden, Pope, and Swift, it has not the mimetic depths of Sophocles, Dante, and Shakespeare. Granted the variety of talent and a hundred other elements, one very important factor remains: the relative limits of their cultural milieu. Brilliant and rewarding as this poetry surely is, it is more sociological in focus. The more profound and mysterious genres of tragedy and epic are not in evidence at the time, despite critical nostalgia for them.

Bate recognizes this limit as one factor among many in the burden which the eighteenth-century poet felt in competing with his predecessors.

The ideal of "generality" brought back to the English mind their own past creative achievement—Shakespeare and Milton especially. Critics could tell them that Waller and Denham had brought to English poets the new, cherished values of "refinement"—cleanliness, smoothness, urbanity, and sophistication. But after admitting this, where was the "generality" (generality in the grander sense of the word—"the *grandeur* of generality," to use Johnson's phrase)? Dryden—however bland, self-controlled, self-confident, and, in the best sense of the word, negligent—had himself slightly chafed beneath this dichotomy. He swung back and forth. But always, in thinking of the rich English past, he was aware of "the giants before the flood" (we see this in the *Essay of Dramatic Poesy*: the dice there are secretly loaded on the side of his great English progenitors), and, in speaking of Shakespeare, he could say enviously that "All the images of nature were *still present* to him." . . . Pope could say that "Nature and Homer were the same"; he could himself translate Homer; and he could contemplate writing a blank-verse epic on a legendary British hero. Nevertheless this gifted poet—certainly one of the eight or ten greatest in the entire history of English letters—settled in practice for the more specialized (and newer) quality of "refinement"; this at least, for the English poet, remained as "one way left of excelling."[2]

Finally, of course, there is always the case of the genius who can subsist on a tradition, even though it is no longer in his contemporary culture the active force it had been, because of a rich interior resourcefulness. Among the artists at this time we think of Mozart, and a little later of Goethe; and among the critics, naturally, of Johnson.

And beyond all this there are always the "freshness deep down things," of which Hopkins speaks, the ability of the human spirit to renew itself, even on the brink of sterility. When a root is blocked in one direction, it gropes in another. This groping may be seen within the vague, seldom truly

2. W. J. Bate, "The English Poet and the Burden of the Past, 1660–1820," in *Aspects of the Eighteenth Century*, ed. Earl R. Wasserman (Baltimore: Johns Hopkins University Press, 1965), p. 251.

efficacious subjective stirrings among the critics, often intellectually unsatisfying because critically unearned. The inadequacy of their ideas of associationism, taste, and sense, pointing though they did to important psychological factors, derived from an univocal and monistic noetic of their own, centered on too exclusive a trust in human emotion. Pope's *Essay on Criticism* showed a generic poetical sense of the need to balance this new spirit with the claims of reason; and Johnson offered a more abiding sense of this need in his practice of criticism. But not until Coleridge was a broad theoretical basis attempted in England, an attempt which turned out to be a fusion of Platonic and Aristotelian metaphysical elements with the associationist and idealist traditions. And despite his struggles, he never quite emerged to a clear theoretical statement; what progress he did make was in good part the work of analogy, even to the point of paradox.[3]

In a very important sense the time was ripe for a recession of the mimetic cultural tradition and an advance of the ways of subjectivity. For more than twenty centuries Western Man had been exploring the many corners of his first great intuition: that things are intelligible inasmuch as they are real. This "given" quality in everything was there to meet the first demands of the questioning mind and to color all its activities. Now man's second great intuition was struggling toward articulation: that all knowledge, and poetry in particular, is also personally creative. Though subjectivity was never really absent from his significant considerations, a

---

3. Coleridge's effort at defining imagination by imitation in his "On Poesy or Art" is an apt example of this method. For a recent history of his struggle for a coherent theoretical statement on the nature of poetry and of his limited success see the illuminating study of Joseph Appleyard, s.j., *Coleridge's Philosophy of Literature* (Cambridge: Harvard University Press, 1965).

more explicit sense of its importance had been gathering special momentum since the Renaissance. From the late eighteenth century onward all the major fields of cultural endeavor would be characterized by a special awareness of this subjectivity. Despite the value of the Classical tradition, such a development was far from unfortunate. One can only regret the limitations and excesses in method that characterized much of the thought in the transitional decades, excesses that left it piecemeal rather than metonymous and alert to analogy. In much the same way one should welcome the scientific revolution of the previous centuries, while regretting the univocal and leveling process whereby it usurped the humane context of culture. The epistemology of poetic theory was probably among the greatest beneficiaries of this new subjective emphasis, and, in turn, its substantial benefactor.

It would be quite false, however, to suppose that it was simply time for a change to subjective cultural emphases, as if the more objective interests had lost their value and importance, especially in the case of poetic theory. It was not that critics had exhausted the possibilities of the tradition of mimesis. The situation, of course, was complicated. But without entering a long discussion of all the causes of Romanticism in England, it is safe to say that at the level of the epistemology of poetic theory, at least, new directions were attempted as much by way of reaction to scientism, skepticism, and near-despair of the mind as from any new or independent discovery. Coleridge's *Biographia* and "On Poesy or Art" are perhaps the best witnesses to this. One finds that some of his greatest gains are the result of strong defense and careful counterpunching. The poor appreciation of mimesis and its function at the end of the eighteenth century was clearly in great part the result of the noetic impact of the Enlightenment and its dehumanizing rationalism.

Perhaps it is a rule of cultural growth that at times of great crisis significant advances are made under threat of disaster, and that what is lost of one's heritage can be best appreciated only through hindsight and subsequent reincorporation. In the centuries prior to the great watershed between the eighteenth and nineteenth centuries, critical comment on mimesis was frequently thin, rhetorical, and moralistic, yet the mimetic literary tradition maintained its vitality. Something quite different happened, however, at the end of the period we have been studying. One must look to the strong impact of the Enlightenment noetic to explain much of it.

In line with Wellek's desire to go beyond mere historicism, these objective and subjective interests in our cultural history reflect the fundamental dynamic we should expect to find at work in the individual human mind, where subject and object are not at odds but in harmony, in analogy with each other for the person's growth, in Eliot's words, "Into another intensity." The intricate pattern of this process, whether in large or in small, is too complex for any ready exploration. Our interest at this point is to stress the importance of the mimetic principle in all poetry, of whatever tradition, which transcends its time of development in the Classical centuries we have been studying, in the same way all history distills a meaning greater and more enduring than the sum of its consecutive moments. This mimetic principle asserts the "given" quality which the Greek mind saw in all reality, hence its imitability; it maintains the stubborn autonomy of form in nature transformed into theme that is independent of private whim, structure that is fruitful in being self-sufficient, and pleasurable contemplation that needs no justification beyond itself. And yet there is always perfect harmony with a valid subjectivity. Without this sense of "the given," imagination has little scope in which to be creative. Goethe once remarked: "a subjective nature has soon talked out his little internal material, and is at last ruined by mannerism."[4] This "given" quality may be at the depths of the poet's psyche, as in most modern literature. No matter. When properly understood, the mimetic principle is operative in the poet who imitates insofar as he makes, and vice versa, as well as in the poet whom Maritain describes as the creative self, not the self-centered ego.[5] The ultimate tension in poetry, then, of subject and object is really the dynamic cooperation of the "creative" with the "given." All true artists show a sense of this mimetic principle in the unselfish regard with which they view even their own work. There is a world of difference between being personal and private.

An abiding sense of the importance of contemplation as the prime function of poetry is perhaps the strongest guarantee that the mimetic principle will not be forgotten, yet it must constantly face one or another of the several pragmatisms that attend us everywhere. It is ironic that the cultural tradition out of which mimesis emerged, with rare exceptions, did not offer adequate critical defense of this function. This was due in part, at least, to an overemphasis of the discursive function of the mimetic mind. But in practice, at least, the concerns of a liberal education, which in great part depends upon this function, were generously fostered. And the abiding paradox of a truly liberal education from the Greeks to our day is its aversion to the didactic.

A recurrent element in the problem of seeing this contemplative function of mimesis, and indeed of any concept of art, has been to relate it adequately to the demands of Christian life. We have already seen that incarnational—as opposed to eschatological—Christianity has always been a friend to the arts. But the fundamental difference between the concerns of salvation and those of culture, though they

4. Quoted in *Criticism: The Major Texts,* ed. W. J. Bate (New York, Harcourt, Brace and World, 1952), pp. 254-255.
5. Jacques Maritain, *Creative Intuition in Art and Poetry* (New York: Pantheon, 1953), pp. 141-145.

confront the same person in a single milieu, has for the most part, in theory at least, been inadequately faced; and a moral pragmatism has too readily pressed its claims, despite the deep contemplative roots of the faith. Yet Auerbach has noted well that mimesis has been deeply enriched by its contact through *figura* with the Judaic and Christian traditions. (This, incidentally, confirms our claims about the metempirical nature of mimesis.) No age has been without efforts to deal with this problem, yet each had its peculiar difficulties. Our own is in many ways most fortunate in this respect. It is heir to the findings of the past. It is also fairly rid of the artificial norms of style of which Auerbach spoke, which derived from the more essentialist limits of the Classical view of rhetoric and from certain sociological presuppositions. Today, too, incarnational theology has a broader and more integral context in which to discuss the problem. In recent years much serious thought has been given it in the work of Lynch, Maritain, Ross, Scott, and Turnell, to mention but a few writing in English.

At all events, it is wise in the end to turn to Samuel Johnson. Of all his contemporaries he was the most keenly aware of the abiding values of the Classical tradition, and most arduous and successful in making them timely. Aristotle at the outset and Johnson at the end of this critical tradition knew well the importance of process, both in life and the thought reflecting it, process, the focus of realistic metonymy. In our own day Philip Wheelwright has recognized the importance of this metonymy for exploring the kind of human experience that issues in depth knowledge, of which poetry forms a significant part, when he speaks of seeking the "intimation of a something more" in the patterns of limit that characterize "Man's Threshold Existence."[6] Giant that

6. Philip Wheelwright, *The Burning Fountain* (Bloomington: Indiana University Press, 1954), pp. 8 ff.

he was, Johnson bore witness to the abiding values of the Classical tradition, while remaining open in so many ways to new, dimly seen forces at work. Process and the method of metonymy find the climax of their significance in his transitional role. The spirit of this role is not that of Shelley's sad cry: "We look before and after, / And pine for what is not." It is rather that of Eliot's paradoxical old men who must be explorers: "We must be still and still moving / Into another intensity."

INDEX

Addison, Joseph, 107-109, 152, 158, 162, 164, 168, 170, 174, 176 f, 214, 222, 239, 252
Adler, Mortimer, 159
Aeschylus, 164
Aesthetics, 2, 35, 44, 99, 113, 117, 122 f, 230. *See also* Aquinas, Art, Horatian formula
Akenside, Mark, 118, 163, 246, 281
Albigensianism, 227
Anacreon, 282
Analogy, 16, 298 ff; in eighteenth century, 76 ff; and ethics, 227; and new science, 122
Anderson, F. H., 82, 83
Anselm, Saint, 235
Aquinas, Saint Thomas, 63, 227, 229, 230-232
Aristophanes, 42, 256
Aristotle, 18-35; and arts, 17, 133; Brown on, 119; on comedy, 160-167; Dryden on, 102; and eighteenth century, 1-6; on epic, 167, 169; on ethics, 224; and form, 49 f, 218-220; on genre, 136-137; and Horace, 38, 39, 42-49; and Horatian formula, 248, 250 ff, 257, 267; on the *Iliad*, 171-172; and imitation, 99-103, 105, 107, 113-129 *passim*; and Johnson, 271-274, 279, 288; and katharsis, 141-149, 151, 154; and knowledge, 5, 30, 55, 77, 129, 184, 192; and language, 184, 186-188, 192; and meaning, 51-53, 132; on music, 113; physics of, 72, 79, 86; and

Plato, 6, 16-18, 219; on pleasure, 24, 44, 99, 139, 252; on plot, 147, 212; on poetic justice, 157; on poetry, 5, 44, 139, 186, 193, 212, 252; and the probable, 56-74, 277; and reality, 53-56; and rhetoric, 38, 39, 142, 188-189, 193; Rymer on, 107; on structure, 16, 130-135, 181 f; style and, 183-187, 189–190, 192; θεωρία, as goal of mimesis, 125; on tragedy, 139-142, 147, 163, 171, 288; Twining on, 121, 154, 267. See also *Metaphysics, Nichomachean Ethics, Poetics, Politics, Rhetoric*
Arnold, Matthew, 298
Ars Poetica (Horace), 35-48 *passim*, 200
Art, 64; and Aquinas, 230-232; and Christian tradition, 229-232, 305; Classical, 9, 17, 25, 44, 51 ff, 124; and ethics, 2, 230, 297; as knowledge, 49; imitation in, 50, 109-118; and pleasure, 71, 72, 73; and psychology, 297; and rhetoricism, 113; theology and, 175, 297. *See also* Aesthetics, Ethics
Associationism, 79, 95-97, 99, 109, 220, 222, 238, 302
Atkins, J. W. H., 8, 13, 15, 45 f, 60, 199 f
Audra, E., 105, 215
Auerbach, Erich, 306
Augustine, Saint, 230
Autonomy:
double (Aristotle), 30, 70, 129; of

309

INDEX

Republic (Plato), 7, 9, 10 ff
Reynolds, Sir Joshua, 266 ff
Rhetoric:
in art theory, 113; in eighteenth century, 4, 38, 44, 299; of the emotions, 119, 259-263; Horace on, 1, 45, 47; imitation in, 210; Johnson's valuation of, 289; and poetry, 119, 181, 191, 193-208; three senses of, 195; *Rhetoric* (Aristotle), 38 f, 142, 187-189, 193
Richardson, Samuel, 1, 285
Romanticism, 113, 116 f, 120, 122 f, 130, 137, 214, 223, 303
Ross, Malcolm, 306
de Rougement, Denis, 64
Rowe, Nicholas, 289
Rymer, Thomas, 106 f, 150, 157, 162, 222, 254 f

Sasek, Lawrence, 242 f
Satire, 175-179, 286 f
Satires (Horace), 38, 42
Scholastics, 77, 109
Science:
Johnson's interest in, 270 f; nature and the new, 79-86. *See also* Mathematics, Physics
Scientism, 79-86, 91, 101, 206, 208, 214
Scott, Nathan, 306
Scottish school:
of critics, 246; of psychology, 203
Sensation, 92 f, 95 f, 102, 108. *See also* Knowledge, Psychology
Sentiment, *see* Emotions
Shaftsbury, Earl of (Anthony A. Cooper), 35, 88, 99, 101, 117, 120, 122, 164 f, 169, 244 f, 255
Shakespeare, William, 60, 104, 159, 223, 272, 277, 282, 288, 291 f, 300 f
Shelley, Percy Bysshe, 35, 307
Shenstone, William, 246
Showerman, Grant, 41 f
Sidney, Sir Philip, 34, 64, 138, 150, 165, 178, 197 ff, 205, 251, 254
Sin, *see* Evil
Skepticism, 77, 84, 176, 239

Smith, John, Boys, 89, 243
Smollett, T. G., 246, 285
Socrates, 6
Sophist (Plato), 15
Sophocles, 147, 157, 164, 172, 300
Sosii, 43
Spectator papers, 1, 109, 152
Steele, Sir Richard, 152, 164, 254 f
Stoicism, 42, 44, 106
Structure:
in poetry, 16, 20, 24, 26, 29, 39, 45, 52, 57, 60, 139-182; Aristotle and Plato, 8, 20 f, 24; element of, 50, 130-182; formalism and, 33; function and, 138-139; genres and, 136-138; Johnson on, 288
Style, 50, 183-217; and form, 186-192; and formalism, 209-216; and function, 192
Subjectivity:
interest and, 304; and mimesis, 98, 117-124; and objectivity, 127 f; and poetic creation, 302 ff; and reality, 304. *See also* Aesthetics
Sublime, Shaftsbury's cult of, 169
Swedenberg, H. T., 168, 170
Swift, Jonathan, 97, 176, 286, 291, 300

Tate, Allen, 2, 33, 44 ff, 69, 192, 205
Tatler, 254
Τέχνη, 6, 20, 51, 299
Temple, William, 149, 174, 263
Terence, 68
Theism, 89
Theodicies, and nature, 86-90
Theology:
Christian, 77, 86; and deism, 88, 89, 106; physics of, 239; and reason, 83, 87, 89. *See also* Christianity, Evil, Rationalism, Voluntarism
Θεωρία, 124 f
Thomson, James, 242
Tillotson, Geoffrey, 106
Tillotson, John, 244
Timaeus, 81
Tindal, Matthew, 88
Toland, John, 88, 239
Tractatus Coislinianus, 161

Tradition, and the poet, 301. *See also* Noetic
Tragedy, 119, 139-140; Aristotle on, 66, 67, 134; autonomy of, 143; and comedy, 163; and epic, 102, 167, 171; Johnson on, 288 f; and katharsis, 153 ff; pleasure in, 147; and poetic justice, 157 ff
Transformation in the probable, 60-62
Trapp, Joseph, 168 f
Troeltsch, Ernest, viii
Truth:
knowledge valued for, 299; poetic, 32, 56, 118, 159; of science, 56; thematic, 23. *See also* Reality
Turnell, Martin, 306
Tuve, Rosemond, 196-199
Twining, Thomas, 33, 114, 117, 120, 123, 154, 166, 267

Unities:
doctrine of, 211, 212; Johnson on, 275, 288
Universal:
Classical, 26, 40, 57, 59, 73, 103, 135, 209, 220 f; of Johnson, 271 f, 277, 290; Pope's, 106
Unrealism:
Johnson on, 290, 293; of Restoration characters, 288. *See also* Reality
Utilitarian views, *see* Pragmatism

Verisimilitude, 211, 257, 285. *See also* Experience, Probable, Realism, Truth
Vida, Marco, 111

Virgil, Pope on, 210
Virtue, *see* Ethics, Evil, Morality
Vivas, Eliseo, 181 f
Voltaire, 88, 213, 234
Voluntarism, 232-233; Christian, 239-243; eighteenth-century, 235-299; and emotion, 244-247; rationalistic, 235-239

Walker, George, 153
Waller, Edmund, 294, 301
Walpole, Horace, 152
Warren, Austin, 149, 196
Warton, Joseph, 179
Wasserman, Earl R., 121 ff, 156
Watson, George, 205
Watt, Ian, 285
Weinberg, Bernard, 36, 180
Wellek, René, 33, 62 f, 149, 304
West, Rebecca, 128
Wheelwright, Philip, 306
Whitehead, Alfred North, 223, 234
Whitehead, William, 162, 164
Willey, Basil, 91
Williams, Aubrey, 105, 215
Wimsatt, W. K., 33, 62, 65, 73, 127, 143, 215, 222, 279
Winters, Yvor, 2
Wit, 213-215
Wordsworth, William, 117, 204, 209, 300
Wycherley, William, 164

Yeats, William Butler, 18, 60, 196, 297
Young, Edward, 118, 153, 262